D0620819

Transforming America's Israel Lobby

RELATED TITLES FROM POTOMAC BOOKS

Crisis and Crossfire:
The United States and the Middle East Since 1945
—Peter L. Hahn

Transforming America's Israel Lobby

The Limits of Its Power and the Potential for Change

Dan Fleshler

Foreword by M. J. Rosenberg

Potomac Books, Inc.
Washington, D.C.

Parts of chapter 8, "Rhetoric (and Paradigms) for the Rest of Us," were originally posted on the author's blog, www.realisticdove.org, on January 10, 2008, and March 28, 2008. Parts of chapter 5, "American Jews, Iraq, and the Fetish of Preemptive War," were originally posted on the same site on October 20, 2007. Revised portions of those posts have been adapted for this book.

Library of Congress Cataloging-in-Publication Data
Fleshler, Dan.
Transforming America's Israel lobby : the limits of its power and the potential for change / Dan Fleshler ; foreword by M.J. Rosenberg. — 1st ed.
p. cm.
Includes bibliographical references and index.
ISBN 978-1-59797-222-2 (alk. paper)
1. Lobbying—United States. 2. Jews—United States--Politics and government. 3. United States—Foreign relations—Israel. 4. Israel—Foreign relations—United States. I. Title.
JK1118.F54 2009
327.7305694—dc22
2008049377

Printed in the United States of America on acid-free paper that meets the American National Standards Institute Z39-48 Standard.

Potomac Books, Inc.
22841 Quicksilver Drive
Dulles, Virginia 20166

First Edition

10 9 8 7 6 5 4 3 2

Contents

Foreword

This book makes a very important contribution to a conversation that all Americans, and especially American Jews, need to have about Israeli policies and the U.S. government's kneejerk support for them. It describes how America's Israel lobby has worked for years to sustain a status quo that has been deadly for Israel and its Arab neighbors and also harmful to the United States. It examines the obstacles to building an alternative to that lobby. And it suggests what can be done to change the political environment that prevents America's elected officials from taking an evenhanded approach to the Arab-Israeli conflict.

I worked on Capitol Hill as an aide to several senators and representatives over a twenty-year period. I also worked at the American Israel Public Affairs Committee (AIPAC) in the 1980s. I can say from personal experience that the pro-Israel lobby has worked to sustain the status quo with a very heavy hand. Members of Congress support hard-line Israeli policies not because they think that these policies are good for Israel or America, but because they are afraid to say no to the lobby.

Back in the 1970s, when I first started working in Congress, legislators simply accepted the lobby as a fact of life. No more. Today, it is hard to find a member of Congress who has anything good to say about the lobby in private, although, because the intimidation factor is so high, it still remains hard to find a member of Congress who will criticize it in public.

It's not a good situation. Elected officials and their aides—in the executive branch as well as Congress—like to feel that they can decide foreign policy issues for themselves. It is not good for the pro-Israel and Jewish communities, let alone America as a whole, when policymakers are made to feel that Israel is the one issue about which they are not permitted to think or to question. Resentment is building.

Dan Fleshler's book provides a valuable service because it spreads the word that most Jews do not share the AIPAC worldview and that there is far less risk in challenging the lobby than politicians seem to think. Despite all the propaganda (put out by both AIPAC and the anti-Israel camp), the lobby has rarely succeeded in defeating any legislator simply because he or she criticized Israel. And one thing is certain: if he or she has the will, any president can pursue Middle East peace without fear of the lobby, because the overwhelming majority of American Jews are not hard-liners, advocates of the lobby's line, or single issue voters (or donors). American Jews are Americans, and treating us as if our only concern were sustaining the status quo in Israel is both insulting and wrong. Few of us take our cues from the lobby.

Still, the lobby is not a paper tiger. Its roar is real, and it does have claws that can harm political and academic careers. So it is not easy to write an accurate, honest book about it. Attacking it almost invariably produces charges of hostility to Israel and/or Jews. Defending it produces the charge that you are a lobby lackey. The safest course is to avoid talking about it at all, and this, until recently, was the course most often followed.

That has changed in the last decade or so. It has changed primarily because activists within the Jewish community are speaking up. No, it does not hurt that Jimmy Carter and Professors Stephen Walt and John Mearsheimer have written provocatively about the Israel lobby. But their efforts might have disappeared into the ether if it hadn't been for voices in the Jewish community that are now saying that the lobby does not speak for them. Those voices have made it easier to criticize the lobby simply by making it impossible to label all of its critics as hostile to Israel and American Jews.

Dan Fleshler is not hostile to Jews or Israel. He has been active in the Jewish community for much of his adult life and obviously cares deeply about Israel. But unlike activists in what he calls "the conventional Israel lobby," he sees nothing contradictory in being, as he puts it "pro-Israel, pro-Palestinian, and pro-American"; he believes that the kind of fair, energetic American diplomacy needed to end Israel's occupation of Palestinian territories is in everyone's interests.

Bottom line: this is a significant piece of work. One can't understand the making of U.S. foreign policy as it relates to the Middle East without getting a grasp of the lobby. Nor can one get it from anti-lobby screeds written by those with little firsthand knowledge of the American Jewish community. Fleshler provides information and insights that will be useful to anyone who wants American leaders to pursue Middle East peace without looking over their shoulders, fearing a backlash from right-wing Jews who don't represent their community.

M. J. ROSENBERG IS THE DIRECTOR OF
ISRAEL POLICY FORUM'S WASHINGTON OFFICE,
A FORMER AIDE TO THREE MEMBERS OF CONGRESS,
AND FORMER EDITOR OF AIPAC'S *NEAR EAST REPORT*.

Introduction

On March 6, 2006, Vice President Richard Cheney received raucous, foot-stomping applause when he addressed the annual policy conference of the American Israel Public Affairs Committee (AIPAC), the legendary pro-Israel lobbying group. In the main ballroom of the Washington Convention Center, Cheney defended the Iraq invasion. He threatened Iran with dire consequences if it stayed on the path to nuclear weapons. He said the United States would give no quarter to Hamas, the Islamic movement that had recently won the election in the Palestinian territories. Nearly 4,500 attendees kept roaring and cheering. They interrupted him forty-eight times and gave him a half dozen standing ovations. This spectacle was broadcast on C-Span and transmitted to living rooms throughout the world, from Jakarta to Tehran to Paris. It buttressed the dark, widespread notion that American Jews are belligerent, militaristic, and working hand in hand with an administration at war with Islam.

In fact, the people applauding at that conference were expressing the views of a small minority of American Jews. The majority of Jews in the United States clearly shared the country's disdain for Cheney, whose popularity ratings that spring were lower than 30 percent, given the chaos in Iraq, the administration's incompetent response to Hurricane Katrina, and other disasters. While they were initially divided about the wisdom of invading Iraq, by that spring most American Jews thought the war had been a mistake, polls showed.

Another anomaly: At that same conference, even louder cheers greeted Benjamin Netanyahu, the right-wing Likud leader who was in the midst of an election campaign, when he recommended the immediate unilateral annexation of large swaths of the West Bank—much more territory than most of his political rivals and most Israeli voters wanted to retain. He called for the construction of "an iron wall around Hamas," defended Israeli settlers and espoused other hard-line principles that appealed to a diminishing minority of Israelis and American Jews. The next month he and his party were soundly defeated at the polls. But Netanyahu clearly had a large and loyal fan club at AIPAC.

Not in the larger Jewish community, though. When it comes to the Israeli-Palestinian conflict, surveys have consistently shown that, compared to AIPAC and other powerful American Jewish groups that purport to represent that community in Washington and the media, American Jews are far more sympathetic to the Israeli left and more supportive of territorial compromise.

All of this raises some of the most befuddling questions in modern American political history: Why have American Jews—one of the most liberal communities in the United States—allowed their global image to be defined by hawks and neoconservatives? Precisely where have all the Jewish doves been hiding all of these years? What accounts for their collective tongue-biting? How did most of Washington become convinced that the only American Jews of any political consequence are those whose mission in life is to close the distance between official American and Israeli positions and to castigate Israel's critics?

These questions have plagued me, an American Jew who has tried to counteract AIPAC and its allies, on and off, since the mid-1980s. As a volunteer and paid media consultant, I have worked with dovish American Jewish organizations that have tried to build domestic support for an end to the Israeli occupation, for a two-state solution, and for a robust American diplomacy that would help to achieve those goals without selling either Israelis or Palestinians down the river. These relatively small groups included Americans for Peace Now (APN), Ameinu, Israel Policy Forum (IPF), Meretz USA, and Brit Tzedek v'Shalom (the Jewish Alliance for Justice and Peace). I also briefly represented the Israeli consulate in New York City when it was having a difficult time selling the Oslo peace process to many American Jews.

For years my camp has tried to convince more American Jews to speak out forcefully against a spreading occupation that we believed was a moral and strategic disaster for Israel as well as the United States. We took our cues from Israelis who believed that America's passive acceptance of Israel's settlement expansion and rule over another people was hurting Israel and rendering it more difficult to preserve Israeli democracy and fundamental Jewish ethics. By and large, of course, we failed. We blew it. In the battle for attention from Washington's political elite, the hawks in my community have usually won and the doves have usually lost. In the spring of 2005 I decided to embark on a quest to find out why.

Stepping back from the activist fray, mostly learning and absorbing rather than applying newfound knowledge, I tried to systematically investigate why AIPAC and other influential right-of-center pro-Israel groups are so good at what they do and what lessons could be learned from their success. I conferred with prominent American and Israeli Jewish leaders, less well-known but equally intriguing American activists who focus on the Middle East, former diplomats, congressional staffers and members of Congress, journalists who cover the American Jewish political scene, as well as other sources. The interviewees included former AIPAC staffers, but with the exception of one off-the-record conversation, several requests for interviews with the current staff were, sadly, ignored.

My ultimate goal was not merely to fully understand and then explain American Jewish power politics. It was to try to come up with concrete, practical prescriptions for altering the domestic political context of America's Middle East policies. What precisely would it take to create an effective lobby for the rest of us, an energized, political bloc of Americans who want the kind of fair, evenhanded Middle East policy that could help Israelis and Arabs to awaken from their shared nightmare? Was it possible to transform the existing pro-Israel community from within and empower those who want America to take a different course in that region? What were the prospects of forging a new coalition with Muslim and Christian Americans who shared many goals with the pro-Israel left? Finally, I wanted to determine whether these were idle fantasies, even less likely than peace in the Middle East, and whether everyone in the tiny, underfunded American Jewish peace camp should just close up shop and go home.

In April 2008 the importance of these questions was underscored with the launch of a promising, well-publicized initiative that is working in tandem with the aforementioned Jewish groups: the J Street project. Unlike those groups, which must limit lobbying activities because of their tax status, J Street is legally entitled to lobby without constraints. And it also has a political action committee (PAC) that can funnel money directly to political candidates and incumbents. In less than a year it attracted close to 100,000 online supporters and raised more than a half million dollars for congressional candidates, more than any other pro-Israel PAC in the country. As a result, it has begun to create at least a bit more political space for American policymakers and politicians who have long wanted to take independent positions on the Middle East and to say in public what heretofore they have muttered to staffers and friends behind closed doors.

Is it remotely possible that any of these efforts could make one whit of difference? In brief, I believe it is possible, but the task ahead is daunting. As this book goes to press, President Barack Obama has just taken office. He and Secretary of State Hillary Clinton are confronted with the need to hit the ground running and deal immediately with the volatile Middle East, two wars in Iraq and Afghanistan, Iran's nuclear program, Israel's tensions with Syria and Lebanon, and the core conflict between Israelis and Palestinians, which fans the flames of regional instability. When it comes to American foreign policy, there is no more important region. The Obama administration needs to know that it will have the political leeway to take a bold diplomatic approach to the entire Middle East. When dealing with the ongoing tragedy of Israel and Palestine, it needs the courage to lean, when necessary, on both sides rather than just one side. This book examines the many domestic obstacles in the president's path and weighs the chances of overcoming them.

The Gray Area

At the same time, this book culls facts from the considerable number of fantasies, half-truths, and misunderstandings about undue Jewish influence that are floating around out there. Until recently, the nuances and subtleties of American Jewish activism were of interest mainly to a narrow circle of scholars and activists who focused on ethnic politics and America's Middle East policy. Now, these issues are at the center of an international intellectual firestorm.

Furious, vitriolic debates about "Jewish power" are hardly new on the American scene. But lately they have become more widespread, more public, and more respectable, thanks in large part to a controversial essay that excoriated the "Israel lobby" by Professors John Mearsheimer and Stephen Walt.[1] Published in the spring of 2006, their paper created the first of several recent controversies over critiques of Israel, including Jimmy Carter's *Palestine: Peace Not Apartheid* and some provocative essays and speeches by Tony Judt, a prominent advocate of a binational state.

The Mearsheimer-Walt essay and a subsequent book-length version, in particular, are bibles and guides for detractors of pro-Israel activism. And they are symbols of irresponsible Israel-bashing to the reflexive supporters of anything and everything Israel does.

As the two professors define it, the *Israel lobby* is a loose assortment of groups and people that, they contend, have effectively controlled America's Middle East policy for decades. This lobby is the main reason why America invaded Iraq. It is the main reason why successive administrations have given Israel free rein to occupy Palestinian land and do virtually anything it has wanted to do. Because of the awesome power of this lobby, criticism of Israel—which has no strategic value to the United States and no moral basis for American support—is routinely quashed in the public arena, and there is little serious political debate about America's intimate relationship with the Jewish state.[2]

Mearsheimer and Walt were savaged for these ideas and accused of committing a host of scholarly errors by a veritable legion of angry critics, including American Jewish stalwarts like Abraham Foxman of the Anti-Defamation League (ADL) and Alan Dershowitz, former American officials like David Gergen, the left-of-center weekly *Forward*, the right-wing cottage industry that monitors attacks on Israel, and columnists and bloggers of every description.[3]

And they were joyfully embraced as heroes in print as well as in the increasingly crowded, anti-Israel, anti-Zionist, and sometimes unapologetically anti-Semitic neighborhoods of the blogosphere and the rest of the Internet. Some of what they claimed—especially about the role of Israel and its lobbyists in the Iraq War—had already been promulgated by an odd alliance of digerati who agree on little except that Israel is an irredeemably evil empire and American Jews who support it are wrecking this country. They include radical libertarians, far leftists, white supremacists concerned about the Zionist-occupied government, well-intentioned people concerned about Palestinian human rights, much of the Arab media, and academics the world over (including some in Israel itself).

After the publication of the professors' paper and subsequent book, people in those two camps squared off and spent much time and energy defending or deploring the particulars of Mearsheimer and Walt's work. The most disturbing aspect of the controversy was that most published analyses were either 100 percent pro or 100 percent con, with no nuances in between. They had the ring of partisan attack ads listing their opponents' mistakes or questioning their motives. They either exaggerated the clout of Israel's supporters in the United States or underestimated it. The gray area where the truth resides was rarely traversed. I try to go there, as much as possible, in this book.

The last thing anyone in the world needs is yet another point-by-point evaluation of the claims made by Mearsheimer and Walt. In the chapters that follow, their arguments and assertions are addressed in passing only when they are relevant to the task at hand. For the moment, suffice it to say that they got many things wrong but they also deserve credit for getting many things right.

It is manifestly true that mainstream Israel supporters can strike fear in the hearts of members of Congress. When Israel attacked the Gaza Strip in late 2008 and early 2009, had there not been a powerful domestic constituency supporting Israel's actions, surely more American politicians would have criticized what most of the world—myself included—believed was an appallingly disproportionate response to Hamas rocket fire.

Needless to say, were it not for Israel's supporters, it is inconceivable that the Jewish state would be the largest recipient of American financial and military aid.

At one point or another, every American administration since Jimmy Carter's has confronted well-organized domestic opposition when it criticized or tried to stop Israeli settlement expansion. As a result, pro-Israel activists in this country have helped to turn the United States into what former Israeli negotiator Daniel Levy calls an "enabler," the equivalent of someone who gives a drunk driver the keys to the car.[4]

The list could go on. But it is not nearly as long or as ominous as the one presented by Mearsheimer, Walt, and their intellectual allies. From personal, sometimes painful experience, as well as from interviews and other research conducted for this book, I know full well what mainstream pro-Israel activists are capable of accomplishing. And I simply don't recognize the carefully organized, ideologically united, shape-shifting, omnipresent, and all-powerful lobbying juggernaut the two scholars and their admirers have depicted.

Israel's advocates in the United States don't have the kind of tight, permanent, and unyielding vice grip on the American government and media that is often attributed to them. They have lost a good many battles over the years, and no doubt they will lose some more. In the rooms in the White House and Foggy Bottom where actual decisions are made, the wishes of hawkish pro-Israel supporters are much less important than is generally believed in the casbahs of Damascus, the editorial offices of *Le Monde* and the *Guardian*, and a large part of the World Wide Web.

But those wishes still matter. Of course they do. The question is, how much? If people object to what many of America's pro-Israel activists stand for and want to change this nation's Middle East policies, they need a realistic appraisal of the role those activists play in the complex, sausage-making—or, if you prefer, kosher-hot-dog-making—process that eventually results in American foreign policy.

That is why, in the first part of this book, I will open up the hood of AIPAC and other conventional pro-Israel groups, poke around, and explain how they actually work, how their staff members and volunteers try to shape and influence Congress and the executive branch. I will gauge the nature and extent of their power. Then I will explore how to counteract the conventional Israel lobby, who is available to do it, why they haven't done it thus far, and what needs to happen in order to create an effective political alternative.

Defining Lobbies

Mearsheimer and Walt have defined the terms of much of the debate over Israel's American supporters. It is likely that for years their work will remain the reference guide for anyone and everyone who wants to attack pro-Israel activists in the United States. So the difference between their definition of the *Israel lobby* and the one used here should be noted at this early juncture.

"To be part of the lobby," they explain, "one has to actively work to move American policy in a pro-Israel direction. For an organization, this pursuit must be an important part of its mission and consume a substantial portion of its resources and agenda. For an individual that means devoting some portion of one's professional or personal life (or, in some cases substantial amounts of money) to influencing U.S. Middle East policy."[5]

Fair enough. But at various points in their book, this definition encompasses right-wing columnists like Charles Krauthammer, who consistently defend Israeli militarism, and liberal columnists like Richard Cohen, who sometimes lambaste Israeli militarism. It applies to neoconservative American officials in the Bush administration like Douglas Feith, who love Netanyahu, and more liberal American officials like Dennis Ross, who openly clashed with Netanyahu. It includes left-wing groups like mine; the settler groups we fight against; media titans such as Mortimer Zuckerman, who are hawkish on Israel; Christian Zionists; and anyone else who "actively works to preserve America's special relationship with Israel."[6]

Because of this sprawling, expansive definition, the *Forward*'s J. J. Goldberg noted, the Israel lobby has "the appearance of a vast, terrifying octopus."[7] I had a different problem with the way this octopus was described than most of the professors' critics. My problem was that it appeared to be so vast, powerful, and terrifying that there did not seem to be any way to stop it.

The definition of a *lobby* that is used here is more traditional and practical. It refers to groups and individuals who support a specific cause or interest and who try to influence public officials to vote a certain way or to make certain decisions. There is more than one lobby within the organized, self-styled, pro-Israel American Jewish community because there are substantial differences of opinion about what Israel needs from the United States. Therefore, elected officials often receive different messages from various organizations within the community.

For example, Brit Tzedek v'Shalom is a grassroots group that calls itself "pro-Israel." It opposes all West Bank settlements, endorses a division of Jerusalem, calls for talks with any group willing to talk to Israel, and bitterly opposed Israel's behavior during the war with Lebanon in 2006. It should not be conflated with AIPAC or groups even further to the right, which have taken opposite positions on those and other issues. Brit Tzedek supports continued American aid to Israel, as do other dovish Jewish groups. But if two organizations agree on one or two policy prescriptions and disagree on ten of them, they can hardly be considered part of the same lobby.

In this book, a large but partial swath of the pro-Israel community in the United States is referred to as the *conventional Israel lobby*, which is defined narrowly enough so that it is possible to discuss how to transform it or build alternatives. The positions of these groups—and individuals within them—have shifted over the years in response to changes in the Middle East. The conventional Israel lobby comprises people who don't agree on everything, but who

1. generally oppose any president who puts any pressure on Israel or argues publicly with Israel;
2. either defend Israeli settlement expansion and the occupation of Palestinian territory or—more commonly—don't lift a finger to try to change this status quo, even if it rankles and disturbs them;
3. either actively oppose negotiations with Israel's most hard-nosed

adversaries—including Iran and Hamas—or don't speak out in favor of such negotiations if the Israeli government wants to completely isolate those adversaries; and

4. either lash out at critics of Israeli policy or, more commonly, do nothing to defend those critics when other groups lash out at them.

As described in detail in chapter 2, which provides a kind of scorecard to American Jewish groups, this conventional Israel lobby includes AIPAC. It also includes many—but not all—of the fifty-two organizations in the Conference of Presidents of Major American Jewish Organizations, the most well-known umbrella group in the community. On most—but not all—issues connected to Israel, this lobby includes the largest and most well-known groups in the Presidents' Conference, such as the Anti-Defamation League, the American Jewish Committee, and the American Jewish Congress, as well as more unabashedly right-wing groups like the Zionist Organization of America (ZOA). On some foreign policy initiatives, these Jewish groups are aided and abetted by Christian Zionists, such as John Hagee's Christians United for Israel (CUFI).

Another characteristic of this lobby is that, over the years, many and often most American Jews have disagreed with it. Name the issue, name the moment, and chances are polls will show that AIPAC and the Presidents Conference were not in step with a large proportion of the community they purported to represent. There are many examples. I've already mentioned the vast distance between the AIPAC rank and file and the rest of the Jewish community on the failed Iraq War. Three others will suffice, for now:

- In the late 1980s public criticism of Israel was still a major taboo in the organized American Jewish community. According to a *New York Times* report in April 1987 about an American Jewish Committee survey of Jews in the United States, "some leaders of Jewish groups have argued the criticism of Israel should be confined within the American Jewish 'family' because public reproaches serve to help Israel's adversaries. But *63 percent of respondents rejected that view, and only 22 percent agreed* [emphasis added]."[8]

- In 1998 the Clinton administration was having trouble with Israeli prime minister Netanyahu, who had authorized provocative settlement construction and was dragging his feet about further redeployment of Israeli troops from the West Bank, which had been promised in the Oslo peace accords. Predictably, AIPAC and the Presidents Conference—working mostly through Congress—warned against any American pressure on Israel. But a poll of American Jews sponsored by Israel Policy Forum found that, by a 9-1 margin, American Jews wanted the administration to take an "evenhanded" approach to the Israel-Palestinian dispute and 84 percent agreed that the United States should "pressure" both Arafat and Netanyahu.[9]
- More recently, in June 2008, 87 percent of American Jews polled by Gerstein Agne said they wanted the United States to play an "active role" to help resolve the Israeli-Palestinian conflict. Of those, 75 percent supported active American engagement even if it meant the United States publicly disagreed with both the Israelis and Arabs. That is not the kind of engagement the conventional Israel lobby can tolerate.[10]

The sentiments of a majority of American Jews are generally expressed by a nucleus of left-of-center groups with connections to Israel. They already present an alternative to the conventional Israel lobby. There are many more Jewish individuals in other mainstream organizations who are not involved with those dovish groups, and others who are unaffiliated, who have the same or a similar take on American diplomacy in the Middle East. One of my tasks here is to examine whether it is possible to galvanize and mobilize these disparate American Jewish elements—along with other Americans—so that our nation's leaders are less beholden to those who cannot stomach diplomacy that is fair to both Israelis and Palestinians.

Power Puffery

After Congress tried to stop Clinton from pressing Netanyahu, an Israeli friend in New York City sympathetic to Israel's Peace Now movement took me aside, clearly annoyed, and addressed me as if I were a symbol of the muffled, passive American Jewish majority. "How can they get away with that!?" he demanded to know. "How can you let them?"

One answer comes from Jimmy Breslin. "All political power," he wrote, "is primarily an illusion . . . Mirror and blue smoke, beautiful blue smoke rolling over the surface of highly polished mirrors. . . . If somebody tells you how to look, there can be seen in the smoke great, magnificent shapes, castles and kingdoms."[11] My wife, Lisa, is in the advertising business, and she describes the conventional Israel lobby's efforts to promote the image of its clout as "power puffery." Convincing the political elite that it represents American Jews is only one of its promotional accomplishments.

In Washington, the line between the perception that you can accomplish something and your ability to accomplish it is virtually indistinguishable. The conventional Israel lobby, especially AIPAC, has thrived in part because of the widespread belief that its money controls the political system and that any president or politician who disagrees with it will be verbally and financially pummeled by well-organized, angry American Jews. In fact, I will show, while it is sensible for politicians to have queasy worries about messing with AIPAC, those worries are often overblown, and that suits AIPAC fine.

For example, the conventional wisdom that confronts congressional incumbents and candidates is that AIPAC can make or break political careers because of the campaign gifts its financial network either proffers or withholds. I will demonstrate that the financial impact of the AIPAC-influenced money machine on congressional races is not as large as is commonly believed. Most members of Congress only glimpse the magnificent shapes, castles, and kingdoms that money from right-of-center Israel supporters supposedly provides. And AIPAC's ability to launch successful revenge campaigns that drive political enemies out of office is exaggerated in the minds of people who should know better, notably politicians and their handlers.

The "reputation of power," wrote Thomas Hobbes in *Leviathan*, "is power."[12] This is a good description of the conventional lobby's impact on the executive branch. There, the lobby's clout owes more to fear, nervousness, and untested assumptions about the Jewish community's reaction to policies than to actual overt pressure. It is based on the perception of what the community *might* do and the punishment that it *might* exact.

Some administrations have ignored or overcome those fears and anxieties. "History shows that when presidents are determined to do something in U.S. interests, the lobby folds," said Samuel Lewis, a former U.S. ambassador to Israel who has held several other State Department posts related to the Middle East. "As [George H. W.] Bush demonstrated, the White House can win the fight. Carter had all kinds of problems with the Jewish community, but that didn't stop him from going forward with our Middle East policy. The lobby didn't have any substantive impact on Carter. To the extent that he was influenced [in Israel's favor], it was by the Israelis. . . . Clinton stood up to them, to some extent. Presidents actually have a lot more freedom than they feel like they have. If a president wants to stand up to the lobby, he can."*

Obviously, if there is to be an effective alternative to the conventional Israel lobby, it will need to find a way to limit or counteract worries about political fallout and instill more courage in America's leaders. That is a tall order. But there is no need to rid the United States of some kind of right-wing Zionist puppeteer that is pulling the strings of American policy; that puppeteer does not exist.

Some analysts go so far as to dismiss the legendary power of the conventional Israel lobby as a "useful illusion,"[13] as David Verbeeten puts it, one that is propped up by different people for different reasons. According to this view, an exaggerated idea of "Jewish power" is a political asset not only to pro-Israel lobbyists. It allows Arab leaders to justify their inability to influence American policy or to address the Palestinians' plight. It gives America's elected officials an excuse for not doing what they want to do, such as take exception to some Israeli policies. It gives Israel's most vituperative critics material for endless speeches, essays, and blog posts. And, needless to say, power puffery enables some Israel-focused organizations to raise a lot of money.

That theory dramatically understates the conventional lobby's clout, which is most certainly not an illusion. If it were, there would be no reason

* Quotes not identified with endnotes are from interviews with the author. A list of interviews is provided at the back of the book.

to write this book. When we get to the end of the yellow brick road in our search for the truth about the lobby, we find that there are actual, powerful, well-heeled wizards behind the elaborate machinery of its influence.

Still, one can detect in the conventional Israel lobby some distinct elements of a little-known, Zionist tradition of power puffery, an ability to take advantage of deep-seated, nearly universal myths of Jewish power, reach, and money. Understanding these illusions is a prerequisite to assessing the limits of the conventional lobby's power and figuring out what, if anything, can be done about it.

Today's lobby has inherited some of the panache and bold self-promotion of Chaim Weizmann, the chemist who, while based in London, successfully and almost single-handedly lobbied for the Balfour Declaration in 1917. That was the statement in which Great Britain promised the Jews a homeland in Palestine. According to Israeli historian Tom Segev, Weizmann made this happen by taking advantage of British officials' fantasies that a powerful network of Jews turned the wheels of history.

Weizmann led them to believe that the Zionists were an integral part of that network and that "in standing with the Zionist movement . . . they were winning the support of a strong and influential ally. . . . In fact, the Jewish people were helpless; they had nothing to offer, no influence other than this myth of clandestine power."[14]

Knowing that British censors were monitoring his mail and sharing it with the Foreign Office,

> every so often [Weizmann] would send out letters that looked as if they had come from the center of world power: "American friends must strain every nerve to influence our Russian friends' favour of vigorous support [for] British and Entente policy and counteract all adverse forces there," he once cabled a Zionist activist in Washington. "We are doing the same here. Wire steps you are taking." . . .
>
> Weizmann's principal achievement was to create among British leaders an identity between the Zionist movement and "world Jewry."—Lloyd George referred to the "Jewish race," "world Jewry,"

> and "the Zionists" as if they were synonyms. . . . Yet none of it was true. The movement that was at the center of world influence in fact occupied four small rooms in the Picadilly Circus in London; its entire archives were kept in a single box in a hotel room. Most Jews did not support Zionism; the movement was highly fragmented, with activists working independently in different European capitals. Weizmann had absolutely no way of affecting the outcome of the war. But Britain's belief in the mystical power of "the Jews" over-rode reality.[15]

Obviously, compared to Chaim Weizmann and his tiny band of allies, Israel's right-wing and centrist supporters in the United States have much deeper pockets, more direct and firm connections to the political elite, and an exponentially larger, better organized, more entrenched network of supporters. The comparison is not meant to equate the two; it is meant to convey similarities in style and affect. The Zionist leader's remarkable ability to "conjure up the myth of Jewish influence and power," as Segev puts it, is something the leaders of the current conventional Israel lobby have inherited, knowingly or not. And they have not hesitated to use it.

In my experience, exaggerated notions of this lobby's power discourage American Jews who disagree with it from opposing it. As I was reading Mearsheimer and Walt's work, I worried that it would prompt potential recruits in a Middle East peace bloc to throw up their hands in despair, assuming that no one could stop AIPAC and its allies.

For years I have listened to American liberals—including those who once helped Middle East peace groups and became disillusioned—fume quietly about the success of the conventional Israel lobby. And I have watched them sigh, or throw up their hands in despair, or murmur phrases like "there's nothing we can do" or—as one of them once sneered to me—"good luck, Rabbi Don Quixote." If they are based in Washington or involved with domestic politics, sometimes they flash that telltale exhausted grin that appears on the faces of people who were once idealistic Student Council presidents and now must spend their days rationalizing and defending injustice and realpolitik.

In fact, there is much that they can do. Jeremy Ben-Ami, one of the founders of the J Street project, told me about a dinner party he attended with Washington cognoscenti—media people, academics, political operatives, etc. "Everyone was talking about this issue and American policy, about what ought to happen. Everyone reached the same conclusion: the policy won't change because of the American Jewish lobby. The conversation about the Middle East in this town usually shuts down at that point. But I exploded. I told them, 'We can't think in conventional political terms! We've got to change the political dynamic!'"

My hope is that if American Jews and other Americans, especially in Washington, learn there is a little less to the conventional Israel lobby than meets the eye, if they understand that it is, say, a four-hundred-pound gorilla rather than an eight-hundred-pounder, they will be emboldened to do something about it instead of passively accepting its predominance.

Underlying Assumptions

The reasons to care about any of this can be found in the Middle East, in the exhausted, agonized faces of Palestinians digging for their loved ones in the ruins of homes destroyed by the Israelis in Gaza City, or in other Palestinians forced to wait for hours at checkpoints before they can move from one West Bank village to another. They can be found in the cemeteries visited by still-grieving Israeli parents of suicide bomb victims and soldiers killed in battle, or in the beleaguered young Israelis at checkpoints who are enforcing an occupation many of them hope will end. They can be found in the most heartbreaking summary of this conflict that has ever been written, a few words from the Israeli poet Yehudah Amichai: "The howl of the orphans is passed from one generation to the next, as in a relay race: the baton never falls."[16]

But they can also be found in the streets of Tallahassee, Cleveland, and San Francisco. One of my underlying assumptions is that *it is vitally important for America to help solve the Israeli-Palestinian conflict because it is in our interests to do so.* It is almost bizarre that it is necessary to take the trouble to point this out because the assertion is self-evident. But while the following truism is recognized by practically everyone in the world, Israeli leaders and many of their American supporters either deny it or try to wish away:

America's unquestioning, unyielding support for Israeli policies is by far the most important reason why Muslims throughout the world despise us. Polls repeatedly show that this is the case. "The Arab world sees Iraq and other foreign crises 'through the Israeli-Palestinian prism,'" says Shibley Talhami, a Brookings Institution fellow who has done extensive polling in the Middle East. "It is their prism—in the same way that, since 9/11, the issue of terrorism has become the prism through which Americans are looking at the Middle East and the Islamic world. I've done surveys in five Arab countries. The vast majority of people say the Palestinian issue is the single most important issue to them."[17] His surveys have also shown that it is American policies, not American values, that are the primary reason for negative perceptions of the United States in the Arab world and that our policies related to the Israeli-Palestinian conflict are the most unpopular.[18]

Why should this matter to the average American? For one thing, since our perceived contribution to the Palestinians' plight is the most important reason for anti-American feeling, it is part of the mix of motivational tools used for recruitment by the tiny dangerous minority of Islamists who would like nothing better than to spill blood within our borders. It could be argued that the Palestinian cause was not a high priority for Osama bin Laden and al Qaeda before the attacks of September 11, 2001; it is inarguable that the Palestinian cause is now helping to transform mere contempt for America into murderous hatred among an untold number of impressionable, young Muslims.[19] The fact that America and Israel are perceived as opposite sides of the same satanic coin also makes it harder for the leaders of Muslim countries to work cooperatively and openly with the United States on other issues crucial to American security, including saving the lives of American troops in Iraq and curtailing Iran. Cooperation with America is not easily sold to much of the so-called Arab street.

Steps to address the Arab-Israeli conflict won't eliminate this hatred of America. Of course the venom has many other sources, including our invasion of Iraq, our support for autocratic Middle Eastern regimes, a burning desire to create an Islamic caliphate, a contempt for all things Western. But progress toward Arab-Israeli—and especially Palestinian-Israeli—peace would diminish the rancor and give Arab leaders much more political cover to crack down on Islamic extremists and help the United States to lower regional temperatures.

That Middle East peacemaking is a vital American interest has long been the majority view in the international diplomatic community. That includes the hundreds of former diplomats, statesmen, and other experts from the United States and the Middle East who were interviewed for a study group sponsored by the U.S. Institute of Peace beginning in 2005. The project was led by Daniel Kurtzer, former ambassador to Israel and Egypt and a longtime Middle East hand in several administrations, and Scott Lasensky, a senior research associate at the institute. Unlike the peanut gallery that disparages American engagement when it becomes too active, many of the interviewees were directly involved in America's Middle East diplomacy and the shaping of foreign policy in general. So the Kurtzer-Lasensky report has impeccable credibility when it asserts,

> For the United States, Arab-Israeli peacemaking is crucial to our own national security interests. Counter-terrorism priorities since the September 11th attacks would be easier to pursue if the Arab-Israeli conflict could be alleviated. Washington's interest in economic and political reform in the greater Middle East is complicated by Arab-Israeli strife. The U.S. interest in mitigating Islamist militancy would also be better served by a renewed peace process as would the need for greater regional cooperation on Iraq and nuclear nonproliferation. Moreover, the conflict has destabilized other parts of the region that remain critical to the United States, such as Lebanon. Most obviously, the U.S. commitment toward Israel's security and well-being is best served by moving toward, rather than away from, a comprehensive Arab-Israeli peace settlement.[20]

Yet, too often, as I will show in chapter 8, Israeli and American Jewish leaders act as if Israelis and Palestinians—as well as Syrians and the

Hezbollah in Lebanon—are engaged in a local neighborhood feud that has no repercussions beyond Ramallah and Jerusalem.

What happens in Israel and the rest of the Middle East is America's business too. And American citizens—Jews and non-Jews—not only have the right to expect certain things of our ally Israel; they also have the obligation, because what happens in the region directly affects their families, friends, and neighbors. Unfortunately, that is still a radical notion in much of the organized pro-Israel community, where the idea of America as the protector of a besieged Jewish state still prevails, and the notion that Israel can help protect the United States is rarely articulated.

Another underlying assumption of this book is that *the only way to fix what is broken in Israel and Palestine is a negotiated two-state solution.* Suggesting that used to bring howls of derision from many in Israel and the organized American Jewish community, but now it takes no bravery to endorse it in front of mainstream Jews. More importantly, it is the answer still endorsed in principle by the silent majority of Israelis and Palestinians. They cling to it even though a shrinking minority on both sides believes it is possible.

Israelis cling to it, forlornly, despite their sense that they don't have a partner for peace who would protect them if an agreement is reached, despite the popularity of Hamas—whose charter contains vile, unapologetic anti-Semitic rhetoric that blames Jews for world wars and financial panics—despite fears that relinquishing the West Bank would give Palestinians a new launching pad for rockets aimed at Tel Aviv and the rest of Israel.

Palestinians cling to it, desperately, despite the inexorable, defiant growth of Israeli settlements, despite the continued development of bypass roads and sewage lines and security barriers to protect Israeli enclaves deep inside the West Bank, despite the fact that, in the words of Gaith al-Omari, a former negotiator with the Palestinian Authority, "Israel is on its way to eliminating the possibility of a Palestinian state that Palestinians could conceivably accept." Or, as Idith Zertal and Akiva Eldar put it in *Lords of the Land*, "The settlement fever and all it involves continues. Almost out of sight and out of mind, it is going on with the full cooperation of Israel and its institutions, as though it were an involuntary, unconsidered movement of a body that has lost its mind."[21]

The truth is, there may be no hope. Some people make a kind of rhetorical blood sport of listing the many reasons why it is impossible to untie the Gordian knot of the Israeli-Arab conflict in our lifetimes. That knot also includes Israel's tense relations with Syria, Lebanon and Iran, but the Palestinian problem remains the most difficult to untangle. It is the one that will get the bulk of my attention here.

The scoffers might be right. The Palestinian state might be yesterday's solution. Pushing for it might be like pushing for the breakup of Bell Telephone or urging construction of a road through a ghost town that was deserted long ago.

Some on the left say partitioning the land was once a good idea but it is too late to make it happen, the Israelis have destroyed the possibility, the settlers cannot be dislodged and moved. In the best-case scenario, these skeptics claim, Palestinians will be confined to Bantustans without economic self-sufficiency, enough water, or the means to protect themselves from the Israelis. Therefore, an increasing number of Palestinian, left-wing Israeli, and other activists believe the only answer is a secular, binational state. People whom I respect endorse this idea, and I would be roaming much too far afield to give it the complex analysis it deserves, but I believe that, among other problems, it is unworkable. It is a recipe for the kind of ethnic bloodshed that would make what happened to the former Yugoslavia seem like a garden party. That is one reason why, despite their desperation, most Palestinians in the occupied territories have not embraced it.

Some right-wing Israelis and their supporters abroad say partitioning the land might have been worth considering at one time, but the Palestinians have destroyed the possibility, they have shown that they will never give up their quest to destroy Israel. Therefore the only answer is, well, uh . . . the right-wingers have no answer.

So we are left with the two-state idea, which—to paraphrase Churchill's view of democracy—is a terrible idea; it is deeply flawed, impractical, a recipe for continuing strife. But it is better than any other idea. And the stakes are too high for Israelis, Arabs, Americans, and the rest of the world to stop trying to achieve it.

"I don't believe it is too late," said Danny Rubinstein, an Israeli reporter who has covered the Palestinian territories for years. "I say, we can still do it. But the price Israel will have to pay is getting higher and higher. Same with the Palestinians. Nobody will pay the price they need to pay unless you [the Americans] tell them to."

This leads to my next assumption: while the United States should not be relied on as a deus ex machina that can swoop in and save the day on its own, *American diplomacy needs to be more bold, forceful, and not wedded to past precedents.* And our government needs to have a much wider range of diplomatic tools at its disposal, including the ability to use sticks as well as carrots when contending with both sides. Active American engagement is an essential component of any peace process in part because, as former Israeli foreign minister Shlomo Ben-Ami has noted, "In the Israeli-Palestinian conflict the possibility of peace without agony was missed long ago. From now on nobody can spare the parties their Calvary."[22]

The Calvary will require both sides to answer, once and for all, painful questions about the future, which—as of this writing—have not been resolved in workable agreements. What will be the precise national borders between the two states? What needs to be done to get Jewish settlers out of most of the West Bank? Who governs which parts of Jerusalem and its holy sites? What will happen to Palestinian refugees from 1948 and their descendants who insist on a "right of return" to their homes in Israel proper?

"You [the United States] are the only nation that can offer bridging ideas neither side is happy about, but both might be persuaded to accept," Ben-Ami told me.

The Calvary also requires both sides to halt behavior that precludes the possibility of peace, especially Palestinian violence against Israelis and Israeli settlement expansion. Only the United States has the leverage needed to persuade them to stop and to ensure that, once agreements are made, both sides keep their promises.

Aaron David Miller, who was on the Middle East team for six secretaries of state, has cautioned that the ability of the United States to fix matters on its own should not be exaggerated. But he suggests an important reason for the kind of engagement that is opposed by many pro-Israel activists: "One of the most important lessons to emerge from the Oslo years is that ignoring bad behavior on either side dooms any chance of serious and successful negotiations. We need to understand and act on this reality. That means imposing costs—political, moral and financial—on each side to dissuade them from their unilateral actions; and, at the same time, working with them on the ground to monitor behavior, solve problems and defuse crises."[23]

The need for more forceful American intervention is expressed here by a broad range of Israelis whom I've interviewed along with Ben-Ami—including former government officials and diplomats, scholars of the conflict, and other experts. I deliberately focused primarily on garnering recommendations from prominent Israelis. That is because, to those who are worried about a serious breach of U.S.-Israel relations, pleas for diplomatic activism from Israelis will be more persuasive than pleas from anyone else. In chapter 7, they offer their own ideas for helpful American interventions, including, in some cases, overt American pressure on Israel.

Regardless of what the United States chooses to do, if it pushes back against Israel in any way, it will be attacked by well-organized American constituencies who believe it is their mission to squelch any disagreements. And that is why a stronger political alternative, a lobby for the rest of us, is needed.

Their Narratives, Our Narrative, My Narrative

These days, when people of good will discuss the Arab-Israeli conflict, they often speak of reconciling two different "narratives." The Palestinian narrative is one of displacement and violence at the hands of the Israelis and betrayal by their Arab neighbors. The Israeli narrative is one of reclamation and survival, against all odds, in a sea of hostile neighbors. Neither side fully understands the historical roots of the other's behavior or acknowledges the other's grievances. To solve this conflict, advocates of dialogue and coexistence education tell us, Israelis and Palestinians must be able to see the world through the eyes of the "Other," they must appreciate that it is possible for a reasonable, ethical person to believe what the Other believes. Those are laudable, sensible goals.

But American Jews whose identities are bound up with Israel also have a distinct narrative. No one seems to care very much about seeing the world, and Israel, through our eyes. Our narrative, too, needs to be much better understood by anyone who wants a new approach to America's Middle East diplomacy. As much as the American Jewish mainstream sometimes infuriates me, I try to honor and respect its narrative in the ensuing pages. It is one that I absorbed at an early age, and it lingers within me.

Everyone who grew up thinking about and caring about Israel obviously has a singular story, a distinct set of associations with Zionism and the Jewish state. It will be useful to take a brief detour to recount my own Israel narrative, as it helps to explain the sensibilities that undergird some of the political ideas presented here.

My maternal grandmother, Pearl Weiner, once told me that she became a Zionist when she was a young girl in Ukraine, shortly after hearing stories about the infamous bloody pogrom against the Jews of Kishinev, in 1904. All of my other grandparents from the former Soviet Union were Zionists to one degree or another, although all of them eventually washed ashore in New York City—where they had relatives—rather than Palestine. One of Pearl's proudest moments was hosting Golda Myerson, a fiery Labor Zionist who later changed her last name to Meir, at a fundraising event in Ohio, where my grandparents spent a few years in the 1930s.

In 1948 my parents, Chana Weiner and Moishe Fleshler, met on a *chava*, a training camp in New Jersey for young idealistic socialists planning to start a Labor Zionist kibbutz in the soon-to-be-born Jewish state. They decided to stay in the United States when my mother became pregnant with my older brother, but many of their friends moved on and founded Kibbutz Gesher Haziv in the Galilee. As a teenager, I attended a camp run by Habonim, a Zionist youth movement. When I was fourteen, I met a woman during visiting day, who, upon hearing my name, said, "That can't be you. You're supposed to be in Israel!"

That was a lingering refrain, I think, of my parents' life when I was young. They loved America, but they were also supposed to be in Israel, where everyone would have called them Moshe and Chana. Instead, my father, aka

"Maurice," ended up as an industrial engineer in northeast Pennsylvania. Instead of organizing the kitchen on a kibbutz, as she had planned to do, my mother, aka "Anna," became a hospital dietician.

So Israel's story was interwined with my own. In the spring of 1967, it could not have meant more to me. Shortly after we moved from Pennsylvania to Queens, New York, in March of that year, my father died, suddenly and without warning, of a heart attack. I was twelve. About two months later, the radio and TV newscasters and the people in my new synagogue were talking incessantly about Israel's desperate straits, about the mobs in the streets of Cairo and Damascus calling for Israel's destruction. Still stunned and shell-shocked from my personal loss, I tried to collect money from my new neighbors to help protect Israel, which, I had been told by any number of grownups, was about to be exterminated unless we helped—unless *I* helped. The metaphor wasn't lost on me as I went from door to door in my apartment building: maybe, with my help, the Israelis would live, even if my dad had not. So Israel's victory in the Six Day War, in June 1967, was literally my victory, too.

Three years later, my mother married an old family friend from Connecticut, Willie Tilow, whom she had known from the "movement." He had crewed on the *Ellul*, one of the boats that brought Holocaust survivors to Palestine's shores, where they tried to run the British blockade against Jewish immigration. One of his proudest moments came when the British arrested him and sent him to jail for a few months in Atlit, on the coast south of Haifa. He eventually returned to the States and for a number of years worked for a New York outpost of the Israeli government, trying—among other things—to arrange private financing for weapons meant for Israel. Willie had three sons, all of whom took a shot at living in Israel, one of whom is still there.

What a heroic, noble story I inherited! All of these tough, ornery idealists, fashioning a new land out of swamp and sand, calling out "Never again!" again and again, to nations that had either tried to slaughter them or done nothing to stop the slaughter.

Oh yes, there was the little bothersome matter of the people who used to live in Palestine. Where were they? What had happened to them? I don't recall thinking about them for more than a few minutes during the first sixteen years of my life. The story I had been fed was that they had run away in 1948 because the Arab leaders had told them to, and they expected to return after all the Jews were annihilated. But they couldn't return. They were nowhere. End of story. Let's help make the desert bloom.

By the early 1970s, another narrative was in the air. It was recounted mostly by the New Lefties, the same intriguing radicals who were spouting rhetoric about Vietnam and the corruptions of the military-industrial complex. They were putting Israel in the same despicable enemy camp as AmeriKa, and any half-awake young adult with liberal sensibilities had to listen and take them seriously. At a Passover seder in 1971, when I was sixteen, my older brother, a Yale student who was dabbling in the Students for a Democratic Society, urged us all to read from a special *Haggadah* that included selections about Palestinians under occupation and a piece by Eldridge Cleaver, the Black Panther. My stepfather glanced at it for a moment, then howled, "Eldridge Cleaver drinks tea with Yasser Arafat!" End of story. Cleaver, and the Palestinians, had no place at the table.

Inevitably and gradually, while sitting at other tables, I learned more about an entirely different story, which was available to those who wanted to hear it. Clearly, something terrible—and, at times, terribly brutal—had happened to an entire people other than the Jewish people, and something had to be done, and no one had an answer.

During the mid-1970s and early 1980s, while at Harvard College and graduate school in Iowa, as a professor in Michigan and then a writer and public relations executive in New York City, I noticed that people who focused on this issue were divided into either fierce defenders or fierce attackers of Israel. I found myself arguing with both of them with equal conviction. Ramming Jewish settlements down the throats of a hostile, occupied Palestinian population in the West Bank was certainly not the answer. Expanding a limited attack on Lebanon into a full-scale war and marching to Beirut and bombing entire neighborhoods were not the answers either. Neither was blowing up Israeli schoolchildren or slaughtering foreign tourists in European airports or throwing Leon Klinghoffer, a disabled American Jew, off a boat in the Mediterranean—all of which, to me, watching from afar, appeared to be the only tactics employed by Palestinian advocates.

It was, paradoxically, concern about Palestinian suffering that coaxed me back to the pro-Israeli cause once again. In the fall of 1982, headlines blared news of the massacre of hundreds of Palestinian refugees in the Sabra and Shatila refugee camps, in Lebanon. Maronite Lebanese Christians committed the crime, but it was apparent from the start that the Israeli army and Defense Minister Ariel Sharon had done nothing to stop the massacre and were probably complicit in some way.[24] It was appalling. The Israelis, more to the point, seemed appalling, beyond repair. Reading the accounts of Palestinian agony, I was furious with the Israelis, furious at all of their knee-jerk apologists in the American media, furious at Likud prime minister Menachem Begin's infamous complaint, "*Goyim* kill *goyim*, and they blame the Jews." But, fortunately, a different, more positive Israel soon presented itself, and the fury abated a bit, when hundreds of thousands of Israelis rose up at a rally organized by the Peace Now movement, demanding Sharon's resignation, insisting that their government be held accountable.

Peace Now had been founded in 1978 by 350 Israeli reserve officers who were afraid Menachem Begin was going to miss the chance for peace that had been offered by Egyptian president Anwar Sadat. I had been only dimly aware of them, but a little research revealed they were speaking out, passionately and sensibly, about the costs of the Israeli occupation and the need to pursue every opportunity for territorial compromise. They didn't have the complete answer either, but at least they were trying to write a different story, to stop what seemed like an utterly mad settlements policy and shape a future different from the one I'd associated with Israel during the years when Likud reigned.

Within a year, I joined a group called North American Friends of Peace Now (which eventually became Americans for Peace Now). In New York City, we met in tiny upper West Side apartments. Along with similar chapters in Los Angeles, Durham, North Carolina, and a few other early outposts, we tried to figure out how to build support within the American Jewish community for eventually giving up the territories, for talking to the

Palestinian Liberation Organization (PLO), and for creating a Jewish state we wouldn't be ashamed of. It was slow going. Few American Jews in synagogues or established organizations wanted much to do with us at first. Few left-wing American Jews who were not Zionists wanted anything to do with us (they still don't). We spent years trying, as the Israelis say, to "walk through the raindrops," dipping and darting, insisting that we worried about Israel's future even as we harangued it for many of its policies.

Professionally and personally, I gradually became immersed in the mainstream American Jewish community. As a media consultant, my clients included a number of different Jewish groups, from B'nai B'rith to Israel Policy Forum. The latter was set up in 1993 at the behest of Prime Minister Yitzhak Rabin, who wanted help in building support for the Oslo peace process among American Jewish leaders, especially those connected with mainstream Jewish community organizations.

When one spends a lot of time with American Jewish clients and causes, one learns the code words and concepts that irritate or frighten Jews in the organized community. I learned, through a hit-or-miss process, what was required to make at least some of them comfortable with helping Israel's peace camp—e.g., using the phrase *Israel's security* in at least every other paragraph in newspaper ads. I learned what the community would not or could not publicly endorse and how far it would go in the direction of Palestinian rights and aspirations. I learned the paradigms of the American Jewish-Israeli relationship, the rules of the game, and the stories that American Jewish leaders told themselves so that they could look at themselves in the mirror every morning. Unless one knows those stories, unless one acknowledges and appreciates that many decent human beings are telling them, one can't get a hearing for other stories.

But it is time for American Jews who care about Israel to find new ways of expressing themselves, new forms of activism to help both America and Israel address today's challenges. And it is time to join together with others in the United States who see no contradiction between being pro-American, pro-Israeli, and pro-Palestinian.

"America and Israel are like an old married couple that do things out of habit and don't even know why they are together anymore," said Jerry

Goodman, former head of the National Committee for Labor Israel and a prominent activist for Soviet Jewry. "You could say the same thing about American Jews and Israel. The world is changing all around both of these couples but they stay in the same old rut."

Israel, the Arab world, and America need them to get out of that rut.

Moving the Pieces

There is a jigsaw puzzle that must be completed in order for peace to have a fighting chance, and the American Jewish community forms a small part of it. The puzzle has many pieces. All of them are on the table, but they are all askew, none of them are where they should be. Some of them need to move farther than others.

This book focuses on a few of them, the domestic political pieces, especially Jewish and non-Jewish American citizens who are passionate moderates, who believe the United States needs to work much harder to break up Amichai's relay race of howling orphans. Fitting them into the puzzle, in turn, will make it much easier for the most important American pieces to move into the places where they belong: the U.S. president, his foreign policy team, and members of Congress.

But even if that happens, the puzzle will be incomplete. Without brave, bold Israeli, Palestinian, Syrian, and other leaders in the region, and without help from the rest of the international community, not much will ever change. There is only so much anyone here can do, good or bad.

Still, the U.S. government needs to do what it can. "If you will it," Herzl famously wrote, "it is no dream." One of the splendid things about America is that it encourages people to believe that anything is possible, including a political climate in which American leaders are emboldened, if and when it is necessary, to press, prod, and challenge Israel as well as its neighbors.

1

Passion, Money, and Smoke and Mirrors: AIPAC and Congress

Although more than a few groups try to represent American Jews in the corridors of power, AIPAC is the main engine of the conventional Israel lobby in Washington. It is the only organization officially chartered to lobby the U.S. government on behalf of a strong U.S.-Israel relationship. And it is the principal target of those who believe there is something unseemly and dangerous about American Jews devoting so much passion and money to help a foreign power. Any effort to gauge the strengths and vulnerabilities of America's traditional pro-Israel forces must begin by opening up AIPAC's hood and poking around.

Jim Besser is a reporter who has covered the American Jewish political scene in Washington for Jewish weekly newspapers since the late 1980s. "When I first started working, someone who'd been around Washington a long time explained the way things worked," he told me. "He said, 'There are three branches of government. The first is the Tobacco Institute. The second is the NRA [National Rifle Association]. The third is AIPAC.'"

But lobbies come and lobbies go in Washington. Power ebbs and flows. The Tobacco Institute is no more, and the tobacco lobby has been gutted. The NRA is still a powerhouse, but at least it is challenged aggressively by gun control advocates. It is not set in stone that AIPAC will retain its bragging rights forever. Right now, though, AIPAC is so formidable that casual observers can be forgiven for believing that it is an immoveable political object that no force can dislodge.

The Greatest Jewish Show on Earth

The most conspicuous and unsubtle demonstrations of AIPAC's power are its storied annual policy conferences in Washington. I have been attending these events for years as an observer and as the Jewish peace camp's equivalent of a Log Cabin Republican, believing that if you can't get a seat at the table with these people, at least you should be in the room and take their measure. Any of the policy conferences could be selected to demonstrate the organization's clout: the one held on May 22–24, 2005, was one of the most memorable, and it is especially illustrative of AIPAC's sway with America's political elite because it occurred at a moment when the organization, believe it or not, seemed vulnerable.

It was a difficult, agonizing spring for AIPAC. A few months before, Larry Franklin, a Pentagon official who had supplied confidential information to two AIPAC officials—Steven Rosen and Keith Weissman—about Iran, had been indicted. Rumors were circulating that Rosen and Weissman would soon receive the same treatment for passing the information on to the Israeli government and an American reporter. The two had been fired before the policy conference convened, but news reports indicated that for years, the FBI had been investigating AIPAC as a whole, not just a few rogue employees. At the time, no one—except, presumably, federal officials—knew if more revelations would be divulged about untoward behavior by other AIPAC officials.

The Jewish media had been running stories that speculated about whether AIPAC would be permanently tarnished, whether the group was losing some of its edge, whether American officials and even members of Congress would be leery of getting too close to its staffers. I heard knowledgeable people in the American Jewish community talking openly about the nature of life in Washington with a weakened AIPAC.

It turned out that the political elite used the conference as an opportunity to practically leap into the AIPACers' laps. For two days a steady stream of American and Israeli dignitaries flowed into the Washington Convention Center and Hilton to trumpet their pro-Israel credentials. The crowd heard from Secretary of State Condoleezza Rice, Democratic Party chairman Howard Dean, Senate Majority Leader Bill Frist, House Speaker Dennis Hastert, Senator Hillary Clinton, and other current or former federal officials and members of Congress in different sessions.

"How much clout does AIPAC have?" asked *Washington Post* reporter Dana Milbank, in an article on the 2005 conclave. "Well, consider that during the pro-Israel lobby's annual conference yesterday, a fleet of police cars, sirens wailing, blocked intersections and formed a motorcade carrying its conventioneers—to lunch."[1]

The entire three-day program was a spectacle of world-class power puffery and political theater, a combination of a manipulative Berthold Brecht play and a schmaltzy Veterans of Foreign Wars convention. In the FBI investigation's wake, the conference was orchestrated to demonstrate that the AIPACers were dyed-in-the-wool, fiercely patriotic Americans. As the *Forward* reported, "One AIPAC staffer, speaking on condition of anonymity, explained that in order to maintain its clout and effectiveness, AIPAC must be seen as a profoundly American group that is primarily interested in America's well-being."[2]

The opening plenary session set the all-American tone. In a large ballroom at the convention center, a gigantic banner behind the stage proclaimed that year's theme: "Israel, an American Value." Attendees sat at tables covered with napkins with designs that commingled the American and Israeli flags.

To be effective, propaganda needs to have many grains of truth, and AIPAC knows how to gather those grains, shine klieg lights on them, and celebrate them. Special recognition was given from the podium to a team of American law enforcement officials—"first responders"—who had recently returned from Israel. A videotape showed AIPAC board members from both parties expounding on the privilege of being citizen activists. They described how thrilling it was to walk the halls of Congress and present their opinions, exercising a right that the rest of the world envied. It was difficult not to be deeply moved because these people, most of them children or grandchildren of immigrants, could not have been more sincere about their gratitude for the opportunity to be living exemplars of democracy.

From the podium, AIPAC executive director Howard Kohr capped off the opening keynote speech by proclaiming, "What a gift we have been given by this country. What a legacy of liberty has been won for us. What a debt we owe Americans, a debt that demands devotion: the same willingness to put service above self and to stand on the side of liberty wherever it is under siege—in America, in Israel and everywhere in the world."[3]

Who, precisely, were these people Kohr was trying to rev up? Much of the blogosphere assumes all AIPACers are right-wing nuts, fanatic militarists, and Likud supporters. It would be much easier to sum up the organization if that were true, but "the participants at the policy conference are not a group of wild-eyed reactionaries," according to Judy Graham, a fellow board member of Ameinu who is a regular AIPAC conference attendee. "[They are] pretty much the people you would be sitting next to at Holy Holidays at a Conservative *shul* [synagogue]. Like most Jews, these are largely Democrats—not the most liberal Democrats, but still Democrats and mostly from New York, California, Chicago, Philly, Southern Florida, but also from the smaller Jewish communities like Tulsa, Salt Lake City, and Orlando. From these smaller communities, it is not uncommon for AIPAC activists to overlap heavily with the [charitable Jewish] Federation and local congregational leadership. AIPAC gives these people (mostly people of considerable wealth) a way to connect to Israel politically and also to connect with their local politicians on behalf of Israel. What AIPAC 'sells' them is a way to be informed about Israel and a way to be involved for Israel."[4]

Graham is correct. Most of the people who show up at these conferences and the rest of AIPAC's members can't be typecast as "neocons" or Likudniks, although AIPAC has its share of those. Most of them are simply worried about Israel. They come to these meetings expecting guidance and instruction from experts about how they—and America—can help to keep Israel safe. And, by and large, they do what they are told. When they cheered for Vice President Cheney in 2006 or Republican presidential candidate John McCain in 2008, they did so not because they were necessarily war-hungry right-wingers or Republican partisans. Barack Obama and Hillary Clinton also received many standing ovations when they addressed the AIPAC conference a few days after McCain's speech. The applause is part of a well-established ritual in which any American leader—whether a Christian Zionist like Reverend John Hagee or a liberal politician like Congresswoman Nancy Pelosi—who displays a resolute toughness toward Israel's enemies and an affection for the Jewish state will be greeted lovingly, as a friend.

On the second night of the 2005 conference, forty-seven senators, 215 members of the House, current and former U.S. officials, governors, and dozens of other dignitaries dutifully trudged to the annual AIPAC dinner. Kohr and AIPAC board members performed the roll call, intoning the names of every member of Congress in attendance along with other notables, occasionally pausing for applause from attendees at tables in every available space in the conference center's large main ballroom. That rite of unapologetic, chest-beating self-promotion occurs at countless dinners throughout Washington, but no group has a longer or more impressive guest list than AIPAC.

The next day, more than two thousand citizen lobbyists fanned out on Capitol Hill to promote tough sanctions against Iran to stop its nuclear research, support for Ariel Sharon's unilateral withdrawal plan from the Gaza Strip, and sustained financial and military aid to Israel. In 2008 about three thousand participated. There is no organization or company in America that turns out so many volunteers for a day's worth of congressional lobbying, each and every year.

The Machinery of Influence

"The thing you need to understand about AIPAC is that it is more about Washington than it is about Israel. It is more about getting a political win and showing political muscle and staying in the game than helping Israel,"according to a former AIPAC staffer.

I have heard several AIPAC-watchers go so far as to say that some of the group's staff members—many of whom are former congressional aides or federal bureaucrats—don't much care about Israel and could just as easily be pushing for breaks for soybean growers or steel manufacturers. That is probably overstating the case, but it is hard to argue with the assessment of Larry Cohler-Esses, a reporter for New York *Jewish Week* who covered Capitol Hill in the 1980s and 1990s: "The old-time American Zionists were Jews who understood that they needed Washington to help them get victories for Israel; the new, AIPAC Zionists are Beltway players who use Israel to help them get victories in Washington."

Capitol Hill is the realm where AIPAC exerts the most influence and makes the most noise and inspires the most fear. Most members of Congress, especially in the House of Representatives, take the path of least resistance when dealing with it. They reflexively endorse documents that AIPAC has drafted or helped to draft. Sometimes they add their own flourishes to existing bills, as M. J. Rosenberg writes: "Routinely, Members of Congress . . . look to score political points by offering amendments designed to highlight their anti-Arab (and especially anti-Palestinian) bona fides. It does not matter to them whether the amendments offered are likely to actually become law, whether they advance US policy goals or whether, if implemented, they would benefit Israel. The point is to go on record as blasting Palestinians in the hope that pro-Israel donors and voters believe that anything that hurts Palestinians helps Israel and that they will reward them accordingly."[5]

There are usually a few of these showboat resolutions and amendments or "Dear Colleague" letters every congressional term. A month after the 2005 AIPAC policy conference, the House of Representatives discussed a resolution (HR144) that noted that Palestinians killed fifty-three U.S. citizens since the September 13, 1993, signing of the Oslo Accords and listed the names. HR 144 mentioned that terrorism "continues to happen . . . despite the recent elections and a new sense of optimism in the region." (The "optimism" followed the election in January of Palestinian Authority president Mahmoud Abbas, a relative moderate, in the wake of Yasser Arafat's death.) During the floor debate, Rep. Steve King (R-Iowa) took the trouble to rise before the C-Span cameras and bravely propose an amendment "condemning attacks on United States citizens by Palestinian terrorists." The amendment was adopted by a roll call vote of 423-0.[6]

Although much of this congressional paperwork does not directly affect policy or compel presidents to do anything, that doesn't mean it is irrelevant. It is part of a constant stream of messages that convey to the executive branch and the rest of the world the impassioned support of Congress for anything and everything Israel does, or at least anything and everything AIPAC and the conventional Israel lobby want. These messages have helped to stoke anti-American sentiment in the Muslim world.

One of the most shameful examples of this was a resolution passed at the height of the Palestinian intifada, on May 2, 2002. It was a time of tit-for-tat, increasingly brutal violence. By any reasonable standard, both sides shared responsibility for the deterioration of relations and the bloody mayhem. AIPAC and others in the conventional Israel lobby were anticipating White House pressure on Prime Minister Ariel Sharon to restrain Israel's response and take steps to calm things down. So, the House passed a bill that called for additional American aid to Israel, held Arafat and the Palestinian Authority completely responsible for the violence, and said not a word about Israel's contributions to the tensions. The vote was 352-21. The Senate passed a somewhat milder bill, 94-2.[7]

Several interrelated reasons explain why AIPAC and its congressional allies are able to drum up support for these one-sided legislative actions so often, and so easily. A look at what makes lawmakers defer to AIPAC reveals much that is unpleasant about decision making on *all* issues that are discussed on Capitol Hill, where votes are influenced by a mélange of factors that include political ambition, greed, cowardice, laziness, ignorance, and, yes, mixed somewhere in there, consideration of what is good for America. Yet it also reveals that some of AIPAC's impact can be attributed to power puffery and widespread misconceptions about the nature and extent of American Jewish influence.

Money and Illusion

Of course, the most important enforcement mechanism for AIPAC and any other successful lobby is money, both given and withheld.

Mearsheimer and Walt offer the uncontroversial idea that "AIPAC's success is due in large part to its ability to reward legislators and congressional candidates who support its agenda and to punish those who do not, based mainly on its ability to influence campaign contributions. Money is critical to U.S. elections, which have become increasingly expensive to win, and AIPAC makes sure its friends get strong financial support so long as they do not stray from AIPAC's line."[8]

The mythic, mysterious power of so-called Jewish money in American politics is grist for the mill of conventional Israel lobby bashers who are less restrained than Mearsheimer and Walt. It is a small step from the two academics' matter-of-fact assertions to the hysterical, sweeping conclusions about AIPAC and money that now clog the Internet. Here is a typical, digital screed from a radical libertarian named Ted Lang: "Our entire government is controlled by Israel! Through a small, rich and powerful Jewish supported tax-exempt lobby, the American Israel Public Affairs Committee, or simply AIPAC, virtually all American domestic and foreign policy is now being controlled by a foreign government entanglement."[9]

And here are the charges former U.S. Senator James Abourezk (D-South Dakota) made in a speech to the American-Arab Anti-Discrimination Committee: "That is the state of American politics today. The Israel lobby has put together so much money power that we are daily witnessing U.S. Senators and representatives bowing down low to Israel and its U.S. lobby. Make no mistake. The votes and bows have nothing to do with legislators' love for Israel. They have everything to do with the money that is fed into their campaigns by the Israel lobby."[10]

In part because they didn't want to associate themselves with such overheated comments for fear of fomenting anti-Semitism, few experts on the role of American Jewish campaign contributions would talk to me on the record about the subject. They were also worried that attaching their names to any quote on this volatile topic would offend AIPAC and the rest of the organized Jewish community. But unless the impact of right-wing Jewish contributions on American politics is assessed—coolly and calmly—and clearly understood, it will be much more difficult to lessen that impact and encourage politicians to listen to other voices.

Despite its name, AIPAC is not a political action committee and cannot legally raise money for candidates. Its individual members contribute or raise campaign funds privately, and they are not supposed to do either one under AIPAC's auspices. And thirty-plus PACs funded by people who generally share AIPAC's take on Middle East issues play an equally important role in the organization's network of influence.

While it can't publicly endorse candidates, AIPAC gives clear signals about who deserves money and who doesn't. One source of guidance is a kind of political report card, the "AIPAC Insider," which gives information on every legislator's voting record on bills, amendments, and other congressional initiatives that AIPAC deems important. Other guidance comes from the advice, importuning, and campaign-related activities of AIPAC adherents acting in their individual capacities. There is some dispute about whether or not the Israel-oriented PACs take cues from AIPAC and communicate with one another, but there is no doubt that concentrated amounts of money from the same PACs flow into the coffers of many of the same candidates during election cycles.[11]

Just how much is this money machine generating for members of Congress? Are the amounts so large that lawmakers can't afford to lose these contributions and thus will always do AIPAC's bidding? In some cases, yes. But when it comes to the impact of political fundraising, AIPAC's most important tool is the widespread *perception* that it is a major source of campaign gifts, which is often not reflected in reality.

It is impossible to quantify with any precision the amount of money the AIPAC network gives to politicians. But it is possible to get a sense of its relative importance in the pantheon of America's political donors.

First, though, it is important to note that Jewish money in American politics should not be conflated with contributions from the conventional Israel lobby. There is no doubt that American Jews contribute much more than their proportionate share of donations to American politicians. One commonly accepted although unproven estimate is that Jewish donors account for about 50 percent of the Democratic National Committee's budget. About 20 percent of contributions raised by Republicans in presidential campaigns also come from American Jewish donors, according to some estimates.[12] But most Jewish political donors give mainly because they are liberals on domestic issues or have strong opinions about matters that have little or nothing to do with Israel.

"As with every other aspect of Jewish politics . . . the [pro-Israel] PAC fascination is misleading," J. J. Goldberg noted in *Jewish Power*. "'Jewish money is certainly the biggest chunk of money in the Democratic party,' says a political consultant who specializes in fundraising. 'But when you talk about Jewish money, pro-Israel money is a relatively small piece of the puzzle.'"[13]

Another common misconception is that the wealthiest Jewish political donors tend to be right-wing. In fact, as a group, they are not monolithic in their support for AIPAC's line or even for Israel itself. For example, individuals and organizations can and do pour millions of dollars into so-called 527 organizations, which are supposed to promote policies and ideas but not specific candidates. The top four individual donors to 527s in the 2004 election cycle were Jews: George Soros, Peter Lewis, Steven Bing, and Herb and Marion Sandler.[14] Soros, Lewis, and the Sandlers are all supporters of ultraliberal domestic causes and, when it comes to Israel, are far to the left of the conventional Israel lobby. In 2007 all three donors or their representatives reportedly engaged in serious conversation with activists who were trying to organize a new alternative to that lobby. This effort eventually resulted in the J Street project.[15]

Finally, and most important, the AIPAC funding network is not as wealthy as is commonly assumed. This becomes apparent if one looks at the website of the Center for Responsive Politics (www.opensecrets.org), which painstakingly analyzes Federal Election Commission (FEC) records. The CRP divides most PACs and individual political donors into "industries" (both corporate and ideological). One of them is called the "pro-Israel industry," which consists mainly of people and PACs in the AIPAC-influenced network.* That industry ranked fortieth out of the top fifty industries that gave to Congress during the 2004 election cycle. It ranked twenty-sixth in 2006.

* *Pro-Israel* is an unfortunate term because I don't believe all of these people or groups are always helping Israel, but for the time being, it will be used for the sake of simplicity.

The CRP-designated pro-Israel industry contributed $5.1 million to congressional incumbents for the 2004 races.* But "lawyers and law firms," the top-ranked industry, contributed more than $86 million, about seventeen times as much as the pro-Israel crowd. Retirees, mainly via AARP, were number two, donating more than $50 million. The real estate industry was number three, with close to $35 million.[16] These three are part of an elite group of major league influence-buying machines in Washington, which includes Big Pharma, the insurers, the defense industry, and other, mostly corporate interests. Compared to them, the AIPAC/pro-Israel network is more like a Triple A franchise that tries to convince people that it belongs in the major leagues. Indeed, if campaign contributions were all that were needed to get congressional obedience, legislators would bow down even lower to accountants and crop producers. Both of those industries routinely outspend the AIPAC/pro-Israel network.

I don't meant to imply that the conventional Israel lobby's political fundraising apparatus is unimpressive. $5 million flowing into congressional coffers during one election cycle is a lot of money. In addition, AIPAC's fifty-odd board members and other people close to the organization are important political players. According to FEC records, AIPAC board members contributed an average of about $70,000 each to campaigns and political action committees in both parties since 2000. One out of five was a top fundraiser for either Bush or Kerry in the 2004 presidential campaign.[17]

Yet, the AIPAC-influenced network does not contribute substantial amounts to *most* individual members of Congress, although it has a big impact on some races. According to Goldberg, who studied this issue closely in the early 1990s, "Congressional races . . . vary widely in their ability to attract Jewish money. Jewish fundraising efforts tend to be targeted at individual legislators with the closest ties to the Jewish community. These may be Jewish

* With a few exceptions, I am using the CRP's data from 2004 to analyze the impact of AIPAC's fundraising network. The data from 2008 are less useful for assessing political contributions from the conventional Israel lobby. That is because the CRP chose to include J Street as one of the PACs in the pro-Israel industry in 2008, even though J Street generally didn't endorse the same candidates as the other PACs.

lawmakers, sympathetic lawmakers in key decision-making positions . . . or simply good friends."[18]

A congressional staffer with decades of political fundraising experience said, "Except when they are really trying to punish somebody, which doesn't happen that much, I would say the AIPAC types contribute, at most, maybe 10 percent of a campaign." Usually, he indicated, they contribute much less. And, usually, campaigns could survive easily without these contributions.

Following the Money

Let's try to follow the money for Representative Dennis Hastert (R-Illinois). The former Speaker of the House, he was and is the kind of powerful political player the cabal watchers claim is beholden to the Israel lobby. In 2004 he was the eleventh-ranked recipient from the pro-Israel industry in the House, according to the CRP.[19] But notice which industry is missing from the breakdown of Hastert's personal top-20 in table 1 (page 41).

The "pro-Israel industry" didn't even make the cut. Moreover, of the $4.8 million Hastert raised for the 2004 race, he received a little more than 1 percent (about $48,500) from that industry.[20]

Now, it is almost certain that the pro-Israel industry's total is artificially low because of the way the CRP calculates it. The CRP defines that industry as the combination of Israel-oriented PACs plus individuals who contribute to these PACs. No doubt some of the financial executives, retirees, lawyers, doctors, and others at the top of Hastert's chart were hawkish on Israel, but they were not categorized as part of the pro-Israel industry. No doubt at least some of them made their views on Israel known to Hastert or his people (who did not agree to be interviewed on this topic).

When I brought this issue up to Douglas Webber, one of the CRP researchers, he acknowledged that they probably "undercounted" explicitly pro-Israel contributions. Asked if it would be possible to double the amount in that category for Hastert, he said, in no uncertain terms, "No, that's not possible. We couldn't be that far off." But even if he is wrong, and even if Hastert received twice or even thrice that amount from Jews who agreed with AIPAC, they still would have accounted for a relatively small percentage of his campaign funds. He didn't need their help.

Table 1. TOP-20 INDUSTRY CONTRIBUTORS TO REPRESENTATIVE DENNIS HASTERT (2004 ELECTION CYCLE)

Industry	Amount
Securities and Investment	$357,075
Retired	$216,850
Lawyers/Law Firms	$202,959
Health Professionals	$189,150
Real Estate	$174,474
Pharmaceuticals/Health Products	$156,750
Construction Services	$143,850
Insurance	$133,249
Commercial Banks	$118,900
General Contractors	$110,250
Oil and Gas	$106,300
Air Transport	$105,300
Agricultural Services/Products	$90,641
Automotive	$85,350
Business Services	$84,825
Miscellaneous Finance	$83,500
Electric Utilities	$82,300
TV/Movies/Music	$75,000
Miscellaneous Manufacturing and Distributing	$73,500
Hospitals/Nursing Homes	$70,996

Source: Center for Responsive Politics, "Top Industries for Dennis Hastert, 2004," http://www.opensecrets.org/politicians/industries.php?cycle=2004&cid=N0000478.

Moreover, there were 424 representatives who received less money than Dennis Hastert from the AIPAC/pro-Israel network in 2004. In other words, *AIPAC actually had a marginal impact on most House races.*

The same thing is true for the Senate, where, for example, the twentieth-ranked recipient from the pro-Israel industry in 2004 was Jim Bunning (R-Kentucky).[21] The industry gave him about $78,000 for the 2004 election. The breakdown of his top-20 contributors appears in table 2 (page 42).

Table 2. Top-20 Industry Contributors to Senator Jim Bunning (2004 Election Cycle)	
Health Professionals	$336,831
Insurance	$320,971
Securities and Investment	$279,506
Retired	$279,011
Leadership PACs	$263,331
Lawyers/Law Firms	$261,334
Real Estate	$207,964
Commercial Banks	$165,463
Lobbyists	$156,471
Electric Utilities	$120,607
Oil and Gas	$116,269
Miscellaneous Manufacturing and Distributing	$107,933
Beer, Wine, and Liquor	$83,418
Pharmaceuticals/Health Products	$82,633
Republican/Conservative	$81,026
Miscellaneous Finance	$77,925
Pro-Israel	**$77,650**
General Contractors	$75,650
Hospitals/Nursing Homes	$75,085
Mining	$72,250

Source: Center for Responsive Politics, "Top Industries for Jim Bunning, 2004," http://www.opensecrets.org/politicians/industries.php?cid=N00003437&cycle=2004.

Even if we assume the CRP undercounted and we arbitrarily double the total Bunning received from the AIPAC network, their help would not have been critically important: they would have accounted for about 2 percent of the $6.5 million he raised for the 2004 race.[22] Furthermore, eighty senators received even less than Bunning from the AIPAC/pro-Israel network that year. So it is hard to make the case that this network "owns" or manipulates the Senate on the basis of financial contributions alone.

The AIPACers do contribute enough so that, when combined with grassroots activism, their money is noticed. No politician would go out of his or her way to turn it down. But, if they *chose* to, most lawmakers could politely disagree with AIPAC or not vote the way it wants on every initiative without taking a big chunk out of their campaign budgets. And yet, of course, most of them don't.

Smoke and mirrors account for some of this resistance. Incumbents and candidates in states and districts with few Jewish voters tend to be especially impressed when they first encounter what appears to be a vast, tightly woven web of like-minded, well-heeled donors.

As one AIPAC staffer explained to me, "Some first-time candidate from Idaho will get a call that invites him to come to New York or Atlanta, meet some Jewish leaders and . . . be guaranteed $10,000. The $10,000 is the minimum amount he would require to get to New York, so he agrees." He meets five people who each give their maximum allowable contribution of $2,000. These contributions are bundled together, "and he gets a very strong message. He's not going to forget those people."

No wonder he is impressed. He is impressed for the same reason that Lord Balfour and Lloyd George were impressed by Chaim Weizmann during World War I. This politician has been hearing all his life about "Jewish money" and "Jewish power," and if he believes he can come to New York and finally tap into it as he runs his race in rural Idaho, he is not going to refuse the help. Their money somehow *seems* more important than money bundled from five local farmers or five local realtors. And, if he is elected, he will think twice about offending the people he met in New York, as he doesn't want to foreclose the possibility of getting even more help from them and their friends around the country.

But the most important reason why most lawmakers don't want to mess with AIPAC is raw, not entirely rational fear.

The Atomic Bomb of Fear

First-time congressional staffers learn the litany of lawmakers whose careers were ruined when, after daring to cross AIPAC's path, money from the Jewish grassroots poured into their opponents' campaigns. The most well-known and resentful victim of the AIPAC network's wrath is Paul Findley, the Illinois Republican who blames Israel's supporters for his defeat in the 1982 election, mostly because he met with Yasser Arafat and called him a "great champion of human rights." In his book, *They Dare to Speak Out*, he details a number of similar revenge campaigns orchestrated in the 1980s by the conventional Israel lobby that supposedly led to the electoral defeats of congressional incumbents and other politicians, including Representative Pete McCloskey of California, Senator Charles Percy of Illinois, and Senator Roger Jepsen of Iowa.[23]

But, surprisingly, the concern that AIPAC and its grassroots troops will target incumbents who take an independent path on Israel is usually unwarranted. "They have an atomic bomb of fear," said Jeremy Rabinovitz, former chief of staff to Rep. Lois Capps (D-California), when I interviewed him about AIPAC. "People think they can defeat incumbents and blow up campaigns. It's a weapon members think they will use. But it's just not true that the Jewish community will sweep in and go after you if don't vote the way AIPAC wants you to. . . . That's a myth."

Most of the widely publicized incidents of the organized punishments exacted by AIPAC occurred in the 1980s. But the legend that the AIPAC network can topple elected officials received a big boost in 2002, when "Jewish money" from all over the country poured into Georgia and Alabama to defeat two African-American members of Congress running in Democratic primaries: Earl Hilliard and Cynthia McKinney. Both had voted against the one-sided, AIPAC-inspired resolution condemning the Palestinian intifada in 2002. Both had called for evenhandedness in U.S. Middle East policy and had otherwise irritated the conventional Israel lobby. When they lost, both blamed the role of out-of-state Jewish PACs and individuals. When McKinney's father, a former congressman, was asked to explain his daughter's defeat, he said, "J-E-W-S."

The role of out-of-state contributions from American Jews in both campaigns is often trumpeted by critics of AIPAC and its allies as proof of inordinate Jewish power. They are probably giving American Jewish donors too much credit. Both McKinney and Hilliard had many other problems before the 2002 primaries. They had lost a large part of their political bases because of redistricting. And both had other issues that drove voters away, including McKinney's controversial statement that President Bush had known about 9/11 in advance.[24]

The most important point about McKinney and Hilliard is that they were targeted for defeat by the AIPACers *because they were politically vulnerable*. The PACs and individuals who are on AIPAC's side pick fights only when they know they can win. McKinney and Hilliard were low-hanging fruit, easy to pick off. They were ideal tools for a rare demonstration project, a warning to the rest of Capitol Hill.

"The amount of [AIPAC-inspired] money moving through most races is actually quite small," J Street's Jeremy Ben-Ami told me. That is one of the reasons why he and his cohorts believe it is possible to have an impact on the political landscape even with a relatively limited budget.

I sometimes encounter or hear from AIPAC-haters who are disgusted by the idea of trying to borrow lessons from its success. They take a holier-than-thou, Pollyannaish view of its tactics; they grumble about the way it takes advantage of the sometimes unsavory combination of money, influence-peddling, media manipulation and other activities that define our political culture. But the rules of the Washington game are the same for any group that wants to have an impact on national policies. "So much of their access is tied into the corruption of our political process, which means money," says Cohler-Esses, describing AIPAC. "That is not something Jews invented, but the only way to counteract it is to buy into that process."

Power, Yearning, and Ignorance

Even in American politics, money isn't everything. Other components of AIPAC's operation must be countered if an alternative political bloc is going to have a chance.

The power of annoyance. AIPAC's staff is unusually adept at exploiting a personality trait that runs deep in virtually every member of Congress, one that I have never seen documented before: incumbents on the Hill have a *deep-seated yearning to not be bothered.* "Members know they'll encounter a high degree of annoying things every day: visits from lobbyists on every issue under the sun, calls from key donors, events they don't want to go to," says Rabinovitz. "They just kind of want to float through the day as much as possible. They want to deal with their pet project. They don't want to deal with calls all the time from people who are upset about something else."

With an easily activated network of enthusiastic, dedicated key contacts in most congressional districts, AIPAC can be exceptionally bothersome. Its network includes major financial contributors, community leaders, and rabbis, but also ordinary folks who are willing to send e-mails and faxes and even roam the halls of Congress if AIPAC directs them to. Since Israel-related issues aren't the primary concerns or priorities of most members, when they are asked to sign something by AIPAC, they'll go along to get along, and above all else, to avoid being annoyed.

The power of energized voters. The impact of persistently bothersome grassroots activism is magnified in districts and states where Jewish votes can have a tangible impact on races. About 89 percent of America's 5 million Jews live in twelve states. They are concentrated in a few large metropolitan areas, and they vote in much higher proportions than other ethnic or religious groups. (For some members, the Christian Zionist vote matters, and that group also tends to veer rightward on matters related to Israel.)

Yet even in districts where Jews are few and far between, members of Congress have exaggerated notions of their numbers. This is another tool that helps AIPAC in the game of perception management. As Jerry Goodman, former executive director of the National Committee for Labor Israel, once joked at a board meeting we both attended, "Congress thinks AIPAC represents all 40 million American Jews."

Still, if polls consistently show that most American Jewish voters are to the left of AIPAC, why do the legislators who represent them not worry too much about these more dovish constituents? One deceptively simple explanation is most American Jews who are sympathetic to Israel's peace camp just don't *care* enough. American Jews, as a whole, have been distancing themselves from Israel. Only about 26 percent of American Jews said they felt very attached to Israel in a 2005 poll by Stephen M. Cohen of the Hebrew University; that percentage has been steadily shrinking during the last fifteen years.[25]

"One of the biggest misconceptions people have is that every Jew in this country focuses on this issue," said Robert K. Lifton, former chairman and one of the founders of Israel Policy Forum, as well as a former president of the American Jewish Congress. "When I tried to raise money for IPF, I constantly encountered people [American Jews] who didn't care very much or weren't all that interested. Some would say, 'Bob, what do I need this for? Let them [Arabs and Israelis] work it out themselves.' In your average affluent club, there are maybe three or four people who have strong feelings about Israel, one or way the other. Everyone else in the club who is Jewish probably wants Israel to succeed but they're not very involved with it."

To American Jewish hawks, Israeli security is often their mission in life, not just their most important political priority. Today, they are the ones who fan out on Capitol Hill and threaten to withhold campaign contributions when politicians don't toe the AIPAC line. And they have mastered the art of annoying politicians and letting them know their votes are being monitored vigilantly.

Liberal American Jews, in contrast, are not single issue voters; they care about a host of issues. A survey of American Jews by the *Forward* in November 2007 revealed that Israel was the most important campaign issue for a tiny minority: "When asked to pick their most important campaign issue from a list of options, 23% of those surveyed named the economy and jobs, followed by health care (19%), the war in Iraq (16%), terrorism and national security (14%), support for Israel (6%), immigration (6%) and the energy crisis (6%)."[26] As a result, relatively few American Jews to the left of the conventional Israel lobby become agitated enough to call or e-mail members of Congress about Israel. More important, they don't care enough to threaten or annoy politicians for voting the wrong way on Israel.

The power of ignorance. Given all the media coverage of the Arab-Israeli conflict and the Middle East in general, and given the region's importance, it would be logical to assume that members of Congress and their staffs have a modicum of familiarity with issues of concern to the conventional Israel lobby. I certainly assumed that when I started to interview people on Capitol Hill for this book. I was wrong. The level of ignorance is, in fact, alarming. If they don't know much about one of the most highly charged, foreign policy issues of our time, I kept asking myself, are they equally ignorant of the nuances of subprime mortgages, global warming or domestic security?

"As far as members of Congress who are well-versed in foreign policy are concerned, most of them have their own positions on Israel and the Middle East," said an aide to a Florida congressman, indicating that the aide's boss, at least, thought for himself. "But there are very few of those. The people who don't have their own positions and aren't well versed, AIPAC has more influence with them."

Bert Rockman, head of the Political Science Department at Purdue, agrees that "very few members of Congress have incentives to be engaged deeply in serious foreign policy debate. Partly that is because such matters are rarely of interest to their constituents or to themselves. And partly it is because foreign policy, like most else on a policy agenda, is political and, hence, a matter of partisan controversy. In a partisan context, slogans work better than serious engagement of issues, and each side comes equipped with plenty of those."[27]

AIPAC helps legislators feel more comfortable with what Rockman calls "brainlocked slogans" because it has a first-rate research staff that is widely admired on the Hill. It simplifies matters with a torrent of easily digested talking points and fact sheets that ease the burdens on beleaguered, overworked, underpaid congressional aides who must advise bosses on complex issues. Some of those aides are Jewish, and of those, some are supportive of AIPAC, which also helps. Finally, through an affiliated foundation, the group also takes lawmakers on trips to Israel, where they see what AIPAC wants them to see.

In recent years alternative groups such as Americans for Peace Now and Brit Tzedek v'Shalom have done a good job of sending talking points and analyses that disagree with AIPAC to congressional staffs, when necessary. There is increasing receptivity to their work from congressional staffers. But most members still think AIPAC speaks for the American Jewish community, or at least the politically important parts of the Jewish community. So AIPAC's e-mails and policy briefings are taken much more seriously.

Breaking Ranks

Even when their seats are not vulnerable, lawmakers believe there is a danger that they could be the next victims of AIPAC's wrath, so most take the safe course and keep quiet if they disagree with Israel. But when AIPAC's attackers and apologists evaluate its power, a mildly promising fact is never mentioned: some members of Congress take independent positions on the Middle East and defy AIPAC, yet *nothing happens to them.* AIPAC knows that these members can't be beaten, so AIPAC doesn't take them on. Surely many more incumbents could follow suit without risking their political careers. For example,

- Senator Robert Byrd (D-West Virginia), the Dean of the Senate, has not hesitated to rail against giving U.S. aid to Israel without any conditions. If anything is sacrosanct to the AIPACers, it is continued aid to Israel. But the conventional Israel lobby has not bothered to try to defeat Byrd because it is a fight they cannot win.
- David Obey (D-Wisconsin), current chairman of the House Appropriations Committee, has been an occasional thorn in AIPAC's side since the early 1990s. In 2004 he told the *Washington Post* that AIPAC has "pushed the Likud Party line and in the process has crowded out other voices in the Jewish community."[28] But there is no way AIPAC is going to engineer David Obey's defeat, so they don't try.
- Representative Jim Moran (D-Virginia) caused a stir in 2002 when he claimed in a speech that, "if it were not for the support of the Jewish community for this war with Iraq, we wouldn't be doing this." Jewish organizations cried foul. If anyone were a logical choice to be a candidate for AIPAC's wrath, it would have been Jim Moran. Yet he had no trouble winning the Democratic primaries in 2004 and then getting reelected twice. In fact, while his main Democratic opponent in 2004,

Andy Rosenberg, said he did receive money from American Jews who were concerned about Moran's statement, he complained, "Compared to the way the Jewish community has helped other candidates running against people, I was very disappointed at the support I received."[29]

- In December 2007, while he was still a Democratic presidential candidate, Senator Christopher Dodd (D-Connecticut) sent around a "Dear Secretary Rice" letter to his colleagues. When I called AIPAC as a member in good standing and asked about it, I was told that the letter was (horror of horrors!) "pro-Palestinian." In fact, it was decidedly (also horror of horrors!) evenhanded. It called for freezing Israeli settlements, dismantling illegal settlement outposts, and reducing roadblocks and checkpoints in the West Bank. It also urged President Abbas to denounce terrorism and recognize Israel's right to exist. Yet AIPAC did not want to burn bridges with an important senator and did not actively oppose the initiative. Dodd somehow emerged unscathed by right-wing Jewish avengers.[30]

Alternative Noises

There are, admittedly, only a handful of members who are willing to be so forthright or candid when they disagree with AIPAC and the rest of the conventional Israel lobby. One of the most important and troubling reasons for this, it must be said, is congressional gutlessness. That does not mean that AIPAC can always get its way with the entire Congress, though. A solid bloc of legislators has shown a willingness not to toe the AIPAC line when events in the region call for moderate messages and presidents decide to push hard for those messages.

"The Middle East is almost always a domestic political issue on the Hill. And right now, that means the Jewish right usually gets its way," said Debra DeLee, the president and CEO of Americans for Peace Now who was formerly the chair of the Democratic National Convention and a Democratic National Committee operative. "But when it is a *policy* issue, there is a much larger group that is willing to examine what AIPAC wants more carefully. They are ready to determine what is best for the U.S., Israel, and the rest of the Middle East."

In fact, in a trend that has gone unnoticed by major media, more and more legislators have decided not to listen to AIPAC all of the time. This was demonstrated on the afternoon of February 1, 2005, during an unprecedented, exhilarating, now completely forgotten moment in congressional history: a resolution on the Middle East was introduced in the Senate *without any input from AIPAC.* It was Senate Resolution 27, which commended "the results of the January 9, 2005, Palestinian Presidential Elections." It called the recent election of President Abbas an important step "towards a free, viable . . . Palestinian state." Brought to the Senate floor by heavyweights from both parties, it passed by unanimous consent. The next day the House approved a similar resolution.

Normally, as part of their command-and-control regimen, AIPAC lobbyists either help to draft or carefully scrutinize anything related to Israel before it is introduced to either house of Congress. This time, the resolution was rushed to the Senate before AIPAC had a chance to change it. In the atmosphere of desperate hope that had greeted Abbas's election and the possibility of moderate Palestinian leadership taking the reins, the Bush administration had pressed hard for this legislation and had worked closely with Congress.[31]

It doesn't matter, for our purposes here, that none of this activity had much bearing on the region, which soon collapsed yet again under the weight of its habitual bitterness. What matters here is that Congress and the White House showed an underreported capacity for independence.

A few months later, in July 2005, a large bloc of representatives again came out of the woodwork and showed that the conventional Israel lobby could not always count on them. They resisted AIPAC's push for legislation (HR 2601) that would have accomplished nothing except to weaken Mahmoud Abbas. The new Palestinian president had been counting on an infusion of American aid to help him compete with Hamas's social service networks. He needed as much money as possible, as soon as possible. But the House resolution split U.S. aid money into quarterly installments, rather than allowing it to be delivered all at once, and put all kinds of restrictions on the funding. Three hundred and thirty representatives voted yes, but 100 voted no.

As one senior House aide said, "If ever there was a time when the side that lost by over 200 votes really won, this was it. Usually, these anti-Palestinian votes are political no-brainers for most Members. The fact that 100 Members could buck this trend and do what they know in their hearts is best for the U.S., Israel and the Palestinians may be a small sign that Congress is waking up."[32]

Since then, at least every once in a while, there have been other signs of congressional awakening. One reason for this is that an increasingly active, dovish, grassroots network has sprung up, thanks in large part to the growth of Brit Tzedek v'Shalom. This organization was founded in 2002 explicitly to develop a larger left-of-center grassroots American Jewish presence that would influence Washington on Middle East policies. On some legislative issues, it has worked in tandem with Americans for Peace Now, Israel Policy Forum, J Street, and other like-minded Jewish groups as well as Churches for Middle East Peace—an umbrella group of mostly mainline churches—and two Arab-American organizations, the American Task Force on Palestine and the Arab American Institute. As will be discussed in chapter 6, these groups don't agree on everything, but they all endorse a two-state solution and have enough in common to work side by side on occasion—and that is good news.

In 2006 this promising, interfaith, multiethnic coalition rallied against a House bill that put even more draconian restrictions on aid to the Palestinian Authority. The House passed the bill by an overwhelming margin, but after phone calls, e-mails, and much explanatory work with sympathetic Senate staffers, the Senate was persuaded to engineer a softer, less onerous version of the legislation.[33] Such is the state of the opposition: it is a major victory when a terrible bill is made less terrible. Since then, the coalition has also rallied behind a few letters and resolutions urging more American engagement in the Arab-Israeli conflict.

✡

"I would say there are about a hundred members who think the way APN and IPF do, and every once in awhile they're willing to vote that way. There are about a hundred who have right-wing views on Israel. There are another two hundred or so who don't really care or know much about the issue," said Rabinovitz.

Political science doesn't offer the tools to gauge precisely how much noise, money and passion an interest group needs to change widely accepted political assumptions, or mindless political reflexes, in Congress. So it is impossible to predict the political tipping point, to measure what it will take to capture the attention and support of the two hundred or so legislators who appear to be up for grabs. According to John Kingdon, who spent three years interviewing public officials and others about how agendas are set in Washington,

> It is difficult to portray precisely how people in and around government arrive at their notion of where the balance of power lies. In part, their calculation involves their perceptions [author's note: there's that word again!] of communications flows. If they hear a lot from one side and not from the other, they assume that the balance lies with the first side. They make this calculation in part because intensity does count for something, and they consider communication to be an index of intensity. In part though, their assessment of the balance turns on their implicit calculation of the various groups' resources.[34]

It is clear, though, that the same mechanisms of influence employed by AIPAC and the rest of the conventional Israel lobby are available to those who want to create or strengthen an alternative political bloc.

There is no secret to any of this. The pro-Israel left and its allies in other faith groups need more people to engage in grassroots and "grasstops" communications with Congress and the White House. "We need the ability to mobilize and reach members of Congress in every congressional district," said Diane Balser, interim executive director of Brit Tzedek v'Shalom. Right now, the organization has a solid presence and the ability to exert its influence in a bit more than forty districts.

Although J Street is off to a great start, this camp needs a much more elaborate campaign finance operation. It needs events that are sufficiently interesting and impressive to cut through the clutter and distractions of the daily news cycle. It needs more Moveon.org-style digital mobilizing, more paid aid, more op-eds, more feature stories that show that its activists are the public face of a much larger movement. It needs to raise a ruckus.

Fortunately, this strengthened alternative political bloc probably need not be as "intense" or have as many "resources" as the conventional Israel lobby. One reason is that an untold number of legislators are sick and tired of AIPAC, so any alternative has at least one built-in advantage.

"Some members of Congress have felt intimidated and resentful and have been forced to take positions against their better judgment, out of fear of retribution," said Victor Kovner, a lawyer who knows the Democrats in Congress well. He and his wife Sara—who served in the Clinton administration—are among the party's leading fundraisers in New York City. He is also an Americans for Peace Now board member and one of the key advisers to the J Street project. "I would like to restore the First Amendment rights of Jewish Americans and non-Jewish Americans to speak their minds on Israel-Palestine issues, without being subjected to baseless vicious calumnies."

A southern congressman, whom I did not even ask to go on the record, told me that when he was first elected, AIPAC sent him a list of its positions on various issues and asked if he agreed with them. He indicated that he didn't agree with all of them and returned it. "Then they got back to me with another document. They said, 'No, this is not what we want you to say. *Here's* what we want you to say.' That pissed me off. I think a lot of members get pissed off by that kind of treatment."

A former senator's aide who is an ally of the Jewish peace camp agreed that "there is a lot of pent-up anger. Lots of staff and some members curse the box that AIPAC puts them in. They feel like they are forced to take positions that they don't believe are in the best interests of the U.S. or Israel. I don't think that progressive voices in the Jewish community have demonstrated the ability to deliver political and financial support for people who step out. But if they did, it might really change the atmosphere around here because they would find members welcoming them." So the angry waters have been rising and pressing against the dam, and perhaps a little more encouragement will open up the floodgates.

We need to retain a sense of proportion here. Despite the energy that is poured into promoting or denouncing all of that AIPAC-inspired paperwork and speeches to the C-Span audience, Congress has a secondary role in most foreign policy decisions. As every schoolchild learns—or is supposed to learn—when it comes to foreign affairs, the president is—to borrow one of the more memorable George W. Bushisms—the "decider." On Capitol Hill, the main challenge to a lobby for the rest of us is to reduce the noise and atmospherics that inhibit administrations from pressing ahead with courageous diplomacy and to prevent sporadic legislation that creates irritating obstacles to that diplomacy.

Nevertheless, sometimes those atmospherics can be bothersome and those obstacles can be cumbersome, so Congress does matter. And since it does, here is a reality check: as of 2008 AIPAC had about 100,000 members, a $100 million endowment, new headquarters, and an operating budget of somewhere between $40 and $60 million.[35] By contrast, none of the left-of-center Jewish peace groups have budgets of more than $3 million.

Much larger organizations with offices in Washington that sometimes disagree with AIPAC, including the Reform movement's Religious Action Center, only occasionally try to stand in the way of its lobbying steamroller, as I will explain in the next chapter. The non-Jewish groups that often agree with my camp potentially have more people and resources at their disposal, but this loose coalition is still a work in progress.

"They are the little skiffs," says Charney Bromberg, former executive director of Meretz USA, referring to the likes of Americans for Peace Now, Brit Tzedek and J Street. "They can move faster than other groups and help to set the course. But they aren't going to be as effective without the battleships." By "battleships," he means the Reform and Conservative synagogue movements and large centrist organizations like the ADL and the American Jewish

Committee. Those groups could certainly make it easier for Congress and the president to chart a more sensible course in the Middle East. To figure out whether that could ever happen and under what circumstances and whether Jews from other sources besides the mainstream establishment could conceivably expand the pro-Israel peace bloc, it is necessary to be familiar with the American Jewish organizational world. I will provide a map of that world in the next chapter.

2

American Jews and Their Lobbies: A Guide for the Perplexed

The Israeli-Arab problem is America's problem. Solving it can and should be a high priority for all Americans. Church groups, Arab-American organizations, and others often weigh in on this conflict. But the conventional Israel lobby has persuaded politicians that it speaks on behalf of the only American Jews who matter and that retribution awaits those who cross it. Like it or not, ethnic and "identity politics" are part of the political game. So, the most effective way to change the current political reality is to demonstrate that another, large, vocal, and—yes, I'm not reluctant to say it—powerful part of the American Jewish community exists, and that it will support American leaders who don't always do what the conventional lobby wants.

"Although there is certainly a need for a broader coalition on this issue, the core of any alternative to AIPAC will need to be American Jews. If you don't speak out, everyone else is going to feel uncomfortable," Ambassador Philip Wilcox told me. Wilcox is the former U.S. consul general in Jerusalem and a longtime State Department hand who now heads the Foundation for Middle East Peace and works closely with the American Jewish peace camp.

Anyone, Jew or non-Jew, who wants to understand, let alone transform, the political environment that affects Middle East diplomacy needs at least some familiarity with American Jewish organizations and where they've come from. But that familiarity is hard to come by. One of the most uncanny talents of American Jews is their ability to invent new organizations and reinvent or sustain old ones, some of which have donors and missions that are virtually indistinguishable even to Jewish insiders, let alone the general public. It is hard to believe that more than a tiny fraction of people who read the *Forward,* the influential national Jewish weekly, could explain the difference, right now, between the American Jewish Committee and the American Jewish Congress.

I suspect that one reason why so many myths and half-truths about American "Jewish power" keep circulating is that it is difficult to adequately describe the organizational landscape without writing an encyclopedia and causing a bleary-eyed stupor in even the most motivated readers. The *American Jewish Year Book* lists over four hundred separate national organizations, and it is heavy going.

The mind-boggling number of separate causes and addresses and acronyms probably helps to explain why few people who expound on the Middle East in the chattering class bother—or are able—to study the Jewish community closely. For example, perhaps understandably, Mearsheimer and Walt did not seem to have a firm grasp of the specific organizations in what they called the "Israel lobby" in their original paper. They barely mentioned groups on the pro-Israel left that supported Israel's peace camp or advocated active, balanced American diplomacy in the Middle East. Perhaps they were duly chastened when critics pointed out that the organized American Jewish community was not monolithic, because they made an effort in their book to show that self-styled pro-Israel American Jewish organizations do not form anything close to a united front. They noted,

> In recent years AIPAC and the Conference of Presidents have tilted toward Likud and other hard-line parties in Israel and were skeptical about the Oslo process . . . while a number of other, smaller groups—such as Ameinu, Americans for Peace Now, Brit Tzedek v'Shalom, Israel Policy Forum, Jewish Voices for Peace, Meretz USA and the Tikkun Community—strongly favor a two-state solution

> and believe Israel needs to make significant concessions in order to bring it about. . . .
>
> Some of these organizations, such as the Israel Policy Forum or Brit Tzedek v'Shalom, actively promote U.S. engagement in the peace process and have been able to win some minor legislative victories in recent years. Yet such groups lack the financial resources and influence of AIPAC, the ADL, the ZOA or the Conference of Presidents, whose right-of-center views are unfortunately taken by politicians, policy makers and the media to be the representative voice of American Jewry. For the moment, therefore, the major organizations in the lobby will continue to advocate policy positions at odds with many of the people in whose name they speak.[1]

The thrust of this passage is certainly true and the last sentence conveys a problem that has been a bane of my existence. But, in the space of a few sentences Mearsheimer and Walt mess up some of the details that are used to back up their argument. They ignore nuances and complexities that are difficult to sum up in general pronouncements.

These should not be seen as petty quibbles over minor organizational distinctions. When figuring out whether and how to create alternatives to the American Jewish status quo, the devil is in these details. Jewish Voices for Peace (JVP), for example, does not support a "two-state solution" and should not be lumped together with groups that do; it takes no position on the shape of a final settlement.

Furthermore, the ADL and even AIPAC should not be tossed into the same undifferentiated, right-wing muck as the more uncompromising ZOA. The ADL could be considered "right-wing" on some issues, as it comes down hard on harsh criticism of Israel, as demonstrated by its attacks on Mearsheimer, Walt, and Jimmy Carter. Because of his visibility, the ADL's executive vice president, Abraham Foxman, often appears to be public enemy number one in the anti-Israel, lefty blogosphere.

But when it comes to the all-important challenge of solving the Israeli-Palestinian conflict, the ADL is, by and large, a centrist organization, at least when compared with other Jewish groups. It publicly supported the Oslo process and other peace initiatives undertaken by the Israeli government. Foxman has repeatedly criticized right-wing settler supporters and other American Jews who have publicly objected to such initiatives. The ZOA's Morton Klein, in contrast, has never met a peace plan or a Palestinian aid package that he could live with. In fact, he consistently criticizes AIPAC and the Israeli government for being too namby-pamby on the Palestinian question and repeatedly violates the so-called norm against speaking out publicly against Israeli policies—a norm that, as we will see, is more often stated than practiced.

Even U.S. officials who should have at least some familiarity with the Jewish groups don't bother to learn much about them. "There is an abysmal ignorance of the American Jewish community in every administration," said Ambassador Wilcox. "That is why they tend to rely on the traditional organizations" for feedback from the community and to help promote policy initiatives even when those organizations are not representative.

One official who was forced to educate himself about the panoply of American Jewish groups was George Shultz, Ronald Reagan's secretary of state. One can sense an undercurrent of long-remembered frustration in his riposte to the Mearsheimer-Walt book.

> Anyone who thinks that Jewish groups constitute a homogenous "lobby" ought to spend some time dealing with them. When Soviet persecution of Jews renewed in earnest after World War II, for example, Jewish groups were all over the place on what should be done. Some called for and funded the creation of a Jewish "homeland" within the Soviet Union. Some supported Israel's approach of quiet diplomacy. Most adopted the techniques of the civil rights movement and made lots of noise. Some advocated and used force. The tension among these groups—all dedicated to saving Soviet Jews—was electric. When the doors swung open, many American Jews wanted to allow the Soviet Jews to choose to come to the United States instead of going to Israel. Israel fought hard against these Jewish groups, arguing, among other things, that U.S. law should not discriminate

> against Israel as a haven for Jewish refugees. Many other examples could be cited, including my decision to open a dialogue with Yasser Arafat after he publicly met longstanding conditions. My decision evoked a wide spectrum of responses from the government of Israel, its various political parties and the many American Jewish groups who weighed in on one side or the other.[2]

In fact, the picture is even murkier than the one Shultz described, because most American Jews have little or nothing to do with *any* of these activist groups. About 44 percent of American Jews are "unaffiliated," which—as defined by the National Jewish Population Survey—means they don't belong to synagogues, Jewish community centers, or other Jewish organizations.* A little less than half of American Jews belong to synagogues and only about a quarter belong to Jewish organizations other than synagogues.[3]

A great many anguished studies and outreach programs have tried to find solutions to this lack of Jewish connectedness and bring these people back into the communal fold. I, for one, would like to bring them into the fold of a Middle East peace bloc. But, for our purposes here, it is the activists who need to be deciphered first. One can't understand this game unless one knows the players, and it is hard to know the players without some kind of scorecard. With that in mind, table 3 (page 62–63) provides a rough, somewhat opinionated reference guide to where American Jewish organizations stand on the Israeli-Arab conflict and what the American government should do about it, circa 2008.

You will be relieved to know that it is not necessary to memorize each and every organization listed in the table. It is meant to provide a general idea of where organizations are situated, *relative to each other*,† in the ideological

* There were more than 5 million American Jews in 2001, as defined by the survey. Statistics on unaffiliated Jews were based on an estimated sample universe of 4.3 million Jews.

† No doubt critics of Israel will take exception to the use of terms like *center* or *center-left* to describe organizations that often support Israeli policies these critics deem to be extremist and right-wing. The categories here are used for the basis of comparison only, as a way to make sense of the organizational landscape, not as a means to express value judgments.

landscape. You can return to it as necessary when specific groups are mentioned later on. The table also gives a concrete sense of what Shultz described: the diverse range of organizations and ideologies and the sheer number of groups that are vying for attention from the media, donors, and often, the U.S. government.

The next time someone starts telling you about the tightly organized Jewish "cabal" that is controlling America, show them this table. Within a few years, no doubt there will be new groups. Current groups will get new leadership that might shift them to the left or right. But this is the Jewish roadmap that confronts the current administration and Congress.

Table 3. THE "ORGANIZED" AMERICAN JEWISH COMMUNITY

Far Left or Religious Anti-Zionist	Pro-Israel Left	Center Left
Israeli Committee Against House Demolitions (USA) Jewish Voices for Peace Jews Against the Occupation Jews for Justice in Palestine Neturei Karta Satmar Hasidim	Ameinu* Americans for Peace Now* Brit Tzedek v'Shalom Israel Policy Forum J Street Project Jewish Labor Committee* Jewish Peace Lobby Jewish Reconstructionist Federation Meretz USA New Israel Fund Progressive Zionist Alliance Rabbis for Human Rights Shalom Center Tikkun Movement Union of Progressive Zionists Workmen's Circle*	Association of Reform Zionists* Central Conference of American Rabbis* NA'AMAT* Religious Action Center* Union of Reform Judaism* Women of Reform Judaism* ________ MERCAZ USA* Rabbinical Assembly* United Synagogue Congress of Conservative Judaism* WIZO Women's League for Conservative Judaism*

Conventional Israel Lobby		
Center	**Center Right**	**Far Right**
America-Israel Friendship League* American Gathering of Jewish Holocaust Survivors and Their Descendants* American Jewish Committee* American Jewish Congress* American Jewish Joint Distribution Committee* American Sephardi Federation * American Zionist Movement* Anti-Defamation League* B'nai B'rith * B'nai Zion Development Corporation for Israel* Hadassah* Hebrew Immigrant Aid Society* Jewish Community Centers Association* Jewish Council for Public Affairs* Jewish War Veterans* Jewish Women International* National Council of Jewish Women * National Conference on Soviet Jewry* National Jewish Democratic Council ORT America* United Jewish Communities*	AIPAC* AMIT Women* Friends of Israel Defense Forces* Jewish National Fund* Republican Jewish Coalition	Agudath Israel Americans for a Safe Israel American Friends of Likud* Committee for Accuracy in Middle East Reporting in America* EMUNAH of America* Jewish Institute for National Security Affairs* National Council of Synagogue Youth National Council of Young Israel* One Israel Fund Rabbinic Alliance of America Rabbinic Alliance to Save Jerusalem Rabbinical Council of America Union of Orthodox Jewish Congregations of America* Zionist Organization of America*

An asterisk means the group is a member of the Conference of Presidents of Major American Jewish Organizations, the most well-known and important American Jewish umbrella group. Along with AIPAC, it is one of the twin pillars of the conventional Israel lobby. The Presidents Conference is sui generis, so it is not listed as a separate organization here, and I will discuss it later in this chapter.

Some of the organizations listed, such as the Jewish Community Centers Association, do not focus on Israel in their day-to-day work. But their voices technically count in the communal debate about Israel because they are members of the Presidents Conference. That designation gives them a seat on AIPAC's executive board, which doesn't have much clout but does vote on general policy directions for AIPAC at meetings twice a year.

Finally, many noteworthy groups are not listed, including the American Jewish World Service, Jews for Racial and Economic Justice, B'Tselem in North America, One Voice, and a motley array of others. They were excluded because they have little to do with Israel and have no seat at the Presidents Conference, or they do focus on Israel but don't consider themselves to be explicitly "Jewish" organization, or they are too small to make a dent in national policy.

Here is how to read the table:

The center. The members of these groups are roughly analogous to the muddled middle of the Israeli political system. These are the troops that everyone wants to capture in the battle for the hearts and minds of American Jewry. In general, they are loathe to air dirty laundry—i.e., their own disagreements with Israel—in public, although some of them have erupted in anger at Israel on occasion, as occurred during the Jonathan Pollard spy scandal. In their official organizational positions, they would be unlikely to abide any American pressure on or harsh criticism of Israel.

The American Jewish center includes some of the most well-funded and influential national groups: namely, ADL, the American Jewish Committee, and the American Jewish Congress. With a self-professed, combined membership of 250,000–300,000, these three are the so-called defense agencies that are concerned with relations between American Jews and the outside world.[4] Their organizational cultures are most comfortable when they can take forceful stances against Israel's "enemies"—e.g., Iran, Hamas, Hezbollah, and far left-wing critics of Israel. They tend to be less comfortable about enthusiastically supporting peace initiatives that require a certain amount of trust in Arab intentions or bold territorial compromises. Nevertheless, like the ADL, the other defense organizations in the American Jewish community did generally support the Oslo peace process in the 1990s, although they did it rather quietly.

Another important group in this category is the Jewish Council for Public Affairs (JCPA), an umbrella organization of local Jewish community relations councils and a few national organizations, including the defense agencies and the Orthodox Union. The leaders of many of the local councils tend to lean to the left on matters such as stopping settlement construction or dividing Jerusalem as part of a final settlement. But the JCPA generally cannot act on those impulses because it is hampered by the need for consensus and by a few cranky donors. Think of it as a reluctantly centrist group.

But, regardless of official organizational positions, within the national centrist organizations—especially the JCPA and the American Jewish Committee—an untold number of *individuals* want to give their government more leeway to chart a different course in the Middle East. Some joined these groups because they tend to promote liberal domestic policies, but such people are not always comfortable with the organization's foreign policy agendas. Some are also members or supporters of explicitly dovish groups further to the left. For example, Martin Bresler, the vice chair of Americans for Peace Now, is the former national vice president of the American Jewish Committee, is on the committee's board of governors, and has long been active in both organizations.

If the time comes when an American president will need support for, say, demanding that both Israel and the Palestinian Authority keep promises made at the negotiating table, there is a swath of people in these groups who, in their heart of hearts, would almost certainly support the president, as long as what he asked for seemed reasonable and in the best interests of Israel and the United States. Some, like Bresler, would be vocal about it and would grab the opportunities for political action offered by the pro-Israel left. Similarly, in the late 1980s and early 1990s, a number of local Jewish federation executives, national organizational leaders, and other prominent American Jews expressed opposition to Prime Minister Yitzhak Shamir's policies.[5] However, judging from past precedents, most doves in this category would voice their endorsement of the American demands in closed-door meetings of their organizations, in chats with friends, and in anguished conversations among themselves. They would do so, that is, unless there were a sudden change in the centrists' paradigm that called for supporting the elected Israeli government when it disagrees with the United States.

The center right. Compared with those in the center, organizations and individuals in this category have been more noticeably squeamish when Israeli prime ministers have offered concessions. And they have been much more reluctant to place hopes in creative diplomacy.

In AIPAC's case, there has occasionally been a willingness among board members to quietly sabotage Israeli peace initiatives or make life more difficult for Israeli governments they don't agree with. They have acted more Israeli than Israel itself. According to Yossi Beilin, one of the most prominent Israeli peace negotiators, "When [in the mid-1990s] Israel asked the United States to lend assistance to cooperative projects in the Middle East and to finance the activities of the Palestinian Authority . . . , AIPAC felt it would be awkward for it to be involved in lobbying members of Congress for such purposes. During those years, AIPAC officials went about their work on the issue of Palestinian aid as if frozen by the sight of a ghost."[6]

Former AIPAC executive director Neil Sher told me that "getting AIPAC to support Oslo, and what the Israeli government wanted to do, was like pulling teeth."

Still, nothing is simple in this organizational matrix; things are not always exactly what they seem. It is possible to list more than a few obstacles that AIPAC has erected to peace diplomacy over the years. But here is an exceedingly inconvenient truth: it is wrong to categorize AIPAC as an inveterate opponent of territorial compromise with the Palestinians or a group that has always been in the thrall of Israel's Likud Party. That is inconvenient to me, at least, because it would be much easier to map out the Jewish community if AIPAC were just plain evil, an enemy of all reason, and a permanent source of bellicose militarism. Don't get me wrong: AIPAC finds it too easy to defend bellicose militarism—Israel's strikes on Syria's nuclear reactor, cluster bombs in southern Lebanon, etc. Still, the pursuit of peace is usually incorporated into its talking points and is even occasionally the focus of its lobbying efforts.

Despite loud protests from the non-compromisers in its midst, AIPAC did eventually throw at least some of its weight behind the Oslo process in the 1990s. Steven Grossman, president of AIPAC from 1992 to 1996 and a liberal Democrat, admitted that there was considerable resistance from some board members and anguished arguments during board conference calls on the Oslo accords. He didn't deny that one of AIPAC's former presidents, Robert Asher actually walked the halls of Congress and lobbied against those accords. But he adamantly insisted, "AIPAC played a very helpful role for Rabin and Peres [in the Oslo process]. In conversations with the secretary of state and others in the executive branch, we made it clear that this was where the community stood, the overwhelming majority of our members were supportive," he said.

Grossman may be gilding the lily a bit. But while the group has long included vociferous opponents of trading territory for peace, they don't control the organization now and it is not clear if they ever did. The idea of "Greater Israel" has gradually lost credibility in the American Jewish community, except among a vocal minority. AIPAC has adjusted, albeit slowly and painfully. And since 2000, while it has thrown up some roadblocks to Palestinian aid and otherwise hampered American diplomacy, it has backed several Israeli governments on controversial ideas and initiatives that the Israeli right despised, including Ariel Sharon's disengagement of Israeli troops and settlers from the Gaza Strip in 2005.

In retrospect, the Gaza disengagement was a complete disaster for a number of reasons, including Israel's insistence on doing it unilaterally, its harsh boycott of the area after Hamas took over, as well as Hamas's insistence on terrifying Israelis with incessant rocket fire and its military buildup after Israel withdrew. Before it occurred, though, the disengagement was supported in principle by much of the Israeli left, who thought the withdrawal from settlements would set an important precedent, while Israeli settlers burned tires and stalled traffic in protest. Thus, AIPAC clearly disassociated itself from the agenda of Likud and the settlers by lobbying Congress to support the disengagement.

So why do America and Israel need an alternative? Because it is one thing to support, however hesitantly or begrudgingly, an Israeli prime minister's peace plan or an Israeli withdrawal from part of the occupied territories; it is quite another to support an American administration that asks Israel to take steps it otherwise might not want to take, or holds Israel accountable for promises, or comes up with diplomatic formulas that are not vetted with the Israelis before they are presented to the Palestinians.

AIPAC and other groups in the center right tend to believe that only direct talks between Israelis and Arabs, without honest American brokerage, can succeed. They are uncomfortable when America plays any diplomatic role other than to exert pressure on Israel's adversaries and strengthen Israel's position with military and financial aid. Any pushback from the United States in response to Israeli behavior or positions is guaranteed to get their troops riled up. It gives them a chance to revel in the idea that Israel is David and the rest of the world is Goliath.

Furthermore, confronting Israel's "enemies" is in the center right's DNA, but subtle engagement with carrots as well as sticks, and negotiations to accompany military posturing and financial pressure, are not. During the Bush administration, AIPAC was on the front lines of the battle to completely isolate Iran, Syria, and Hamas, urging the United States to sanction them without talking to them. To put it mildly, that approach has not worked very well. It is not helpful to the United States or Israel.

Neither is unthinking tribalism. When Condoleezza Rice addressed the AIPAC policy conference in 2008, she mentioned that something had to be done about the "daily humiliations" of Palestinians under Israeli occupation. A stony, uncomfortable silence greeted that comment. That is reason enough to build an alternative pro-Israel lobby, one with the universal values and basic decency needed to acknowledge Palestinian agony out loud.

The far right. These people want Israel to retain the occupied territories, for religious reasons and/or because of security concerns. They are fans of Benjamin Netanyahu and Israeli leaders even further to the right. The noisiest and most noticeable far right Jewish group on the Washington scene is the ZOA, which has some influence on Congress. Most of the rest are Orthodox Jewish organizations with close ties to the Israeli settlement movement.

The most important secular group in this category is the Jewish Institute for National Security Affairs (JINSA), a think tank and advocacy group that claims to have twenty thousand members. It promotes a hawkish American defense posture and, according to its website, spreads the word "about the important role Israel can and does play in bolstering democratic interests." It has a distinctly neoconservative tilt. Some of its advisory board members, such as Michael Ledeen, John Bolton, and Richard Perle, were either directly involved in the Bush administration's Iraq War effort or were important cheerleaders for war, as those who claim it was a "war for Israel" love to point out.[7] A JINSA report on Secretary of State Rice's agenda for the Annapolis peace conference convened by the United States in November 2007 tells you everything you need to know about the institute's attitude toward the Israeli-Palestinian conflict:

> She's pushing and cajoling on behalf of semi-reformed terrorists who disdain America and our democratic principles. She's inviting 49 countries to midwife Palestine—don't mistake this for a conference to establish the legitimacy, security and permanence of Israel in the Middle East. She is wooing Syria, Iran's lapdog and North Korea's partner that is in the process of destroying America's democratic friend Lebanon. . . . Palestine is a terrorist sinkhole, ruled in parts by a corrupt secular dictatorship and a corrupt religious dictatorship—which one rules how much remains unclear, but neither is a proper partner for American financial, military or political support.[8]

There are other, tiny right-wing groups that make Mort Klein of the ZOA look like Mahatma Ghandi, such as the Jewish Defense Organization and the remnants of Meir Kahane's Kach Party. They are not listed in this table because they are so far beyond the fringe that no American politician could conceivably take them seriously.

The pro-Israel left. Many critics of Israel wouldn't mind if it disappeared. The pro-Israel left, where I can be found, wants to make it better. It wants to help Israel survive and thrive. These groups are and will remain the core of an alternative to the conventional Israel lobby, at least within the organized Jewish community.

Most people in this camp believed in a two-state solution before it was fashionable. All of the groups are opposed to settlement expansion, are enthusiastic about bolstering Palestinian moderates, and want the U.S. government to be a neutral, fair arbiter of the Israeli-Palestinian conflict, although precisely what that entails is a difficult, open question. They are all publicly committed to protecting Israel's core security concerns as they define them. For example, unlike groups further to the right, many of the organizations in this category criticized Israel's recent assault on the Gaza Strip as a counterproductive overreaction to the provocations of Hamas rockets. Yet they were also careful to stress that Israel had the right and the obligation to defend its citizens from those rockets.

The organizations usually have the same or very similar positions on Middle East issues. But there are differences, some social, some pertaining to their activities. Americans for Peace Now raises money for the Peace Now movement in Israel and has a well-established legislative outreach program. APN's staff of savvy political operatives, along with an e-mail network of supporters, helped to orchestrate some of the small victories in Congress mentioned in the previous chapter.

Israel Policy Forum is a smaller, more elite group of wealthy or well-connected Jews, some of them from the established mainstream Jewish community. Many are major donors to the Democratic Party, and some are entrenched in mainstream Jewish organizations, especially in New York City.

Brit Tzedek v'Shalom strives to be the grassroots arm of the pro-Israel left, with about forty chapters and thirty-four thousand "supporters" as of 2008, although the number of people who are active is much smaller. Other, smaller groups, including Ameinu and Meretz USA, work in tandem with the rest of the pro-Israel left on the Arab-Israeli conflict but also focus on Israel's domestic issues. Another very important cog is the Reconstructionist synagogue movement, whose rabbis and other leaders are key members a[illegible] supporters of the other organizations in this camp.

A total of sixteen organizations are listed in this section of table 3; each of the groups I haven't mentioned is playing a unique role and deserves to be accounted for here. But, as we still need to deconstruct the rest of the community, the report on this section will conclude with just one more, an intriguing new addition to the Jewish community:

In 2006 efforts were made to cobble together a few of the pro-Israel left-wing groups to form a strengthened alternative lobby that would be more than the sum of its parts. Eventually, when it was clear these organizations were not going to merge, the J Street project was created. As mentioned before, J Street funnels money to incumbents and candidates through a political action committee. It also lobbies on a range of issues, including the Israeli-Palestinian conflict and Iran, and speaks up about others, such as the unfortunate embrace of Christian Zionists by the conventional Israel lobby.

"The most significant [contribution of J Street] is bringing the political reality of the American Jewish community, including contributors, into the political arena in Congress," says Jeremy Ben-Ami, J Street's executive director. In 2008 JStreetPAC endorsed forty-one candidates, three for the Senate and thirty-eight for the House. Of those, thirty-two won.[9]

J Street's additional financial and political muscle, if it develops, will come from a combination of major donors and the kind of "Netroots" community that Moveon.org, Obama's 2008 campaign, and other tech-savvy organizations have demonstrated can raise large sums from many small contributions. It is testing the vitally important question of whether unaffiliated, younger American Jews who have not been helping other groups in this camp could be persuaded to get involved.

The center left. These organizations, most of them from the Reform and Conservative synagogue movements, collectively represent more American Jews—more than 3 million—than those in any other category. Their national leaders and other rabbis share and express many of the pro-Israel left's political goals, but their organizations are more cautious about taking official, controversial stands because not everyone agrees with them.

Rabbi David Saperstein of the Religious Action Center (RAC), the Reform movement's political action arm, told me, "All the [Jewish] peace groups have members who join because they endorse the general outlook of the organization. We are a different kind of entity with different kinds of responsibilities. Our members have different viewpoints, different kinds of sensitivities." That, he says, constrains the RAC from pushing too far to the left on matters related to Israel. The RAC also has a host of legislative priorities, and Israel is only one of them. That is another reason why the group only occasionally joins with the pro-Israel left in trying to galvanize its grassroots for legislative battles related to the Middle East.

Nevertheless, Rabbi Saperstein and Rabbi Eric Yoffie, the leader of the Union of Reform Judaism, have been outspoken opponents of the Israeli settlement movement because of the dangers settlement expansion poses to a democratic Jewish state. Yoffie even told a *Haaretz* reporter in November 2003 that he was "calling on American Jews to exert their political influence in the U.S. in order to make the American administration prompt Israel to do what it cannot do on its own."[10]

"Is it possible for an American government that is clearly supportive of Israel and a two-state solution to be, at the same time, activist and deal with the settlement question?" Yoffie asked. "In my view, yes. . . . If the Israeli government is putting settlements in place in a way that leads the American government to conclude a two-state solution is no longer possible, then it's reasonable to say the United States needs to take action." He would not comment on what kind of action is warranted, but he didn't hesitate to say that "getting tough means getting tough with both sides."

Under what circumstances would the Reform movement as a whole be directly engaged in political activity that involves a more forceful American role? "The American Jewish community is more moderate than we are given credit for. If there is a sensible viewpoint put forward by the American government, you will find a significant number of American Jews will be supportive. We'll be involved," said Yoffie.

I hope I am wrong, but I strongly suspect he is being overly optimistic. When national Reform leaders take forceful stands on issues, that does not necessarily mean that many congregations will engage in controversial political activity, especially if it involves Israel. But individuals within this movement, like those in centrist organizations such as the American Jewish Committee, are clearly an important potential source of activism.

A separate, distinct group of organizations in this category (e.g., MERCAZ USA, Rabbinical Assembly, etc.) are part of the Conservative synagogue movement, which is more traditionalist in its religious practices than the Reform movement is. It would not have been inaccurate to place them in the centrist category as well, as Conservative Jews are deeply divided on Middle East peace issues. But their leaders and a percentage of their members have the potential to help strengthen the pro-Israel peace camp, so I've optimistically kept them in the company of the Reform movement.

In March 2007 Rabbi Jerome Epstein, the executive vice president of the movement's umbrella synagogue group, United Synagogue of Conservative Judaism, got into a lot of hot water for signing a letter to Secretary of State Rice that was organized by the National Interreligious Leadership Initiative for Peace in the Middle East (NILI), a coalition of more than two dozen Jewish, Christian, and Muslim leaders. The letter called for the release of Palestinian prisoners and the dismantling of roadblocks and objected to the "security barrier" in areas "that infringe on Palestinian land," among other things. It irked some Conservative Jews, who complained to the movement's leadership.[11]

"Until recently, 'pro-Israel' has meant an Israel-right-or-wrong approach," said Rabbi Epstein. "Anyone who has challenged Israel or made suggestions to Israel, including U.S. officials, has been considered unfriendly to Israel. But there are cracks in that now. More people in the congregations, especially younger people, agree that they can support Israel and not agree with everything Israel does. If one says to them, 'The American government also needs to be concerned with the health and welfare of the Palestinians,' it is not seen by them as anti-Israel. But many older people don't agree."

The Far Left. At the other outer edge of the community are Jewish groups that don't hesitate to call Israel an "apartheid state" and to urge the United States to take harsh measures to stop the occupation. This segment of

American Jews contains a vocal contingent who share the Star Wars vision of the conflict that is popular in the rest of the far left. This contingent believes the concept of a Jewish state is inherently racist, Israel is an evil empire, there is no way to redeem it, and the prime minister of Israel—no matter what his or her views might be—is equivalent to Darth Vader.

Organizations in this category are outside of the communal tent and have poor or nonexistent relations with all other groups in this chart, including those in the pro-Israel left. But that doesn't mean *all* of these people have markedly different goals for the Middle East than those in my camp.

Jewish Voice for Peace is an interesting case. Founded in 1996 as a Berkeley-based group, it has grown into a national organization with more than twenty thousand people in its e-mail network. Mitchell Plitnick, its former policy director, said, "The problem with Americans for Peace Now and Brit Tzedek is there are issues they just won't touch and things they won't say because they are worried about the mainstream community. . . . And they think every negotiating position needs to be based on what Israel will be able to accept politically. Someone has to be out there saying, 'All settlements are *wrong*. What needs to happen is for Israel to give them up.' . . . People need to be able to say the Wall is *wrong*. People need to be able to say the occupation is *wrong*. . . . In Gaza, Israel behaved appallingly. There needs to be a group that can say that, in no uncertain terms."

JVP advocates steps that infuriate the rest of the organized Jewish community, such as divesting from American corporations doing business in the West Bank or withholding American military aid to the Jewish state. It takes no position on the end-game, endorsing neither a two-state solution nor a binational secular state, in part because it wants to take a big-tent approach and attract as many people as possible. As a result, it has become a magnet for American Jews who seethe with a permanent rage against all things Israeli.

"A lot of [JVP's] people are committed anti-Zionists," said Plitnick, who now runs the Washington office of B'Tselem, the Israeli human rights group. "They're more concerned that Israel not be a Jewish state than concerned with the Palestinians." He left the organization in 2008 mainly because too many of his former colleagues refused to admit that Israel had legitimate security concerns. "They think all Israel has to do is kick out the settlers and walk away from the territories, and everything will be solved," he said.

Nevertheless, many of JVP's members support a two-state solution. I know some of them. Their objectives are not much different than mine, although we differ on tactics. "It's possible to find the occupation morally reprehensible and still be pro-Israel," according to Plitnick. By all rights, it also ought to be possible for the pro-Israel left to find common cause with at least some of these individuals, along with their ideological allies in the non-Jewish left-wing groups, such as United for Peace and Justice (one of the main organizers of the anti–Iraq War protests).

The groups I am associated with openly shun JVP. That is unfortunate because, although I often disagree with it, JVP plays a valuable role, in my judgment. It can hit different pressure points in our political system. As far as I am concerned, those who want peace in the Middle East should let a hundred flowers bloom. The environmental movement contains tree-huggers as well as people comfortable collaborating with BP, and it is more effective because of that diversity.

If the moment comes when more passionately moderate Jewish voices are needed to bolster evenhanded American diplomacy, there are people in the non-Zionist left of the organized Jewish community who may well be persuaded to join the chorus, much like free-thinking centrists who would join my camp from the opposite direction.

Babel's Leader

Presiding over much of the fractious organized community like a cranky mother hen is Malcolm Hoenlein, the vice chair of the Presidents Conference and the organization's principal staffer since 1986. For more than sixty years, the conference has been the group charged with representing the "consensus" views of the American Jewish community to the executive branch and the media. It hosts Israeli leaders and foreign dignitaries, brings radio talk show hosts to Israel, and—when issues are pressing—organizes rallies and protests. When Hoenlein tries to call the highest levels of the State Department to express concern or provide an interpretation of events in the Middle East, his calls are taken. Or at least that's what he says.

On its website, the Presidents Conference calls itself "the voice of organized American Jewry, speaking and acting on the basis of consensus on issues of vital international and national concern." That is a bit like someone from Babel, after God exacted his punishment, claiming to speak for and coordinate all of the people in that multilingual tower.

As exemplified in the above passages from Mearsheimer and Walt, this group is often described as a right-wing, hawkish, or Likud-leaning "organization," which implies a unified front of Jewish leaders. The truth, predictably, is more complicated. The conference includes dovish and left-of-center groups, such as Americans for Peace Now, Ameinu, and various organizations associated with the Reform and Conservative synagogue movements. It supposedly makes official statements only when its members reach consensus.

There have been recent occasions when it was possible to detect such a consensus and the conference responded. For example, it rallied support for people in northern Israel shelled by Hezbollah and helped to organize a rally at the United Nations to protest the appearance of Iranian president Mahmoud Ahmadinejad (although some of its member groups, such as Americans for Peace Now, have not supported the conference's confrontational approach to Iran). But on the thorny issues of Israeli settlements and how to address the Palestinians' plight, nothing close to a consensus has existed for decades. As a result, often the conference has officially stayed on the sidelines rather than address these issues directly.

Nevertheless, Hoenlein is often cited as the answer to the question of why the American Jewish establishment does not reflect majority-Jewish opinion. So it is worth spending some time to decipher him. Frequently accused of putting his own right-wing stamp on the organization, he has become a lightning rod of criticism from both the pro-Israel left and anti-Zionists.

Michael Massing, who has written widely quoted magazine pieces analyzing and criticizing AIPAC and the Presidents Conference—and is cited at length by Mearsheimer and Walt—lays out a commonly accepted case against Hoenlein:

> Hoenlein is supposed to reflect the broad consensus within the conference. And, when there actually is a consensus, he gives it an effective voice. It's when there's not that the trouble begins. The problem in part reflects how the conference is organized. . . . The smaller conservative groups in the conference decisively outnumber the larger liberal ones and so can neutralize their influence. And that leaves considerable discretion in the hands of Malcolm Hoenlein. . . .
>
> Hoenlein's statements tend to echo [Ariel] Sharon more than [Ehud] Barak. "Jews," he noted, "have a right to live in Judaea and Samaria, part of the ancient Jewish homeland—just as they have a right to live in Paris or Washington." The catchphrase "Judaea and Samaria" is a biblically inspired reference that Likud Party supporters use to justify the presence of Jewish settlers on the West Bank. Hoenlein, in fact, has long been involved with the settlers' movement. For several years in the mid-1990s, he served as an associate chairman for the annual fundraising dinners held in New York for Bet El, a militant settlement near Ramallah that actively worked to scuttle the peace process by provoking confrontations with neighboring Palestinians. [Author's note: Hoenlein has denied that charge and has said his name was listed without his permission on an honorary fundraising committee for Bet El.]
>
> Such activities have fed the impression among some conference members that Hoenlein has given the group a strong conservative tilt.[12]

This impression has been reinforced in the past decade by the election of two right-wing Jews as conference chairmen: Mort Zuckerman and Ronald Lauder. (Hoenlein has insisted that he has little to with the election process.)

It isn't so much what Hoenlein and the conference have done but what they haven't done that sets people off. When Likud's Yitzhak Shamir was prime minister in the late 1980s and early 1990s, the conference let loose with a steady stream of statements supporting nearly every Israeli policy, including the expressed policy of breaking the bones of Palestinian protestors during the first intifada. In contrast, when the Oslo process began under the government of Yitzhak Rabin, there just wasn't much activity by Hoenlein and the conference. A story in the New York *Jewish Week* in 1994 about accusations of the conference's "resounding silence" on the peace process captured the flavor of that controversy: "In the ten months since Yitzhak Rabin and Yasir Arafat shook hands on the White House lawn, American Jewry's leading umbrella organization has not faxed out one new release to hail Israel for the risks it has taken for peace with the Palestinians. . . . By contrast, in one week last year, the group, the Conference of Presidents of Major American Jewish Organizations, used three news releases hailing Israel for granting asylum to 84 Bosnian Muslim refugees."[13]

In 1995 the consul general of Israel in New York City, Colette Avital, grew so frustrated with Hoenlein's lack of enthusiasm for the Oslo process that she organized several behind-the-scenes meetings with leaders of major American Jewish organizations and pleaded with them to start speaking out more aggressively for the policies of Yitzhak Rabin. As a consultant to the consulate in New York City, I attended a few of those meetings, and they made little headway, mainly because no one wanted to circumvent the Presidents Conference.

Rabbi Yoffie and others also voiced complaints against Hoenlein after Ariel Sharon announced his Gaza disengagement plan, and it took more than a year for the conference to endorse the plan.

The legendary Israeli diplomat Abba Eban, also frustrated with the rightward tilt of the conference under Hoenlein's watch, once half-jokingly proposed the creation of a Conference of Presidents of Minor American Jewish Organizations. Periodically, people in my camp talk about breaking away and setting up an alternative. Rabbi Yoffie and others have called for drastic structural reforms in the conference to give more power to larger organizations.

Whatever his individual views might be, Hoenlein is in an unenviable, possibly untenable position, given the divisions within the community. When

I sat down with him at his office in midtown Manhattan, he insisted that he had done what he could to help every Israeli government, right and left. "People complained that I didn't smile" at the famous signing ceremony on the White House lawn, where Arafat and Rabin shook hands. "So what? I didn't think there was anything to smile about. Neither did Rabin. I knew it was a risky, tricky business. There were big problems that had to be overcome. That doesn't mean we didn't try to help him. . . . During Oslo, we spoke up. We supported the government. Rabin never once complained about us. . . . He complained about AIPAC, not about us."

Hoenlein seemed equally upset about left-wing and right-wing critics during our conversation. "I get it from the Left and I get it from the Right," he said. "I am not an ideologue. . . . My job is to support the policies of the Israeli government. People on the right still blame us for supporting Oslo, even today. And they blame us for supporting the Gaza disengagement."

He clearly wishes that all of the member groups would adapt the same, circle-the-wagons mentality and never relinquish it. One probable, understandable reason for this is that the divisions make it impossible for him to do his job effectively. But there is more to it. He made the classic case for American-Israeli solidarity and Jewish unity as twin, tactical weapons. It stems from the mind-set in which the world is nothing but a battlefield where the enemies of the Jews are forever swarming. Knowing full well that I have worked with groups pushing for the United States to lean on Israel on occasion and knowing that I was writing this book, he offered something between an argument and a plea: "There should not be daylight between Israel and the U.S. government. That doesn't mean they have to march in lockstep. But every time there appears to be a wedge, Israel's enemies drive a Mack truck through it. They exploit it and misinterpret it as Israel's weakness." Leaning forward across his conference table, he implored me, "People need to be very careful about what they say. . . .

"One precondition of every success the American Jewish community has had is unity. Every success has depended on it. . . . You name it. Raising money during the Six Day War. Freeing Soviet Jewry. Getting refugees out of Ethiopia [to Israel]. Standing up strong for Israel."

Asked to give advice to American Jews who wanted America to take a more forceful role in the Israeli-Palestinian conflict, he said, "If you believe in Jewish unity, let that guide you when you take a stand." In other words, he was asking us to shut up.

This argument—and the worry about Israel that is at its core—should not be dismissed lightly or scoffed at by anyone who hopes that more mainstream American Jews will endorse evenhanded American policies in the Middle East. I have heard the argument supported by the example of American Jewish divisions in the late 1930s and throughout World War II, when ideological and organizational fissures were among the reasons why the community never effectively mobilized on behalf of a clear plan for rescuing European Jews.

But if the most powerful umbrella group in the Jewish community is unable to endorse the kind of American diplomacy that could rescue both Israelis and Palestinians, that argues for different groups, different arrangements. Indeed, I find hope in table 3, because it means there is not just *one* lobby trying to press Israel's case in this country. "We have several lobbies," Mark Rosenblum, the political director of Americans for Peace Now and one of its founders, told me. "American Jews aren't like the oil industry, or the trial lawyers, or even the gun owners, who can get their act together and unite behind a position."

A Note about Everyone Else

So they are out there: hundreds of thousands of American Jews who belong to synagogues or are affiliated in other ways and don't agree with AIPAC or Malcolm Hoenlein or the ZOA. Many more American Jews have nothing to do with the organizations in table 2.1 and have untapped potential for political engagement.

One fascinating and, to me, promising statistic from the National Jewish Population Survey is that 48 percent of unaffiliated Jews feel emotionally attached to Israel.[14] We also know that, as a whole, unaffiliated Jews are less enamored of the policies of the last few Israeli governments than affiliated Jews.[15] Younger Jews in this category are especially intriguing. Many of them bear some resemblance to Dan Fleshler, circa 1984, but with crucial differences:

In a report that assessed the connections of American Jews younger than thirty-five to the Jewish people and Israel, Ariel Beery and Hindy Poupko remarked on the differences between this generation and those who hold the reins of power in mainstream American Jewry: "Having come of age during the first intifada . . . many of these youth came to believe that if anyone in the Israeli-Palestinian conflict was to be given the mantle of victim, it certainly was not the Jews. The cognitive dissonance caused when the historic image of Israel as the oppressed came into contrast with the contemporary image . . . as oppressor caused many of this new generation . . . to either tune out from relating to Israel whatsoever, or to tune into anti-Zionist claims."[16]

In that generation, while some are actively involved in the anti-Israel far left, others have embraced Israel and are providing fresh blood to the conventional Israel lobby. But in their interviews, Beery and Poupko also identified a "middle group" that was neither permanently hostile to nor happy about Israel. "This group often described their relationship to Israel as 'love/hate' and expressed growing concern for Israel's 'immoral' behavior. Yet, while they maintain a somewhat critical approach to Israel, they still felt that Israel is in fact the Jewish homeland and plays a critical role in their Jewish identity."[17]

Their ties to Israel, however frayed or tentative, would be enough to disqualify them as candidates for political activism in the judgment of people who think positive feelings about the Jewish state are tantamount to positive feelings about South Africa under apartheid—or worse. But the American Jews they scorn could be effective new messengers for evenhandedness to elected officials. I will have more to say about these potential new recruits in chapter 10.

"There Is No Cohesion"

Until now, a small fraction of both affiliated and unaffiliated American Jews have cared enough, or been convinced enough, to help out the little skiffs on the pro-Israel left. But relatively new mechanisms now exist to let them weigh in with grassroots communications to Congress and U.S. officials, even with targeted political donations. Many more of them must be galvanized to offer meaningful support to a U.S. president who is willing to push and prod Israel on the settlements and other matters, even as he presses the Palestinians to deter violence that only convinces Israelis that they cannot take a chance on withdrawing from more territory.

If American Jews who are part of the organizational world are concerned about splintering the Jewish community, they should be able to find reassurance in the history of the community's relationship with Israel and Zionism. Hoenlein was correct when he cited examples that showed the value of American Jewish unity. But those were the exceptions, not the rules. Our tradition of schisms and arguments is as rich and venerable as our tradition of power puffery, yet somehow the American Jewish community and Israel have survived and thrived.

Much of the world now considers American Jews and Israelis to be long-standing partners and coconspirators. But, from the late nineteenth century through World War II, Zionism was one of the most divisive ideas in American Jewish life. That was true during the heyday of Theodor Herzl, founder of political Zionism. According to the historian Walter Laqueur, in the late 1890s, "For rabbis and laymen alike, Zionism was a disturber of their peace of mind, an offense to their Americanism, an obstacle to Jewish adjustment in a democratic environment."[18] It just didn't have much appeal for most American Jews, who were doing their best to carve out lives in a country that may not have accepted them completely but was certainly the best alternative the world had to offer.

To the defiantly assimilationist Jews of the Reform synagogue movement, it was also theologically offensive. In 1885 a national convention of Reform rabbis in Pittsburgh famously declared, "We consider ourselves no longer a nation but a religious community. And therefore expect neither a return to Palestine . . . nor the restoration of any laws concerning the Jewish State."[19] Similarly, the American Jewish Committee was stridently anti-Zionist when it was founded in 1906 by a small group of wealthy German Jews reacting to pogroms in Russia and Ukraine. Dedicated to protecting the civil rights of Jews around the globe after World War I, the committee "gradually came to support the rebuilding of Palestine for religious and cultural reasons, but shunned any nationalistic overtones in that work; it endorsed *Zion* but not *Zionism*," according to Melvin Urofsky's wishfully named *We Are One! American Jewry and Israel.*[20]

The idea of a Jewish state had more appeal to Eastern European immigrants who arrived en masse before World War I and imported fierce intellectual disputes over Zionism, socialism, and Bundism. But it was a minor distraction to most American Jews. By 1914, out of America's 2.5 million Jews, only about twenty thousand belonged to Zionist organizations, although the membership rosters began to steadily increase during World War I, thanks mainly to the leadership of Louis D. Brandeis, who became a powerful advocate of American Zionism.[21]

Gradually, during the 1920s and especially during the advent of Nazism in the 1930s, what had been the cause of a passionate minority gained more support. Clearly, something had to be done to rescue the Jews of Germany and Austria, and then the rest of Europe. The option of Palestine as a place of refuge became more convincing to the Jewish mainstream. Still, concerns about the nature of that place of refuge continued to bring painful, unresolved disputes about Jewish nationalism into sharp focus. Between the world wars, according to Urofsky,

> Anti-Zionist leaders feared that a Jewish homeland would raise political questions about their loyalty to the United States. . . . How, they asked, could an American citizen be loyal both to the United States and to a foreign Jewish state? What would happen were the United States and the Jewish one ever come into conflict . . . ? Would their true allegiance to America be recognized by their non-Jewish fellow citizens or would they be ostracized, as had German nationalists in 1917 and 1918. . . . They had chosen who and what they wanted to be—Americans who practiced the Jewish religion—and the whole idea of Zionism, of Jewish nationalism, threatened their status.[22]

These questions were shunted aside by many American Jews by the war's end, as newsreels showed the evidence of Nazi horrors and the gates of Europe and even America were closed to Holocaust survivors.

Yet even after the war, even after Auschwitz, there was *still* a deep-seated reluctance among a broad range of American Jews—including the American Jewish Committee Brahmans and many Reform Jews—to explicitly call themselves Zionists.[23] Nor was there anything resembling unity among American Zionists. To read the chronicles of Zionist leaders in the United States at mid-century is to hear the echoes of furious disputes over long-forgotten documents and events—the Cos Cob conclave, the Biltmore conference—turf battles, and wrestling matches between men with oversized egos. There were profound differences over whether and how much to confront the British, whether to press explicitly for a Jewish state, how hard to press the Roosevelt administration to do something about concentration camps and desperate Jewish refugees. More detail about the specific issues that divided them is not within my purview here. But it is worth noting that these pre-state schisms had something in common with contemporary disputes over the Israeli-Palestinian conflict: they drove even friendly American policymakers batty, as it was difficult to figure out which American Jews were worth listening to or what, precisely, the community wanted.

One account of that period notes, "Sympathetic Americans despaired at the conflicting signals with which they were bombarded; legislators who took stands in response to the arguments from one camp would find the Jewish vote diverted from champions of the other. Diplomats hostile to Zionism were cheered by the disarray."[24]

Breckinridge Long, one of the Zionists' chief antagonists in Roosevelt's State Department during the war and an unapologetic anti-Semite, happily scribbled in his journal, "The Jewish organizations are all divided amid controversies. . . . There is no cohesion nor any sympathetic collaboration—rather rivalry, jealousy and antagonism."[25]

This was the environment in which the conventional Israel lobby was born.

The Birth and Tormented Youth of the Pro-Israel Lobby

The current formal conventional lobby's roots go back to the American Zionist Emergency Council, which was formed during World War II to press for the Jewish state,[26] aided and abetted by Israelis led by Nahum Goldman, a leader of the World Zionist Organization based in the United States. After Israel's war of independence, the group's organizers understood that the philanthropic largesse of American Jews was not sufficient to help the fledgling Jewish state absorb newly arrived refugees and stay afloat in a hostile Arab sea. With insufficient sympathy from the Eisenhower administration, which was careful not to offend Arab leaders by noticeably tilting in Israel's direction, the Zionists had no choice but to ask Congress for help. In 1954 one of the Emergency Council's key activists, Canadian journalist Isaiah (Sy) Kenen, became the head of a new lobbying organization that was not tax-exempt and could legally make Israel's case to the U.S. government. It was called the American Zionist Committee for Public Affairs.[27]

Kenen slowly began to build a network of Jewish community leaders in congressional districts around the country. To do so, he had to find allies in a chaotic mess of existing national and local groups, most of which still exist today and are on display in table 3.

According to his memoirs, throughout the 1950s, Kenen had to scratch and claw for the right to represent Israel's case in Congress, contending with battles over turf as well as ideology. ADL staffers wanted their group to be responsible for grassroots organizing. A Reform rabbi in San Francisco publicly questioned Kenen's right to speak for American Jews. But he fought them off, and the network of key contacts kept expanding.[28]

In 1959, to attract more help from the *non-Zionists*, he changed the name of his group to the American Israel Public Affairs Committee.[29]

If you are already getting a little dizzy from the communal infighting and jockeying for the right to speak for American Jews, imagine how U.S. officials must have felt.

The Conference of Presidents

In 1954 Henry Byroade, an assistant secretary of state with the Middle East portfolio, was growing tired of giving identical briefings to one American Jewish organization after another. Wanting one address where he could explain the Eisenhower administration's views on Israel and where the

Jewish community would represent its views, he asked for the help of Nahum Goldman and another young Israeli in the United States, UN Ambassador Abba Eban.

After Byroade showed them his calendar, which included meetings with five different Jewish groups in five days, the Israelis helped him to set up a group designed to convey the community's consensus to the executive branch. Originally called the "Presidents Club," it consisted of the leaders of a dozen organizations who met periodically and sought to create one voice for the Eisenhower administration.* It should come as no surprise that, even at the outset, according to Eban, the leaders of individual groups continued to bang on the State Department's doors and arrange their own private meetings when they were unhappy about something.[30]

In 1959, this group became the Conference of Presidents of Major American Jewish Organizations.

Jewish Glasnost

Despite some turf battles, AIPAC and the Presidents Conference eventually carved out a reasonably clear division of responsibilities. By mutual agreement, the conference, under the direction of Yehuda Helmann from 1959 to 1986, focused on the White House and on making Israel's case in the media. AIPAC worked the Hill. A third group, the National Jewish Community Relations Advisory Council (NJCRAC, now the Jewish Council for Public Affairs) and its local, member organizations, supplied or supplemented grassroots troops when AIPAC needed them.

Kenen's operation relied on a list of a few hundred Jewish community leaders, businessmen, rabbis, and others. It was a reasonably well-oiled machine. And it was, by and large, a quiet one until the mid-1970s. Kenen's credo was to "stand behind legislation, not in front." Emphatic but private pressure by a relatively small roster of individuals was the order of the day

* It is common in Jewish circles and in media accounts to ascribe the founding of this organization to a grumpy Secretary of State John Foster Dulles. But there is no evidence that Dulles himself initiated the group. The legend may be another example of American Jewish mythmaking that has created a perception of more direct access to power than actually exists.

until he retired in 1974. Kenen's replacement, Morris Amitay, recalled that when he took over, he and his staff had to explain even to people in the Jewish community—let alone public officials—that AIPAC was not the same thing as OPEC.[31]

Under Amitay, the list of activists expanded and was computerized. When quiet phone calls weren't enough, when major letter-writing campaigns, ads, and protests were called for, AIPAC, NJCRAC, and the Presidents Conference sometimes managed to work closely together and tap into the rest of the organized community.

Thanks in part to a glasnost between the national groups and a growing sense of confidence and political maturity, the affiliated Jewish community started getting noticed in Washington as a formidable *public* political presence in the 1970s and even more so in the 1980s. It didn't always achieve its policy goals. But it became a force to be reckoned with—prompting the United States to help free Soviet Jews, orchestrating a dramatic expansion of U.S. aid to Israel and taking the sting out of the Arab boycott of Israel, among other successes.[32]

J. J. Goldberg explains how, in 1980, the components of the Israel lobby (there was only one lobby back then) functioned in its storied fight against Ronald Reagan's proposed sale of five airborne warning and command systems (AWACS) to Saudi Arabia:

> The campaign against the AWACS was waged by a broad consortium under the umbrella of NJCRAC working with AIPAC and the Presidents Conference. The Presidents Conference oversaw the efforts of national agencies to flood the media, forge interfaith coalitions and create a national mood of urgency. NJCRAC delivered its armies of local community leaders to call their representatives and talk tough. AIPAC did what it had always done: it lobbied. It supplied lawmakers with facts and figures, helped them identify fence sitters and hand-delivered promises and threats in the name of the Jewish community. In effect, it was the campaign's public face to Washington.[33]

The grassroots army grew even larger after 1981, when Thomas Dine, a liberal staff aide to Senator Edward Kennedy, replaced Amitay at AIPAC soon after the AWACS battle. For all of the Jews' passions and organizing skills, they had lost that battle, and Dine and his lay leadership wanted an even more formidable grassroots operation. So they built their own. AIPAC's membership roster, eleven thousand when Dine took over in 1980, was expanded to fifty-five thousand by the time he stepped down in 1993.[34] Yet, paradoxically, in the 1980s, when AIPAC and the rest of the Israel lobby reached its zenith of actual as well as perceived power, when American Jews appeared to be among the most tightly organized, dedicated citizen lobbyists in the country, the consensus that had arisen around Israel was slowly eroding.

Having finally resolved the debate about the wisdom of Jewish nationalism and the Jewish nation-state, in the decade leading up to the Oslo peace process American Jews were dragged, mostly unwittingly, into a debate that few felt qualified to participate in. That began in 1977, when more than thirty years of Labor Party rule in Israel were overturned by the election of Menachem Begin, who declared his fealty to "Greater Israel" and sanctioned a dramatic expansion of new "facts on the ground" in the West Bank.

An internecine war of ideas broke out among American Jews with competing visions of Israel and the best way to support it. Fought mostly behind closed doors, occasionally spilling into the streets or the op-ed pages and ads of non-Jewish newspapers, it will be described at greater length in chapter 4, where I explain why the doves, for the most part, lost it. For now, suffice it to say that American Jews took up the same questions that were hotly debated in the Jewish state beginning in the 1980s. They involved a host of issues, from the wisdom of attacking Lebanon—more than once—to the wisdom of giving the PLO a chance to govern. But the debate always came down to a confrontation between two fundamentally different visions of the world, belief systems based as much on psychology as on logic or ideology.

Broadly speaking, those on the pro-Israel Jewish left felt that maintaining the status quo ante of the occupation and a state of constant contention with the Arabs was more dangerous than attempting to change the status quo. They wanted to explore every possible diplomatic opportunity and to find and encourage Arab negotiating partners. Some were motivated purely out of concern for the survival of a majority-Jewish state and didn't much care one way or another about the moral costs of ruling over another people; others, like this author, were concerned about those costs.

Those on the right felt that changing the status quo was too risky, that Arab intentions were too suspect to test. Some of them felt territorial compromise was contrary to God's law. All of them were adamantly opposed to American pressure on Israel.

Those in the center shifted between the two camps depending on the news of the day.

The same war of ideas is still going on. As before, a crazy quilt of disparate ideologies and organizations confronts the White House. Which will it pay attention to? How much, in the long run, does it matter what any of these groups do or say? To figure that out, we need to examine how and why activists for Israel interact with the executive branch.

3

Lamp Salesmen and Secretaries of State: Lobbying the Executive Branch

To try to get what it wants from the American government, the conventional Israel lobby makes noise mainly in the media and in Congress. And one source of hope, one reason why it might not be necessary to match the lobby's volume in these arenas, is Congress doesn't control foreign policy. It has the power of the purse string and can impose sanctions on foreign countries. It approves treaties and key appointments. It is supposed to provide consent as well as advice on military actions. It can create the kinds of political atmospherics that make it either easy or difficult for presidents to achieve their foreign policy goals. However, according to presidential scholar Bert Rockman, "In the end, when presidents are really determined to have their way, they usually do, especially where they can take the initiative and force Congress' hand."[1] The key words here are "really determined." Interest groups can certainly dampen enthusiasm for taking—or even considering—bold foreign policy initiatives.

To figure out how much conventional pro-Israel activists matter to the executive branch—and to gauge how much an alternative lobby *could* matter—it is important to understand the mechanisms of the activists' influence, the different points of contact and modes of interaction between them and U.S. officials.

✡

"It's mysterious how it works," said Samuel Lewis, when I asked him to explain how the conventional Israel lobby exerts influence on the executive branch. "It's easy to see bits and pieces of it, but it's hard to get the whole picture. It works through different channels, not one well-coordinated lobby." If anyone should be able to see the whole picture, it is Lewis, a State Department hand who dealt with the Middle East in several administrations. Yet the nature of American Jewish influence-building seemed, at its core, ineffable to him.

Still, certain aspects of its approach are straightforward. In addition to Congress, the mainstream American Jewish community has used individuals and organizations with access to successive presidential administrations to make its case about Israel. Traditionally, the executive director and chairperson of the Presidents Conference are key ambassadors from the organized Jewish community to the State Department and White House.

"I always had access if there was a crisis," said Seymour Reich, the chairman of the conference in 1989–90, who eventually became president of Israel Policy Forum. "[Secretary of State James] Baker was always available to Malcolm [Hoenlein] and myself." That was true even though the Bush team was reputed to have less concern about—and patience with—Jewish pro-Israel activists than any administration since Eisenhower's.

But access didn't mean Reich got the results he wanted. He recalled the angst in the Jewish community when the first President Bush made a statement that was critical of Israeli settlements, including those in Jerusalem. At the time, a united Jerusalem was sacrosanct to Reich and other mainstream Jewish leaders. The construction of new Jewish neighborhoods that rimmed the city was thought to be a natural expansion of the capital. So, Reich and other leaders expressed outrage publicly and privately to the State Department. Eventually, he recalls, "[National Security Adviser] Brent Scowcroft set up a call with Bush. I shared my concern about lumping Jerusalem in with settlement activity. Bush assured me that the issue would be clarified. . . . But they did not retreat. The next statement that came out was worse."

Over the years, along with leaders of the Presidents Conference and other key organizations like ADL and the American Jewish Committee,

Jewish donors and friends of various presidents have tried, usually in informal settings, to represent the community's views or Israel's positions. As former Israel ambassador Avraham Harman explained in 1979,

> One of the most important influences, especially in a large country like the United States . . . is getting a man's time. If there is somebody like an Abe Feinberg [a banker who was a friend of Presidents John F. Kennedy and Lyndon B. Johnson] who has access to the President, doesn't overstay his welcome or abuse it, but reserves use of this access to matters of greatest importance, then he has gained Presidential attention on this matter. . . . If you go through diplomatic channels, the information gets there—eventually. Mr. X is a man who has the President's confidence. . . . He has access to the President. . . . He sees the President socially over a drink—the conversation wanders—the President is relaxing with him . . . , then he can effectively discuss Israel's problem.[2]

Every high-powered lobby looks for the same inroads to every White House. At times, American Jewish friends have made a tangible difference to presidents' policies. At other times, they have had little impact.

Movie executive Arthur Krim and his wife were close friends of Lyndon and Lady Bird Johnson and regular White House guests. Just after the Six Day War, when Johnson was working on an important speech that would define his Middle East policy, he reportedly read drafts of it to Krim and other guests at a dinner party and accepted "comments and suggestions from around the table" that helped to shape its tone and content.[3] Max Fisher, a major Republican donor and fundraiser, served many different roles for the Nixon and Ford administrations and was sometimes used as an unofficial emissary to the Israelis. When Secretary of State William Rogers proposed an ambitious peace plan for the Middle East in December 1969, Israeli prime minister Golda Meir and her cabinet were not happy. Nixon authorized Fisher to communicate privately with the Israelis to let them know the administration would not impose the Rogers plan on them.[4]

So, one clear lesson is that dovish Arthur Krims and Max Fishers are needed, friends and confidantes who can bolster a president's confidence to do the right thing. To some extent, as we'll see, that is what happened during the Clinton administration.

Not satisfied with this hit-or-miss approach, and searching for a way to sustain good relationships with the Reagan administration, in the late 1980s AIPAC began a concerted effort to lobby the executive branch, led by Executive Director Tom Dine and Research Director Steven Rosen. Until then, the White House was the purview mainly of the Presidents Conference and a few national groups with Washington offices. But, following the communal tradition described in the previous chapter, AIPAC cut into their turf.

An entire department was set up to focus mostly on mid-level State Department and Pentagon officials and to influence the recommendations that eventually reached decision makers. (In 2006 AIPAC's legislative and executive departments were combined.) Interactions with these officials also helped to shape AIPAC's congressional agenda, as it gave the group a way to discern an administration's positions on potential or existing legislation.

This operation has gotten international publicity as a result of the espionage indictment of Rosen and Weissman. What has not gotten attention is another important reason for the growth of AIPAC's executive lobbying arm: *it gave key board members something to do*. While this part of the operation increased the group's influence in many ways, it also created new, inherent limitations on what it could accomplish.

During the Reagan-Bush years, AIPAC made a concerted effort to find and make use of wealthy political players with at least some direct access to the White House. The most well-known were some hard-knuckled conservative businessmen who served in succession as AIPAC presidents beginning in 1980: Larry Weinberg, Robert Asher, Edward Levy Jr., and Mayer "Bubba Mitchell." Known to Jewish insiders as the "Gang of Four," they were active volunteers who became involved in the nuts-and-bolts of the operation and wanted the chance to personally influence American policy. While previously there had been individual American Jewish donors who had sought to play that role, AIPAC's enterprise was more organized and elaborate.

At first glance, the spectacle of high-powered, wealthy American Jews talking about foreign policy with American officials is grist for the mill of conspiracy theorists. It would not be surprising if some of them took the preceding quote from Ambassador Harman and spattered it all over the Web as proof of a sinister network of Jewish control. But the reality was often less impressive. Sometimes it was downright embarrassing. "In one notorious incident," according to J. J. Goldberg, "Ed Levy, who headed AIPAC from 1988 to 1990, went to the Pentagon to lobby for a Hawk missile the Pentagon was trying to acquire. But he forgot which version of the Hawk he was asking for, and ended up demanding the wrong one."[5]

Douglas Bloomfield, AIPAC's director of legislative affairs during much of the 1980s, called the Gang of Four and other wealthy board members "affable millionaires who expected to get access. At first, they would meet with members in the House but soon that wasn't important enough. Then meeting with senators wasn't important enough. Then assistant secretaries of state weren't important enough. . . . They ended up going up the chain of command and having strategic conversations about topics they knew nothing about. Steve [Rosen] adroitly played to their egos," Bloomfield said, referring to top donors and board members.

This illustrates a fundamental, poorly understood rule of not-for-profit life in this country: whatever else motivates them, the single most important goal of advocacy groups is to perpetuate themselves, to give their board members a sense of purpose, and to ensure that their staffs keep their jobs. In a recent study of interest groups and their motivations for lobbying, political scientist David Lowery nailed this point: "Virtually all studies of interest organizations begin with the simplifying assumption that they are motivated actors whose prime purpose is to influence public policy. This assumption is incorrect. Rather, interest organizations are motivated actors whose primary purpose is to survive."[6]

At any rate, Bloomfield and other AIPAC staffers who were on the scene at the time scoffed at the group's new focus on executive lobbying, believing that members of Congress were the only people with enough clout to personally lobby administration officials. "To political appointees or the

Secretary of State, you're going to talk policy?" asked Morris Amitay, Dine's predecessor, in an entertaining interview with author Dan Raviv in 1991. "You're going to send in lamp salesmen and real estate developers to talk policy? In the White House or State, they can't be bamboozled. It was ridiculous for AIPAC to start on that course."[7]

Dine told me he thought Amitay's attitude was "overly contemptuous" of AIPAC's lay leaders. "In any nonprofit, you have board and professional staff. When you visit NSA [the National Security Agency] or the president, you take your leadership. That doesn't mean they were everyday executors of policy."

Regardless of the effectiveness of individual board members, AIPAC's executive lobbying operation clearly had an impact on military matters related to Israel. Describing the origins of the operation, Dine said, "Originally, our main concern was to find out about arm sales, what was being planned for the Arab states. The other concern was to bring the militaries of the two countries closer. So, we wanted to find out what was being contemplated in the Pentagon, the State Department, and the NSC [National Security Council], especially about military priorities. From these contacts, we developed a new way to enhance bilateral relations. Tactical issues were discussed in a relaxed way, and we could share ideas and get ideas."

In 1987 the *New York Times* reported on AIPAC's "cadre of weapons experts and strategic analysts who have become a small think tank. . . . They understand weapons systems, know the literature and have many contacts in the Pentagon and other agencies. . . . Mr. Rosen has reportedly worked to flesh out the strategic [U.S.-Israel] relationship by encouraging joint American-Israeli naval maneuvers, the use of target ranges by U.S. Navy planes and the like. Despite initial opposition from the Pentagon, the relationship has become institutionalized."[8]

It is still institutionalized. One of Dine's main rationales for this and all of AIPAC's other activities was to "make Israel stronger so it would have the option of making peace," he said. Back then, that was a common justification for arms sales, for American financial aid to Israel, and for strengthening relations between the two countries. The idea was that if the Arab states understood that the United States would remain in Israel's corner, they would stop seeking ways to destroy the Jewish state and be more amenable to diplomatic solutions. It may be hard to fathom for those who believe there can be no possible noble motive for arming Israel, but Dine, Bloomfield, and others who helped to solidify the defense relationships believed that they were helping to foster peace.

Whatever webs of influence might exist in the Pentagon and other parts of the defense establishment, the diplomatic corps and the White House have been much less amenable or susceptible to direct lobbying from AIPAC and other Jewish groups. Congress was and is the main vehicle used to press for what the conventional Israel lobby wants in the way of diplomacy. "I would trade ten billionaires for one senator anytime if I wanted to influence the White House," Aaron David Miller said.

"AIPAC by the late '80s moved to influence the executive branch. I don't recall a single example in which anyone listened to them or changed their minds," recalls a former State Department official who was there at the time. "Steve Rosen would invite you to lunch because he wanted to express the concerns of the Jewish community and find out what's happening. . . . But I am not aware of any case where we were headed in one direction where Rosen or Malcolm Hoenlein or David Harris [of the American Jewish Committee] came in and then we changed directions. In most cases, there aren't dramatic shifts in policy no matter what external sources say or do."

None of this is meant to imply that, except for the influence attained via congressional ties and military contacts, the conventional Israel lobby has had little direct impact on the executive branch. But when it comes to the all-important matter of presidential decision making on Middle East diplomacy, the lobby's effect has usually been subtler than its accusers claim. Its impact appears to have been based mainly on *memories or impressions* of past confrontations, rather than overt pressure or sophisticated political analyses. So here, too, power puffery has played a major role.

Another Atomic Bomb of Fear

"Pro-Israeli groups are often most influential when they do nothing at all to influence policy," wrote William Quandt. "The law of 'anticipated reaction' governs here. . . . Alternative courses of action are frequently rejected because of the expectation of negative reaction from pro-Israeli groups and their supporters in Congress. Caution may result in internal vetoes over policy, based on the . . . assumption that the proposed action would be too controversial. Real tests of strength are rare, so the 'anticipated reaction' is often as effective in shaping policy as the mobilization of support in a confrontation would be."[9]

The theme of self-imposed restraints, of initiatives not taken, of statements toned down or never made, of creative ideas squelched at their inception is a consistent one in accounts by public officials and knowledgeable observers when discussing the impact of the conventional Israel lobby on different administrations. "The Jewish lobby has the capacity to constrain the executive branch through Congress and with public signals, and to some degree with direct intervention with people in the White House," said Samuel Lewis. "They [the conventional lobby's activists] can and do set limits on the freedom of action that the White House feels like it has." Note the striking similarity with the psychology of legislators who also "feel like" they are completely restrained from saying what they wish to say by formidable Jewish power, although their fears are in many cases exaggerated.

Unlike the blame-the-Israel-lobby-for-everything theorists, political scientists have identified a great many factors that enter into foreign policy decision making: the philosophy and ambitions of the president, bureaucrats, and the bureaucratic process (i.e., aides disagreeing and squabbling), organizational groupthink (i.e., aides not disagreeing or squabbling), and domestic politics, to name but a few. Foreign policy aides at different levels of the bureaucracy clearly play a key role, and it is in the minds of these people where the "anticipatory reflex," as Aaron David Miller calls it, is especially active.

Within the State Department bureaucracy, much of the nervousness about confronting the lobby is left unspoken. In the administrations of Reagan and George H. W. Bush, Philip Wilcox said, "In most confidential conversations of the State Department, people didn't talk about the Jewish lobby. It wasn't said that 'we can't do this' because of the lobby. But there was an understanding that domestic politics were important."

An official who served in the foreign policy teams of George H. W. Bush and Clinton remembers the silent message conveyed to the State Department bureaucracy when Clinton appointed Martin Indyk, a former AIPAC staffer, to be ambassador to Israel and kept Dennis Ross and Aaron David Miller—both of them Jewish—on his Middle East team: "It was definitely a signal to everyone that he [Clinton] didn't want a war with the Jews."

Of course, the challenges posed by the conventional Israel lobby are also openly discussed, sometimes to an absurd degree. When the second intifada began in 2000, the Clinton administration's view was that Israel's response was often disproportionate, recalled Robert Malley, executive assistant to Samuel Berger, Clinton's national security adviser, and then a Middle East adviser to Clinton himself:

> There were almost no Israeli casualties, at first, and many Palestinian casualties. I remember countless meetings over what statements we should use to describe Israel's response. We had to think if we were going to be accused of "moral equivalence" if we came down too hard on the Israelis. Should we say their reaction was a "hindrance to the peace process" or "a major obstacle"? You don't want to go through the pain of overreaction from the community if it can be avoided. . . . So, yes, there is a form of self-censorship. You have to think three times before you can say anything. It does influence what you say and perhaps what you think, but it is hard to calculate how much it really matters. It is hard to separate out its role in policymaking because everything is intertwined—how Israel will react, how the Palestinians will react, how the EU and UN and the [American Jewish] community will react.

Malley described the political calculus involved in deciding whether or not to annoy the conventional Israel lobby: "It's a matter of keeping down background noise [author's note: *noise* was his choice of words, unsolicited and unprompted]. We had to work on a number of issues and if we alienated an important group on Capitol Hill over relatively minor issues, or because of our word choices, it would be harder to accomplish what we wanted to." He also insisted, however, "When we dealt with something important to the national interest, when it was something we really wanted to do, like whether or not to favor the division of Jerusalem, I don't think the community had much of an impact."

Of course, no one on the earth knows precisely why they do anything. And former government officials can't be expected to explain or accurately gauge the extent to which domestic interest groups mattered to them. We are in the realm of imprecise, speculative psychology here. But clearly, the memory of past confrontations with the American Jewish community hangs over every White House like a sword of Damocles. That has contributed to what Daniel Levy aptly calls "initiative recoil . . . , when the U.S. government preemptively holds back from making a move or seizing an opportunity based on the calculation that is not worth the domestic political fallout."[10]

Kurtzer and Lasensky describe the legacy of George H. W. Bush's battles with Israel and American Jewish groups in 1991 and its effect on subsequent administrations:

> The political fallout from the sharp disagreements with the Yitzhak Shamir government, particularly over settlements—and the White House decision to dig in its heels over their continued expansion—*had a searing effect that far outlasted the Bush Administration, reverberating well into the Clinton and Bush 43 years and causing the next president* [i.e., Clinton] *and his team to overcompensate in ways that created a different set of problems* [emphasis added] . . .
>
> When presidents lead in Arab-Israeli diplomacy, Congress and public opinion follow; as legislators from both parties told the study group, Congress is especially willing to line up behind a president, provided the administration's strategy is sound and Israel's security is protected. . . . But this truism is sometimes lost even among U.S. negotiators as the so-called anticipatory reflex sets in and policy choices are preemptively constrained. *At times, U.S. policy on settlements and Jerusalem has reflected this phenomenon* [emphasis added].[11]

The Wild Card: Presidential Will

M. J. Rosenberg has been watching State Departments and presidents chicken out for decades. He thinks that, especially during their honeymoon period, American presidents could stifle their fears, take a deep breath, and state a bold case for a new direction in American Middle East diplomacy without major political damage. According to Rosenberg,

> AIPAC is most afraid of a president who gives a speech that says, "This is what we want to do because it is in the best interests of America and of Israel."
>
> Any new president can do anything he wants for about a year, especially if he can show that America needs it to happen. . . . The lobby will fold. Congress will fold. What inhibits this is fear, a lack of will.
>
> What you have, inevitably, are people around every president who supported him during the campaign and think they know the Jewish community. That includes Jewish donors but others, too. They will say, "Don't do it." But they are wrong. Think of the power of the American president! He can do whatever he wants! It's not what the lobby will or won't do that matters. It's whether the president has the will to say to friends and allies in the [American Jewish] community and to the American people, "I'm doing this because America needs me to do it and so does Israel."

Rabbi Eric Yoffie thinks that even AIPAC might not create terrible problems if, for example, a president articulated a clear American and Israeli interest in stopping settlement construction and then insisted in no uncertain terms that Israel do something about it. "As for AIPAC, we'll see. I am not sure they will object the way they would have in the past. While they're capable of being wrong, and they've certainly taken positions I've disagreed with, they are also pretty realistic. They know how to read the tea leaves. If we have a strong administration that's prepared to push forward, they're going to ask themselves, 'How are we going to get on the right side of these folks?'"

Those might be heartfelt wishes more than well-grounded predictions from Rosenberg and Yoffie. By the time you read this, it may well be that their hopeful readings of the domestic political landscape will have been tested by the actions of the Obama administration or one of its successors. But even if Rosenberg and Yoffie are right, that would not diminish the importance of continually drumming up political support for balanced Middle East diplomacy, in order to encourage American administrations to suppress their anticipatory reflexes and take political risks. The problems in the region are far too complex to be solved unless U.S. presidents are willing to take such risks.

The Two-Way Street

It may be a "truism," as Kurtzer and Lasensky put it, that presidents can stand up to the conventional Israel lobby and still get what they want out of Congress. But it is certainly not conventional political wisdom that presidents can do so without serious political damage. Jimmy Carter and George H. W. Bush, for example, certainly showed political backbone and accomplished a great deal in the Middle East despite furious confrontations with the organized American Jewish community. But both lost Jewish votes when they ran for reelection.

Carter received 64 percent of the Jewish vote in 1976, but that total plummeted to 45 percent in 1980, the lowest percentage of Jewish votes of any Democratic presidential candidate since James Cox in 1920. Bush's Jewish vote count went from 35 percent in 1988 to only 12 percent in 1992.[12] Both probably would have lost their elections anyway. Both were held responsible for economic downturns and other problems, and neither could match the charisma of their opponents, Ronald Reagan and Bill Clinton. But if there had been any doubts in the political elite that a war with the Jews was costly to an American president, the experiences of Carter and Bush put them to rest.

Chipping away at that assumption is probably the single most important challenge facing an alternative pro-Israel lobby and its allies. This will require some help from the top. A president needs more than guts and energetic political support for Middle East policies from a core constituency. He or she needs more than a lobby for the rest of us. A president also needs the political skills to reassure the center and center left of the American Jewish community that the United States will protect Israel's core security interests.

When Mearsheimer and Walt and their fans discuss the supposedly awesome power of the Israel lobby, they seem to assume that presidents are just sitting around, waiting to be manipulated, and have no responsibility or ability to lessen American Jewish hostility. But lobbying is a two-way street. It is not simply a matter of oil company executives or trial lawyers or pro-Israel American Jews pressuring Congress and the executive branch to do certain things. Every administration needs to sell its policies or plans to relevant domestic constituencies as well as to Congress.

A number of administrations have used unofficial Jewish liaisons to explain policies to the community and act as a sounding board for its concerns. But regardless of how political capital in the Jewish community is developed, a president who has it is another important piece of the jigsaw puzzle. And that is another lesson from the Carter and George H. W. Bush administrations. Both presidents made matters worse for themselves because of their inability to build support—or their lack of interest—in the American Jewish community.

The most famous single confrontation between an American president and the conventional Israel lobby occurred on September 12, 1991. After about twelve hundred American Jewish volunteers descended on Congress to press for immediate approval of loan guarantees to help Israel settle Soviet refugees, President Bush held a press conference. He invoked "powerful political forces" arrayed against him. He said, "We're up against very strong and effective groups that go to the Hill. I heard today there were something like a thousand lobbyists on the Hill working the other side of the question. We've got one lonely little guy over here. I think the American people will support me." He even slammed his fist on the podium once, and angrily described the amount of money America was shelling out to Israel "despite our own economic problems."[13]

Bush and Secretary of State James Baker had been trying to cobble together an international Middle East peace conference in Madrid. They believed the loan guarantees would muddy the waters and had been trying for many months to ensure that the guarantees would not be used to free up money for settlement construction. So Bush had asked for a 120-day delay before Congress considered the loan guarantees. Israeli prime minister Shamir, reassured by AIPAC and Likud operatives in Washington that Israel could win a fight in Congress, had tried to go around Bush and secure the guarantees right away.

Bush's annoyance on that podium was sparked mostly by Shamir, not the American Jewish lobbyists. But the rebuke of "powerful political forces" and his anger on that podium infuriated American Jews in the organized community, who felt that he had come close to anti-Semitism and had attacked them for exercising their democratic rights. Tensions eventually eased a bit as the White House tried to soothe the community, but they never disappeared.

Bush and Baker exacerbated the problems with their language and seeming lack of concern for what the Jews thought. "Baker may not have said 'F— the Jews, they don't vote for us,'" a member of Bush's Middle East team told me. "But even if he didn't use the F-word, he probably said something like it. . . . It just wasn't part of their makeup to sell [policies] to the Jewish community," although certainly meetings with American Jewish leaders were held constantly and mid-level State Department officials made outreach efforts.

"Bush was just tone deaf," said Steven Spiegel, a UCLA professor who is an expert on domestic politics and Middle East diplomacy. When Bush stepped off the podium after the "lonely guy" press conference, according to Spiegel, one of his aides reportedly warned him that he would have trouble with American Jews. Completely surprised, Bush answered, "Why?"

It is true that Bush and Baker, in general, did what they wanted to do despite American Jewish opposition, whether quiet or vocal. They demonstrated this during public fights with Shamir before the loan guarantees battle, as when Baker announced the White House phone number and said the Israelis should call when they were serious about peace. Congress folded over the loan guarantees and did not obstruct the administration. Bush and

Baker were not prevented from dragging Shamir kicking and screaming to the Madrid peace conference in 1991. But the legacy of the confrontations, as we have seen, affected future administrations. And those confrontations could have been less bitter and less prolonged with more skillful outreach to Jewish leaders, according to Spiegel, whose advice to presidents is, "You've got to reassure them with rhetoric. Then do the right thing."

As for Carter, "the most revealing characteristic . . . of [his] foreign policy team was its lack of connection to, or understanding of the Jewish community. . . . He did not fully comprehend the American Jewish value system," wrote David Howard Goldberg in a study of ethnic interest groups and foreign policy.[14]

Carter was president before the PLO gave even tentative signs of recognizing Israel and renouncing terrorism. Direct negotiations with Arafat and a Palestinian state were unthinkable to most American Jews and Israelis. In their minds, the phrase "Palestinian homeland" was synonymous with a terrorist state on Israel's borders. Yet Carter seemed to ignore all of this from the start of his term, when he said, "Palestinians need a homeland," provoking attacks from American Jewish leaders. He either didn't realize or didn't care that he was using an inflammatory codeword. And he continued to antagonize the organized pro-Israel community by openly challenging cherished principles, as when he intimated in different ways that it was time to include the PLO in negotiations.[15]

Jewish groups organized incessant, vitriolic protests throughout his administration. Some of the worst occurred in October 1977, when a joint U.S.-Soviet communiqué was announced, committing the superpowers to a conference aimed at a comprehensive settlement. The conference was to include all parties to the conflict, which clearly meant the Palestinians would be part of the mix. In response, American Jews and anti-Soviet activists sent thousands of telegrams to the White House, and furious Jewish leaders besieged Carter's Jewish liaison, Mark Siegel.[16]

Samuel Lewis thinks the flap over the Geneva conclave was a textbook case that demonstrated the ability of an American president to stand up to the Israel lobby and carve out an independent foreign policy. "When we were discussing plans for the Geneva conference, there were plenty of signals of how upset the Jewish community was with the idea of dealing with the PLO," Lewis recalled. "But it didn't deter us. Certainly the White House is conscious of what the [Israel] lobby is doing, but when it decides to make something a priority, the lobby generally can't do much about it."

In contrast, William Quandt, who was also on the scene at the time, indicated that Carter's fights with American Jews hampered his Middle East diplomacy: "Carter . . . paid an *unnecessarily* [emphasis added] high price in domestic political terms" for his aggressive Middle East diplomacy during his first few months of office. "At this early stage in his presidency he was not particularly concerned. Later, however, he found that many in the American Jewish community and in Congress were very critical of his initial moves in the Middle East, with the result that they were unwilling to give him the benefit of the doubt in his confrontations with Menachem Begin."[17]

Carter and his team tried to reassure the community, but they were not very adept at it. "Carter did a lot of good things for Israel," said Spiegel. "But he didn't know how to talk to the Jewish community. He even admitted that he never understood American Jews. . . . He could have done a much better job" of reassuring the community about his commitment to Israeli security.

To be fair, it might not have been possible for either administration to reassure the community, no matter how skillful their efforts. Those were the pre-Oslo years, before much of the American Jewish community began to catch on that within the PLO, there were moderate Palestinians worth talking to. More important, neither Carter nor George H. W. Bush had the benefit of a well-organized American Jewish peace camp with much political clout, although Americans for Peace Now did support Bush's positions during the loan guarantees. As we will see, Israel's settlement policies under Begin and Shamir bothered a great many American Jews and Jewish leaders, but the organized dissent was still perceived by both the community and the American political establishment as coming from a left-wing fringe.

We do know, however, that an alternative political bloc of American Jews sympathetic to Israel's peace camp can muffle the irritating background noise from the conventional Israel lobby. We know that they can give American presidents more wiggle room to do what they want to do on the

Israeli-Palestinian front, even (gasp) to pressure Israel when necessary. We also know that the wiggle room can become larger if a president is popular in the American Jewish community. We know that all of this is possible because it occurred during the Clinton administration.

"Bill's Jews"

Bringing up Clinton in this context might seem paradoxical, as I have noted that worries about the conventional Israel lobby probably inhibited his advisers to some extent. But he himself had the political capital he needed to put most of those worries aside. He wasted that capital by not pushing back hard enough on Israel's settlement expansion and not getting involved early enough in the Oslo peace process. But the fact remains that, during his presidency and the stormy tenure of Prime Minister Netanyahu, the background noise included the word *pressure*, and it was coming from the lips of prominent American Jews who were clearly part of the mainstream community, not ultra-leftists.

During the Clinton administration, for the first time, high-dollar political donors and fundraisers who slept in the Lincoln bedroom included Jews from the pro-Israel left. His pals included wealthy board members of Israel Policy Forum who were also major players in the Democratic Party, such as Jack Bendheim and Alan Solomont, as well as S. Daniel Abraham from the Center for Middle East Peace. He was also friendly with Americans for Peace Now supporters, some of whom were in his administration. "They were 'Bill's Jews,'" said Larry Cohler-Esses. "They gave him a comfort level to push ahead with Oslo."

According to Jonathan Jacoby, former executive director of IPF, "In normal administrations, AIPAC, the Conference of Presidents and maybe a few other groups like ADL have the most access and tell the president what American Jews think. In that administration, Clinton got a lot of input from a much broader spectrum. . . . Clinton did feel that he had considerably more leeway than other presidents."

"There was an effort to meet with IPF as often as possible, and to ask them to endorse certain policies," Robert Malley recalled. "We wanted to show Congress that there was a multiplicity of views in the Jewish community, to counterbalance those who opposed what we were doing." These meetings were also important for internal communications within the administration, as a means to reassure senior policymakers of the support of Jewish leaders. "It did help to write to the secretary of state and let her know that these people met with us," said Malley.

But Clinton didn't limit his outreach to the pro-Israel peace camp. Far from it. Unlike Carter and George H. W. Bush, he won the trust of Jewish centrists because he knew how to speak their language and obviously cared deeply about Israel's safety.

All of these efforts came in handy when the Clinton administration had to deal with Netanyahu. Shortly after he took office, in September 1996, Netanyahu sparked riots by sanctioning the opening of an ancient tunnel under Jerusalem's Old City, alarming Muslims who believed Israel intended to disrupt sacred mosques on the nearby Temple Mount. The State Department reprimanded the prime minister. Two months later, in the midst of negotiations over the status of Hebron, the Israeli leader announced settlement construction elsewhere in the West Bank and was publicly criticized by Clinton. There were other tiffs, other problems, including Netanyahu's reluctance to follow through on further redeployment from the West Bank that had been agreed to by Israel and the Palestinian Authority.[18]

Beginning in the late summer of 1997, Secretary of State Madeleine Albright issued muted but nevertheless public challenges to Netanyahu as well as Yasser Arafat. In September, while in Israel, she called for a moratorium on settlements, which, at the time, was a controversial proposal. While the Presidents Conference and other groups expressed concern and worry, as reported in the *Washington Post*, Albright received backing for this approach from American "Jewish leaders" who "concluded that a much more muscular U.S. role, even if it involves pressure on Israel, [was] necessary to revive negotiations over implementing the 1996 Oslo accords." She also secured a much needed endorsement from an ad—which I wrote—in the *New York Times* headlined "Thank You Secretary Albright," which included signatures of the leaders of the Reform and Conservative movements and "former leaders of such mainstream groups" as the Presidents Conference, AIPAC, and the United Jewish Appeal.[19]

In September Israel Policy Forum released the aforementioned, rather astonishing poll that indicated American Jews wanted an "evenhanded" American approach to the conflict by a margin of 9 to 1; 84 percent endorsed American "pressure" on both Netanyahu and Arafat; and 79 percent supported the idea of a moratorium on Israeli settlements in the territories, which was seen as a direct challenge to the Israeli government.[20]

As recounted in the *American Jewish Year Book*,

> The apparent growth of dissatisfaction with the Netanyahu government in American Jewish circles did not go unnoticed in the White House. On October 6, President Clinton, Vice-President Gore, and Secretary of State Albright held a "working dinner" with a small group of American Jews that lasted for three hours. Unlike such meetings in previous administrations, the guest list was not arranged by the Conference of Presidents of Major American Jewish Organizations; rather, the names were individually selected by the White House. Leaders of the mainstream Jewish organizations were there, but no noted "hawks." Conspicuous by their presence were three dovish activists: Jack Bendheim of the Israel Policy Forum, S. Daniel Abraham of the Center for Middle East Peace and Economic Cooperation (neither organization belonged to the Conference of Presidents), and Sara Ehrman, a close personal friend of the Clintons who was on the board of Americans for Peace Now [author's note: she was also in the administration at the time].
>
> Clinton and Albright came away from the session convinced that Jews were not unanimously enamored of Israel's current government, held diverse views about the specific matters in dispute between Israel and the Palestinians, and would not necessarily react with outrage if Washington gently pressured Israel to make concessions for the sake of peace.[21]

Did this political protection matter? Yes. At least it mattered a little. The Clinton administration eventually forced Netanyahu to agree begrudgingly to a phased redeployment from the West Bank in negotiations conducted at the Wye River Conference Center in Maryland. It pressed him to confront right-wing Israeli settlers, who had previously adored him, and to withdraw from Hebron. But it didn't matter enough. Netanyahu never implemented the entire Wye River agreement. Hebron is now a cauldron of tensions between an isolated, entrenched Jewish settler population and Palestinian residents, some of whom have been forced out of their stores and homes under the watchful eyes of Israeli soldiers. Clinton and Albright clearly did not exert *enough* pressure on Netanyahu, especially on the issue of settlement construction.

Of course domestic politics, and nervousness about American Jewish reaction, must have played at least some role. During Netanyahu's tenure, at times conservative parts of the pro-Israel community rose up with a fury, demanding that the administration stop trying to impose its will on the Israeli prime minister. But the main reason Clinton didn't push Netanyahu harder was his reading of Israeli politics, his understanding that the Likud prime minister could go only so far without prompting a collapse of his government. "Bill Clinton faced less pressure from domestic politics than any other president engaged in serious Arab-Israeli diplomacy. In fact, if there was any pressure from the Jewish community it came from groups like [Americans for] Peace Now and the Israel Policy Forum that were pushing him to go fast," according to Aaron David Miller.[22]

So, one lesson from the Clinton years is that if there is an unyielding Israeli government and a president with support from domestic constituents that he trusts and cares about, the effect of public rancor from American Jews uncomfortable with any U.S.-Israel disagreement can be minimized, if not eliminated. Accomplishing that didn't require a large army of liberal Jews who were comfortable with interventionist American diplomacy. Surely a larger, better-funded, more muscular alternative to the conventional Israel lobby would give future presidents more room—even if the alternative is a two-hundred-pound gorilla instead of the four-hundred-pounder that currently has dominion.

Another important lesson from the Clinton years: when Israeli and Arab leaders do seem ready to negotiate seriously, as occurred at different junctures during the Oslo process, and if an American president has the toughness and tenacity to mediate, most of the American Jewish community will either be supportive or won't do much to interfere, despite the inevitable annoying squalls created by right-wing organizations.

Alas, it might be a long time before the kinds of opportunities available during the Clinton years emerge again. Indeed, they may never emerge. Certainly for the foreseeable future, in the absence of visionary leaders among either Israelis or Palestinians, there will be a need for America to tell all sides "no!" from time to time in order to stave off further disaster. There will be a need for creative bridge-building proposals that call for difficult sacrifices from all parties. It is not politically costly to tell Palestinian and other Arab leaders no or to suggest ideas that they find hard to swallow. Treating the Israelis that way, of course, is another matter.

✡

To gauge the readiness of Jews in the United States to mobilize on behalf of a different American approach to the Israeli-Palestinian conflict, it would be helpful to consider a specific diplomatic scenario:

Let's say the United States, EU, Russia, leading Arab states, and the UN come up with a comprehensive diplomatic package. It includes specific suggestions on final status issues and simultaneous confidence-building steps that will show each side that the other is, at long last, truly serious about pursuing peace. Initially, the Palestinians—including, yes, Hamas—are required to strictly enforce specific security measures, which will be monitored by the United States and other third parties. For its part, Israel must freeze all settlement construction in the West Bank. Unlike in the past, though, the United States insists that there will be *no* exceptions, no more new homes in or near existing settlements, no more new buildings in disputed territory on the outskirts of Jerusalem.

And let's say it becomes clear that the Israeli government has no intention of taking these steps. In response, rather than resorting to its standard, ineffectual complaints, the United States lets it be known that it is seriously considering the imposition of tangible costs on Israel unless it complies.

In that event, the conventional Israel lobby would, of course, raise hell. Some members of Congress would scream bloody murder. What about the rest of us? Americans of all creeds and colors would need to support the American positions, if there is to be any hope of countering the right-wing Jewish and Christian Zionist furies. But, the most consequential core of an alternative would still need to come from American Jews.

Among American Jews as a whole, there is much broader support for creative diplomacy and pressure on both sides than exists in the organized community. Polls about the Middle East are only snapshots at given moments in time and can vary widely depending on events in the region, but surveys have indicated that a large bloc of American Jews want their government to take a more evenhanded, activist approach to the conflict. There are several others in addition to the IPF poll in 1997.

For example, just before President George W. Bush was scheduled to meet with Prime Minister Sharon in Crawford, Texas, in April 2005, 75 percent of American Jews polled agreed that the "U.S. should push both sides towards a peace agreement, even in the face of objections from Israelis or Palestinians," according to a survey commissioned by Ameinu.[23]

As mentioned in the introduction, Americans Jews overwhelmingly supported aggressive U.S. leadership to resolve the Arab-Israeli conflict in the summer of 2008, according to a poll by Gerstein Agne that was commissioned by J Street. Eighty-seven percent of those polled said they supported the United States playing an "active role" to help the parties resolve the conflict. Of those, 70 percent said they would support that active role if the United States exerted "pressure" on both sides.[24]

Whether enough American Jews who feel that way would give the conventional lobby a run for its money, support the administration, and buck up its courage would depend on a number of variables. As noted, the president would need to sell his policies as both pro-American and pro-Israel. It would help if at least part of the Israeli public gave broad, vocal support for the American stance.

The extent to which this bloc could be mobilized would also depend on how tough the United States wants—or needs—to be. Ken Bob, the president of Ameinu, spends a lot of time reaching out to affiliated Jews in synagogues and other settings. "My reading is that there is a willingness to get behind the U.S. if it says 'no' publicly. But I don't see much appetite for using the really big sticks. There may be a willingness to think about some things around the edges, but not the main stick, like withholding military support. Anything connected to Israeli security is a red line, nonnegotiable."

That does not mean that it is impossible to drum up support for some of the other suggestions for gentler U.S. leverage that are made by Israelis in chapter 7, such as an American refusal to protect Israel from denunciations by the UN Security Council. It might even be feasible for organizations in my camp to take what would be a truly groundbreaking step and support targeted financial penalties, as APN did during the loan guarantees fracas. There is certainly a much larger grassroots constituency to support a president who did what George H. W. Bush did than existed in the early 1990s.

The biggest potential sources of new grassroots support for any tough-minded American diplomacy are the Reform synagogue movement and the younger parts of the Conservative moment. But it is certain that, no matter how gentle the American nudging and prodding of Israel, and no matter how forcefully the movements' leaders support it, many congregants will be upset and worried if there are serious disagreements between the United States and Israel. These battleships cannot move quickly or efficiently when matters of great import are controversial because they must take into account the wishes of diverse crews. I hope that Rabbi Yoffie is correct in his prediction that his movement "will be there" if the United States acts more aggressively to address the settlements and that his congregations can be mobilized. That support is not something any Congress or any administration should count on, though.

Regardless of what the organizations do, what might be possible is the mobilization of many more iconoclastic *individuals* from the Jewish mainstream (including those from the American Jewish Committee, the JCPA, local community relations councils and federations, and synagogues), people who choose not to worship on the altar of communal unity anymore, who understand that it is time to stop sitting passively and letting Hoenlein and the AIPACers speak for them. Sooner rather than later, they need to get off their duffs and take advantage of the opportunities for political activism now provided by the pro-Israel left. So do unaffiliated individuals outside of the community who have a connection to Israel but are not willing to give it a free pass to do what it wants in the territories. In order to create an effective counterweight to the conventional Israel lobby, lingering, deep-seated inhibitions about chastising Israel and fears about American diplomacy that could harm the Jewish state need to be overcome. Many, many more silent Jewish doves need to become vocal ones. The next chapter examines why not enough of them have done so, thus far.

4

THE SILENCE OF (MOST) AMERICAN JEWISH DOVES

"Each Man Had to Wrestle with Himself"

As far back as the late 1970s, Ted Mann was appalled by the policies of Likud Prime Minister Menachem Begin, his fealty to the Greater Israel concept, his public alliance with the religious settlement movement—Gush Emunim—and his unwillingness to budge on the Palestinian question. In April 1977 Mann, then-chairman of the National Jewish Community Relations Advisory Council, was one of eight Jewish leaders who traveled to Israel to meet with Begin and warn him about the impact of Israeli policies on America. They were the emissaries of an organized Jewish community that was, according to J. J. Goldberg, "on the verge of panic" because of "Israeli intransigence."[1]

After supporting for decades an Israeli government dominated by the Labor Party, which they assumed—rightly or wrongly—had gone out of its way to extend its hand for peace, much of American Jewry was utterly flabbergasted by Begin and his Likud-dominated cabinet. The new Israeli government was suddenly in the hands of people who had inherited the tradition of the uncompromising "Iron Israel" advocated by Begin's mentor, the Revisionist leader Ze'ev Jabotinsky.

It was a tradition few knew anything about. For the first nineteen years of the state, Begin, Arthur Hertzberg explained, was "a figure on the fringe. In the 1950s he had threatened negotiators of the reparations agreement with Germany . . . with death. Before, in 1947, after the United Nations resolution establishing a Jewish state in international law, Begin had declared permanent 'war' against the partition of Palestine. Until 1967, most Jews in Israel, and elsewhere, regarded such ultranationalist rhetoric as absurd. After 1967, the rhetoric and practice of aggressiveness, in the name of Jewish nationalist purpose, seemed ever less absurd to more and more Jews."[2]

In the prevailing American Jewish narrative, Israel had always offered its hand in peace to the Arabs and had consistently been rebuffed. After its victory in the 1967 war, for example, Labor prime minister Levi Eshkol had offered to negotiate the fate of the West Bank and Gaza Strip with Arab leaders. Their response had been the infamous "three nos" of the Arab League's Khartoum Resolution: "No peace with Israel. No recognition of Israel. No negotiations with Israel." But Begin appeared to be matching the Arab League's recalcitrance by announcing his intention to expand settlements in occupied territories.

Likud's ascendancy created a "crisis of allegiance for American Jewry," as Samuel Freedman described it. With the exception of two years, Likud prime ministers led Israel from 1977 to 1992, "when Israel's eternal right to Judea and Samaria was government policy. . . . The venerable formula of supporting Israel no longer applied because there were two Israels vying for that support—Peace Now's and Gush Emunim's, Labor's and Likud's—and the votes in the Knesset elections split almost equally between them."[3]

In the organized American Jewish community, within a year of Begin's election, "local leaders found themselves forced to defend Israeli positions they could not understand. Contacts with non-Jewish dialogue partners—church leaders, civil rights leaders, labor leaders—were becoming testy. Synagogue rabbis reported distress among their congregants at what looked like Israeli reluctance to make peace,"[4] Goldberg recounted.

Like Israelis, like much of the world, American Jews were astonished and moved in November 1977, when Egyptian president Anwar Sadat made his historic visit to Jerusalem, addressed the Israeli Knesset, and declared his interest in peace. But by the spring of 1978, Israeli-Egyptian talks were not showing signs of much progress. Begin's intransigence appeared to be the principal explanation to American Jews who followed such matters.

So, Mann and seven other leaders traveled to Israel to express their dismay. "We all thought the construction of settlements at the time the president of Egypt was trying to make peace made no sense. We were all very upset," he said. He was accompanied by Albert Chernin, executive director of the National Jewish Community Relations Advisory Council; Naomi Levine and Howard Squadron, executive director and president of the American Jewish Congress; Bertram Gold and Richard Maas, executive vice president and president of the American Jewish Committee; and Benjamin Epstein and Burton Joseph, national director and president of the Anti-Defamation League.

According to Mann, *none* of his traveling companions accepted the idea that the settlements, or clinging to the West Bank, were essential to Israel's security, which was the justification that the Begin government was trying to sell to its own public and the rest of the world. "All eight of us believed that, if there were a partner on the other side, Israel needed to seek a solution that involved two states. Some of us may have favored the Jordanian option, others a Palestinian state. But even back then, we thought Israel had to find a way to get out of the Palestinian territories," Mann recalled.

But none of them said it publicly at the time. And none of them except for Mann raised public objections against Likud-led expansionism throughout the Begin-Shamir years. Mann said he did not think less of those who refrained from speaking out in the pre-Oslo era.

> Each man had to wrestle with himself about what to say about policies that he thought were just stupid. . . . It wasn't clear to any of us what the rules should be. The feeling among Jewish leaders was that they were the experts on American politics and Israel's image in America, not experts on Israel's security or internal affairs. . . . There was a sense of Israel as an embattled country, and Israeli prime

> ministers had to make life-and-death decisions, and we didn't have to live with the consequences of those decisions. PLO terrorists were attacking Israel, let's remember. Russia was arming the Arabs.

During the 1978 visit, "all we could tell Begin was that it would very hard to sell to the American people the idea that the settlements were needed for Israeli security. . . . None of us had the guts to tell him we didn't agree with the idea, either."

Mann soon lost his hesitancy. In 1980, as the outgoing chairman of the Presidents Conference, he spoke out against Begin's settlement policies. In 1987, as president of the American Jewish Congress, he and Executive Director Henry Siegman led a delegation to Israel that resulted in a report warning of the occupation's adverse demographic consequences to the Jewish state. In 1988 he was one of the founding co-chairmen of Project Nishma, which sought to expose the mainstream American Jewish community to Israeli military officials and experts who thought the occupation was an intolerable security risk. That group eventually merged with Israel Policy Forum in 1997.

"My attitude was I never believed in supporting every American policy whether it was right or wrong," Mann said. "Why should I believe that about Israel?"

Myths and Taboos

There weren't enough Ted Manns back then, and there aren't enough now.

But he was hardly the only liberal American Jewish organizational leader who raised objections to Israeli policy in the 1980s and beyond. I will soon explore why the doves who opposed settlement expansion and wanted to give diplomacy every possible chance didn't make much headway. But first it is important to give American Jewish opposition a bit more credit than it is receiving these days. Mearsheimer and Walt, for example, provide several examples of the "norm against public criticism" and "efforts to marginalize dissenting voices" among American Jews, depicting a community in which only a few lonely, brave voices have vigorously dissented against Israeli policies.[5]

Similarly, online columnist Anthony Loewenstein wrote on February 6, 2007, that a "growing number of concerned Jews in the U.S. are no longer staying silent in the face of Israeli policies in Palestine and Lebanon," as if that were a new, long-awaited development. "For too long, Jews in many Western nations have shunned and intimidated fellow Jews who speak out against the illegal settlements or of the cruelty of the 40-year occupation."[6]

Mearsheimer, Walt, and Loewenstein are exaggerating. There has never been an unbroken wall of silence from the organized Jewish community when confronted with controversial policies that troubled the Israeli left. To be sure, there are still those in the United States and Israel who *want* a taboo against criticism to be accepted and enforced, who believe that American Jews should keep their mouths shut no matter what Israel does. They share Hoenlein's sentiment that the wagons should forever remain in a circle. And there certainly have been too many examples of American Jews coming down hard on dissenting voices within their own community.

In one incident, AIPAC's Steven Rosen helped in the early 1990s to orchestrate the dismissal of a liberal editor at the *Washington Jewish Week*, Andrew Carroll. The paper had been reporting with uncomfortable candor about AIPAC and American Jewish critics of the Shamir government. Rosen told another Jewish weekly that "keeping the paper in the hands of the 'alternative' crowd was unhealthy."[7] That was *my* crowd he was talking about, of course.

But American Jews have violated the taboo against criticizing Israel so often—and so vociferously—in the last three decades that it can no longer be taken seriously as a predictor of the community's behavior. It was defied repeatedly by American Jewish right-wingers like Mort Klein of the Zionist Organization of America, who loudly opposed and even lobbied against the Rabin government in the mid-1990s. Even before that, left-of-center Jews who considered themselves pro-Israel refused to passively accept everything Israel threw at them. The dissent came not only from the small peace groups with which I've been associated, such as Americans for Peace Now, but also from at least a few leaders of important, mainstream institutions, such as the venerable American Jewish Congress or the Union of American Hebrew Congregations (now the Union of Reform Judaism).

In *Irreconcilable Differences? The Waning of the American Jewish Love Affair with Israel,* Steven Rosenthal devotes nearly a whole book to documenting examples of public criticism of Israel by the American Jewish establishment. He chronicles a slow process beginning in the mid-1970s—even before Begin's election—in which nearly universal public support for Israel among American Jewry gave way to bitter and vocal dissent.[8] Mostly, the sentiments were kept in-house. But the anger and anxiety kept simmering, bubbling, and occasionally boiled over with such force that it was noticed by the mainstream media, even by the holy *New York Times.* (Based on my experience as a public relations consultant, I can attest that in the minds of some American Jews in the Northeast, if an event wasn't covered in the *New York Times*, then it didn't happen.)

What follows are a few snippets from the *Times* archives.

"Our Way Is Not Their Way." As far back as December 30, 1976, the *Times* ran a headline that announced, "American Jewish Leaders Are Split over Issue of Meeting with PLO." The article described a controversy over meetings between a group of American Jews and PLO leaders who were touring the United States under the auspices of the American Friends Service Committee. The Jews included several members of Breira (Alternative), an organization established by rabbis and community activists who were alienated both by the anti-Israelism of the New Left and the American Jewish mainstream's unwillingness to consider territorial compromise.

Nearly every established American Jewish organization boycotted and shunned both Breira and the American Friends Service Committee for these meetings and other activities that challenged the organized community's conventional wisdom about talking to the PLO and the importance of recognizing Palestinian aspirations. The Jewish organizations' actions were shameful but hardly surprising. By my reckoning, this was about ten years before it was possible to have a polite discussion in more than a few synagogues about whether there were any moderates affiliated with the PLO, which had emerged on the world stage with spectacular terrorist operations beginning in 1970. But, as Rosenthal put it, "The cat was out of the bag—the fact that not all Jews were marching in step had been emblazoned on the pages of the most influential newspaper in America."[9]

The norms of discourse gradually (*very* gradually) began to change and paradigms began to shift. On July 2, 1980, the *Times* reported that fifty-six prominent American Jews had released a statement "protesting Israel's resistance to territorial compromise and Jewish extremists within the Israeli government." The statement, which had been released weeks before by 250 academics under the auspices of Peace Now, was entitled "Our Way Is Not Their Way." Three of the signers were former chairmen of the Presidents Conference: Ted Mann, Reform Rabbi Alexander Schindler, and Rabbi Joachim Prinz. "Also included were three former Chairmen of the United Jewish Appeal's Young Leadership Cabinet, five members of the World Zionist Executive, five former presidents of the United Jewish Appeal's women's division and dozens of rabbis, according to the *Times* article.

The statement read, "Extremists in the public and within the Government, guided by secular and religious chauvinism, distort Zionism and threaten its realization. They advance the vicious cycle of extremism and violence, which nurture each other. Their way endangers and isolates Israel, undermining our ethical basis for our claims to a life of peace and security."

The reaction from much of the community was furious and swift. Howard Squadron, then-chair of the Presidents Conference, called the statement "regrettable." He said that for Jews in the United States to engage in public debates about Israel policy was "always unjustified and divisive." AIPAC's Morris Amitay said the statement was ill-advised because "American Jews . . . have more important things to do," including "encouraging American aid to Israel to bolster Israel's economy, limiting the flow of arms to the Arabs and assuring the election of legislators friendly to Israel." This was an instructive comment: It appears that Amitay was annoyed mainly because people weren't dutifully helping AIPAC win the Washington game, as opposed to being annoyed for ideological reasons.[10]

"We Were Used Like Cows." On July 15, 1982, five weeks after Israel invaded Lebanon, another *Times* headline proclaimed, "Discord Among U.S. Jews over Israel Seems to Grow." The article noted, "Although the Israeli government and the major American Jewish organizations insist that virtually all American Jews support Israel's invasion of Lebanon, there is evidence of

disagreement as the attacks go on. . . . As in Israel itself, opponents of the policies of Prime Minister Begin and Defense Minister Ariel Sharon are beginning to engage in skirmishes through articles, statements, letters and newspaper advertisements."[11]

All major American Jewish organizations supported Israel's initial decision to carry the fight to the Lebanese. But the discontent noted by the *Times* could not be contained. It exploded in September 1982, when Christian militiamen under Israel's watch massacred Palestinian civilians in the Sabra and Shatila rescue camps. Footage of the massacre and the bombed-out rubble of Lebanese houses on television was too much for some national and local American Jewish leaders, as it was for this author. Rabbi Arthur Hertzberg, vice president of the World Jewish Congress, wrote an op-ed in, shockingly, the *New York Times* titled "Begin Must Go."[12] Rabbi Alexander Schindler, the head of the Union of American Hebrew Congregations who had supported Begin throughout his tenure, flew to Israel to express his concern and was rebuffed and insulted by Israeli officials. When he returned, he told *New York* magazine, "We were used like cows. We were milked, both for moral and financial support—and for the influence we could bring to bear on Washington—and when we were used up we were put out to pasture. . . . But we've crossed a watershed now, and our open criticism will continue and increase."[13]

Don't Expect "Reflexive Loyalty." On March 21, 1988, a *New York Times* headline proclaimed, "Shamir Assails His U.S. Jewish Critics." The lead: "Prime Minister Yitzhak Shamir lashed out yesterday against American Jews who have been pressing the United States government to force Israel to accept an international conference to resolve the Arab-Israeli dispute." The article recounted Shamir's speech to a meeting of the Presidents Conference during a visit to quell opposition among both American Jews and some members of Congress. It noted that, while he was greeted with thunderous applause by most Jewish leaders, "Albert Vorspann, senior vice president of [the Union of] American Hebrew Congregations, argued that Israel could not always expect the 'reflexive loyalty' of American Jewry. He said it was 'dangerous to imply that honest disagreements represent disloyalty.'"[14]

Private Doves, Public Hawks. There were other examples of public American Jewish opposition to Likud policies and Israeli behavior. But sporadic protests from liberal American Jewish leaders about Israel—and more sustained, well-intentioned campaigns by small dovish groups like Americans for Peace Now—just didn't matter all that much to official Washington in the pre-Oslo era of the 1980s and early 1990s. They were not backed by a grassroots movement with any clout or by donors with much money. They were drowned out by the voices of American Jews who would not relinquish old modes of loyalty to the democratically elected Israeli government, even the dysfunctional, "disunity governments" led mostly by Shamir.

As far as the American media, American politicians, the Israeli and Arab public, and the rest of the world were concerned, the face of American Jewry was not Vorspann and certainly not Peace Now acolytes, but the throngs that greeted Shamir during his visit in March 1988, as recounted in the *American Jewish Year Book*:

> About 100 enthusiastic supporters met him at dawn at Kennedy Airport, bursting into "Hatikva" when they saw him alight from his plane. Though his meetings at the State Department brought no diplomatic movement, his speeches before Jewish audiences evoked enthusiasm. In Washington, a crowd of 3,000 at the National Young Leadership of the United Jewish Appeal repeatedly interrupted Shamir with applause and cheers as he reiterated his refusal to cede territory in exchange for peace; in New York, close to 1,000 pro-Shamir demonstrators rallied across the street from his hotel; and in Los Angeles, despite a boycott by some community leaders who disagreed with his views, 1,600 people turned out to hear the Prime Minister speak and others had to be turned away.
>
> . . . Upon his return to Israel, Shamir enthusiastically reported that "the vast majority" of American Jewry "enthusiastically and faithfully supports Israel and stands by the government of Israel unreservedly."[15]

In fact, nothing close to a "vast majority" supported Shamir, according to a *Los Angles Times* poll of American Jews published the next month. While "Jews divided just about evenly over whether Jews 'should support Israel in public even when they disagree in private,' younger Jews approved of public criticism by a three-to-two margin," according to the *American Jewish Year Book* summary of the poll. More than 60 percent backed the international peace conference that had been rejected by Shamir.[16] What's more, Jewish leaders were even more dovish. In September 1988, 84 percent of Conservative rabbis told pollsters they were willing to give up land for a secure peace.[17]

"So many [Jewish leaders] during the 1980s and '90s were private doves but public hawks," said Thomas Smerling, the executive director of Project Nishma and later head of Israel Policy Forum's Washington office. "Contrary to common belief, polls showed that the higher up you were in American Jewish leadership, the more dovish your views were. That was because you had more contacts, more information about Israel. The Jewish leaders at the top knew the truth but didn't tell people. . . . There was a disconnect between what they knew and the public relations their organizations were churning out about why the West Bank was vital to Israel's security or why there were no Palestinians to talk to."

Project Nishma and Americans for Peace Now did have a few successes with timid Jewish leadership. As Shamir was preparing to visit the United States in 1991 to address the General Assembly of American Jewish Federations, Smerling and Mann persuaded forty-one American Jews—many of them prominent leaders of local Jewish federations around the country—to sign a letter telling him not to mistake the warm welcome he would receive with support for his policies. They told the prime minister, "Profound differences exist with respect to the principle of land for peace with secure borders, a principle which some reject outright, but, we believe, most American Jews do not reject."

American Jews believed that this letter was written and delivered because it was reported in the *New York Times*.[18] But the letter was an aberration. For most of the signatories, it was a momentary lapse of self-censorship that was rarely repeated. In the pre-Oslo era, the vast majority of American Jews—

both inside and outside the communal establishment—said nothing, did nothing, and pretended to see nothing, as the occupation kept expanding and diplomacy kept failing. As is the case today, much of that had to do with a comparative paucity of intense feelings about Israel.

As Samuel Freedman put it in his description of the pre-Oslo years: "America's doves on the whole didn't care about Israel nearly as deeply as did its hawks. Asked general questions about their emotional tie to Israel in various polls, the doves did proclaim it. But in specific measurements of the bond—multiple trips to Israel, friendships with Israelis, Hebrew fluency—the liberals showed far less connection than the conservatives." Their passivity continued when, in the 1990s, Israeli governments under Yitzhak Rabin and then Ehud Barak tried to negotiate a two-state solution. "Even as Ehud Barak won the election in 1999 in a platform of peacemaking, liberal American Jews had already lost the peace issue to their conservative foes, less through defeat than by lassitude and abdication."[19]

"It's an amazing story and no one's ever really told it before," Smerling said. "How could a community that was liberal, mostly Democratic and leaning toward Labor allow to speak on their behalf people who were conservative and learning toward Likud? . . How could a community known for its intellect end up saying so many stupid things?"

"You'll Never Get to Me"

One standard explanation for American Jews' ferocious support for Israel is the shared memory of the Holocaust. The importance of this memory became apparent in the weeks leading up to the Six Day War, when overt threats from Egypt, Syria, and other Arab states persuaded American Jews—rightly or wrongly—that a second Holocaust was distinctly possible.

In the nineteen years between the State of Israel's founding and 1967, American Jews had mostly taken its existence for granted.[20] While Israel had attracted the community's philanthropic dollars, it was not the linchpin of identity, the cause that mattered most, the central beneficiary of political passion. On the eve of the Six Day War in 1967, in fact, AIPAC was almost broke, according to Sy Kenen.[21]

But the mobs in Cairo and Damascus calling for Israel's destruction, and Nasser's closure of the Straits of Tiran to Israeli ships, prompted a sudden, unprecedented surge of fund-raising and political activism on Israel's behalf. Israel became what Jonathan Woocher dubbed the "civil religion" of large numbers of American Jews. Melvin Urofsky gives one, although certainly not the only, reason for this newfound zeal, which found ready-made mechanisms for expression in the institutions that Nahum Goldman, Sy Kenen, and other Zionists had built in the 1950s: "The memory of the Holocaust and the guilt Western Jews felt for not having done enough to rescue their brethren awoke a need for action, for identification, for unity. Israel, God willing, would not perish, but no matter what happened, no one must be allowed to say that American Jews had again stood by passively. Here, more than in any situation, the cry of 'Never Again!' rang loudest and truest. . . . As Elie Weisel so poignantly wrote, behind the army of Israel stood another army of six million ghosts."[22]

Palestinians have long argued, understandably, that they should not have been forced to pay the price of the European Holocaust. Those who have some familiarity with the United States also get miffed that the extinction of the 6 million has motivated American Jews to support Israel. No doubt they will be even angrier when I explain how the same syndrome, the same determination to never desert Jews under siege, contributed to the reluctance of a whole generation of otherwise left-leaning American Jews to hold their tongues when confronted by questionable Israeli policies. Mark Rosenblum, one of the founders of Americans for Peace Now and its precursor—North American Friends of Peace Now—calls them the "gilt-and-gelt generation."

Rosenblum recalled a yacht ride near Miami, around 1991, with a prospective donor, a wealthy businessman who was "way to the left" on most domestic issues. "He was born in the early 1930s. He remembered how angry he was when he discovered that his father wasn't lifting a finger to stop the Nazis. . . . That's what I was up against, that mentality." Undaunted, Rosenblum expounded on the price of the continuing occupation, the importance of exploring every opportunity to trade territory for peace. He had been making the same arguments for a decade, and he is still making them now, barnstorming the country, trying to drum up both grassroots support and major donors to Peace Now in Israel and its American counterparts.

During a recent interview, Rosenblum could not remember precisely what he told this prospect, but he said that, as the sun faded over Biscayne Bay, he almost certainly talked about his hero, Gen. Yehoshafat Harkabi. A former head of Israeli military intelligence, in the mid-1980s, Harkabi began telling Israelis that clinging to the territories would be more risky than relinquishing them. He urged Israelis to be "Machiavellian doves," to press for territorial compromise with Palestinians because it was in Israel's interests to do so, not out of any profound love or sympathy for Arabs in the West Bank and Gaza Strip.

In Florida, no doubt Rosenblum made the demographic argument that Harkabi and many others frequently trotted out, the stock speech that, while old hat to Israelis by the early 1990s, still wasn't in common parlance within the American Jewish community: These days the same argument is echoed by conservative Israeli leaders like Ehud Olmert and Tzipe Livne. In 1992 it represented a radical shift in thinking for many American Jews: If Israel continues to rule over the Palestinian people, it will have two choices. It could cease being a Jewish state because eventually Palestinians would be in the majority from the Jordan River to the Mediterranean. Or it could cease being a democracy because Palestinians in the territories, deprived of the right to vote, would be permanently disgruntled second-class citizens. Either way, it would be committing suicide.

That boat ride took place just after the Madrid peace conference, in which Palestinians affiliated with the PLO participated, albeit indirectly, by conferring with a Jordanian delegation. The Israelis of Peace Now believed it was time for Israel to sit down with its enemies.

But, Rosenblum recalled, "All the logic, all the facts I gave him, didn't mean anything to him. There was no way this guy was going to call for Jews in a Jewish state to surrender anything, ever. Case closed. There were people who couldn't utter a negative public word against Israel because they were still feeling guilty. They had their own 'Never again!' 'Every year,' he told me, 'I give a gift to Israel during Yom Kippur. . . . I know I'm going to have a bad year unless I do something for Israel. . . . ' He wasn't willing to ask Israel to back down from its enemies. There was no way to make up for the guilt. 'You've got all the facts,' he said. 'You'll never get to me on this one.'"

Today, that generation, and overt guilt about the Holocaust, is fading. But Hitler is still routinely invoked by Jewish leaders in this country. The powerlessness of American Jews in the 1930s and 1940s remains a powerful mobilizing tool. If I had a hundred dollars for every time Jews who argued in favor of talking to Arafat, Abbas, or Hamas have been compared to Neville Chamberlain, I would have enough to be a major Jewish philanthropist (and more people would listen to me). The combination of Hamas, Hezbollah in Lebanon, and, of course, Iran's reckless president and nuclear weapons program has provided plenty of ammunition for those who want to believe it is 1939, or whose organizations have a good reason to exist as long as it continues to be 1939.

It is not only the AIPAC crowd, or the man whom Rosenblum failed to persuade in Florida, who share the primal fear that is the basis of too much American Jewish political thought and action, the psychic space in which Auschwitz, all the Palestinian suicide bombings, what the pharoahs did to us in Egypt, the Iraqi Scuds falling on Tel Aviv, the Spanish Inquisition, and hundreds of other chapters all mingle together. To some extent, my crowd—those who hope Israel will do everything possible to pursue meaningful compromise with the Palestinians—shares it as well.

It is easy to lapse into the practice of what Avram Burg, a former Labor politician, calls "catastrophic Judaism."[23] Against my better judgment, I have found myself succumbing to appeals to raw fear over the years.

During a plenary session of the 2006 AIPAC Policy Conference at the Washington Conference Center, I was among the five thousand people who watched a videotape that juxtaposed footage and photos of the Nazis and their decimated Jewish victims with images of Hamas and Iranian president Ahmadinejad. Then Executive Director Howard Kohr took the stage, in front of a tableau of giant photos of Israel's disparate enemies.

After making pat comparisons between the Third Reich and the mortal dangers pictured behind him, he made an argument that was so powerful, so vivid, that for a moment even I—a PR guy who knew full well that he was being manipulated and spun—was won over, even I was revved up, even I applauded. Kohr told us,

> In 1943 ten years and two million European Jewish deaths after Hitler rose to power, a group of American rabbis traveled to this city in an attempt to get a meeting at the White House. Their goal: to make a direct appeal for the United States to save their Jewish brothers and sisters from the gas chamber.
>
> The meeting never happened. White House officials sent word that they were too busy to take a meeting.
>
> My friends, decades later, in our nation's capital, at a conference of a size and diversity our forefathers would have found inconceivable, the Vice President of the United States will come to us in what will be the largest American Jewish audience that any Vice President has addressed. . . .
>
> My friends, think back to that moment during World War II to the meeting that never was. How much could action at that moment have changed history? How many could have been spared the horror? These are the questions that haunt a generation. . . .
>
> This time, we must make sure the world listens. We must use the strength we have built to change the course of events. *Now* is the time to stop Iran. *Now* is the time to confront Hamas. *Now* is the time for leadership. Ladies and gentleman, *now* is the time for action![24]

Kohr's rip-roaring speech was the last presentation of the evening. The next morning, Vice President Cheney received the aforementioned rousing reception from thousands of fearful, inspired AIPACers, who had been convinced—like that twelve-year-old Jewish boy with his collection cup in Queens, New York, just before the Six Day War—that it was up to them to prevent the next Holocaust.

How can America's Middle East peace camp possibly compete with *that*?

✡

Revisionist historians now claim that Israel has consistently exaggerated the threats to its existence and its citizenry, that Israel was never in danger of extinction in 1948 or 1967 or even 1973. The notion that fears about Israel are a kind of elaborate scam is increasingly common on the anti-Israel blogs. Here, for example, is a typical comment from "Ed" on Mondoweiss, a blog by Philip Weiss that worships Mearsheimer and Walt and deplores much of the pro-Israel lobby: "It seems to me that the mask is slowly slipping from the face of organized Judaism and behind the mask is a twisted, contorted, fascist entity with an outsized victim complex masquerading as a put-upon, besieged community of innocents."[25]

"If you ask these people [Israel-bashers on the far left], they'll say, 'Certainly it's wrong to kill an Israeli.' But in their political calculus, it's not a concern," said Mitchell Plitnick. "They see it as something that doesn't happen that often and that's not what they're interested in combating. The idea that Israel might be behaving the way it does because of threats, there just is no appreciation of that in their minds."

In fact, American Jewish and Israeli fears have generally been based on harsh reality, nothing terrifying enough to warrant Holocaust invocations, but real nevertheless. The fears do not necessarily justify Israeli actions; in my judgment, they certainly did not justify the bombs that carpeted densely packed neighborhoods in the Gaza Strip in late 2008 or the subsequent Israeli ground invasion. Nevertheless, the rockets from the Gaza Strip that were aimed at Sderot and Ashkelon were not imaginary demons. Neither are Palestinians who would like the same weapons in their arsenals in the West Bank. The idea that Iranian nuclear weapons might some day be poised to strike Tel Aviv is not a concoction of Israeli and American fearmongers; neither are the suicide bombers who have slaughtered mothers and babies in shopping malls.

Palestinians have been traumatized by endless conflict, and they have suffered much more than Israelis by any reasonable standard. Research indicates that as many as 60 percent of the 1.3 million residents of the Gaza Strip demonstrate signs of post-traumatic stress disorder (PTSD), and that was before the recent carnage. But Israelis have been traumatized too, and the organized American Jewish community is afraid that they will continue to suffer. In one study of three thousand primary care patients in Israel, 23 percent indicated that they had experienced traumatic events; of those, 39 percent reported experiencing PTSD.[26]

Yet even if the scoffers are accurate, even if Israeli and American Jewish fears are exaggerated, that analysis offers nothing useful to explain the psyches of American Jews who feel a connection to those Israeli mothers and babies. My concern is how American Jews have perceived reality, how that perception has shaped their political activities, and how to prevent the perception from stifling dissent.

The Secondhand Narrative

Another important aspect of American Jews' Israel narrative is that it is secondhand. It is someone else's story, a chronicle overheard and then retold to one another and then to the rest of America. Until recently, before online reports from *Haaretz* and other direct news sources became readily accessible, that story was conveyed mainly by Israeli propagandists, their allies in the United States, and media images.

Except for the Orthodox, few Jews in the United States understood Hebrew during the Begin-Shamir years. Even fewer understand it now. Only a fraction of American Jews visit Israel and of those who do, few visit more than once. It used to be that the small minority who were truly interested in the inner workings of Israel had no option except to subscribe to the weekly English-language *Jerusalem Post* or to read the one story from Israel that appeared each week in their local Jewish newspapers.

As a result, American Jews and Israelis are usually out of sync, separated by a vast information gap, which has made mobilizing for peace an uphill battle in this country. After a once-verboten concept is discussed openly in the Israeli media, the American Jewish community is invariably caught in a kind of rhetorical time warp; it generally takes years before we catch up to the Israelis and discuss controversial topics outside of our living rooms: e.g., "Palestinian state," "talking to the PLO," and, more recently, "negotiating with Hamas." American Jews who follow Israel closely sometimes refer to this phenomenon as *Diaspora lag*.

This information gap helps to account for the lack of sufficiently enthusiastic American Jewish support for the Oslo accords. Both inside and outside the organizational world, they had been taught for years that Arafat was a terrorist demon and that the PLO had nothing but bad intentions and was not to be trusted. When Rabin turned the tables and shook Arafat's hand on the White House lawn in 1993, they were as bewildered as they had been when Begin was elected. ("The biggest obstacle to the doves in the American Jewish community," said Douglas Bloomfield, "was Yasser Arafat.")

I encountered this Diaspora lag all the time when I first became involved in Middle East peace work in the 1980s. Back then it was illegal for Israelis to meet with the PLO. Debates about whether to negotiate with the PLO were all over the Israeli media, but in the United States, North American Friends of Peace Now and a few other tiny groups, such as New Jewish Agenda, were the only ones who dared to raise the issue in Jewish settings.

In the spring of 1989, I spoke to an audience at a Reform synagogue in Brooklyn about Peace Now and its efforts to end the occupation for the sake of a democratic Israel. According to my diary, at the outset, the crowd was polite and I could spot some people nodding their heads in agreement when I invoked Harkabi and other Israeli security experts. As usual, though, a few belligerent characters were wriggling in their seats, obviously infuriated. Then I got to the notion of talking to the enemy. And I lost them all.

At that time, Peace Now leaders and other Israeli activists were making a concerted effort to establish contacts with Palestinian leaders who also believed in a two-state solution. Some, including Hanna Seniora, Faisal Husseini, and Sari Nusseibah, were from the West Bank and, while not formally connected to Arafat's PLO, were clearly part of the family. In turn, Peace Now's supporters abroad had been reaching out to Palestinian and other Arab-American counterparts in the United States and Europe. I played a very small role in this process.

The outreach culminated in a conference called "Road to Peace" at Columbia University in March 1989, a few weeks before my speech in

Brooklyn. It was sponsored by the Israeli magazine *New Outlook* and the Palestinian newspaper *Al Fajr* and partly organized by Friends of Peace Now. The conference gave Israelis, some high-ranking PLO officials such as Nabil Shaath, and American Jews and Arab Americans an opportunity to call for immediate talks between Israel and the PLO and to endorse two states for two peoples. (I know this actually happened not only because I was there, but more importantly, because Celestine Bohlen of the *New York Times* covered it.[27])

So, I told the crowd in that Brooklyn synagogue a little bit about the Columbia conference and why it gave me hope. I said some nice things about Faisal Husseini. I mentioned that Arafat and the PLO had accepted relevant UN resolutions (242 and 338) that clearly implied a two-state solution. I said it was worth exploring whether they were serious. None of that went over very well, even with those who had been nodding their heads in agreement. To them, anyone connected with the PLO or any other Palestinian group was a cartoon villain.

In the question-and-answer period, I was repeatedly asked to defend not only the concept of Israel negotiating with bloodthirsty terrorists but also my own behavior. The belligerents kept interrupting me. At one point, I lost my patience and shouted, "If I had to spend the rest of my life on a desert island, and I had to choose between spending it with the Palestinians I met at the conference or you, believe me, I'd take those Palestinians any time!"

That didn't go over very well, either. There was a moment of absolute, stunned silence. Then the catcalls commenced, and it became impossible to continue the presentation.

If I had said that to a centrist Israeli audience, they might have denounced me, but they would have tagged me as a Peace Now type, the kind of impassioned leftist they were familiar with and who was an accepted participant in the ongoing dialogue about what Israelis have dubbed "*hamatzav*" (the situation). But even in a relatively liberal synagogue in Brooklyn, I was greeted as if I were an alien being, and a hostile one at that.

Today, anyone who wants to know what Israelis are saying and thinking can find it easily on the Internet. But, at least in my experience, few American

Jews are willing to put in the time and stay current; they continue to rely on received wisdom and a carefully controlled flow of news and opinion from the conventional Israel lobby.

The Need for Simple Answers

A related challenge has been the lack of easily justifiable, simple causes to rally around. This is a complicated business. The Jewish peace camp here and in Israel has focused on demonstrating the necessity of compromise, but only if and when a reliable partner for peace can be found. It is difficult to mobilize on the basis of "if and when." We have tried to garner support for maddeningly conditional, murky goals, Israeli policies that required leaps of faith, knowledge of the nuances, and a willingness to take calculated risks—e.g., trusting former terrorists to be neighbors. It is hard to ask people to get excited about the idea of an enduring peace when it is much easier to show them why there is absolutely no hope, and Israel's only recourse is grim, bloody conflict management. "It is easier," Henry Siegman told me, "to *shrei gevalt* [to cry out one's woes]" than to push for compromise. "The Right always has it easier because they can always be against something."

This lack of clarity and easy answers in turn reinforces the natural tendency toward me-too-ism, a desire not to stray far from conventional communal wisdom and risk ostracism. Why step outside the circle of wagons for the unpredictable, shifting terrain of negotiated compromises and criticism of Israeli policies?

"People don't swim against the current in an environment of uncertainty," said Rosenblum. "You can be penalized, not get invited to the right dinners. It's a problem in a small community with an existential connection to another country. . . . To resist it, you have to be 100 percent more certain, you have to have a lot of evidence. You have to have all your references in order to withstand political attack and isolation. . . . Unless you are part of a small community of intellectuals who live on the street of critical inquiry and can feel confident about making complicated arguments, you aren't likely to find a home in an organized political movement [like the American Jewish peace camp]."

Me-too-ism certainly came into play during the famous loan guarantees tussle between American Jews and President George H. W. Bush. Many of the Jews who helped Shamir by lobbying for the loan guarantees were not especially passionate about the Israeli prime minister's agenda: keeping settlements intact while he freed up money to help Israel absorb Soviet refugees. It was the refugees who motivated them, as helping Soviet Jewry was a cause that had united much of the community throughout the 1980s. More than a million of those stranded, beleaguered Jews needed to get to Israel and they needed American assistance. But, to some, Bush and Baker appeared to be using Soviet Jews as hostages in a dispute with the Israeli government.

"It was one of those historic moments," said Rabbi David Saperstein, who helped to organize the lobbying effort. "It was like the '67 war or the Yom Kippur War, when there was overwhelming unanimity in the Jewish community on behalf of a cause that would link Israel and the United States. The community was split—and conflicted—about many of the policy issues in Israel. . . . But on this issue, everyone across the board, all the doves and all the hawks—all were in favor of the loan guarantees."[28]

Not quite. What has not been mentioned in any chronicles of the loan guarantees battle is that it forced American Jewish doves to make painful, wrenching choices. Ted Mann remembers agonizing over whether to object publicly to the lobbying effort as the leader of Project Nishma. He had been speaking out against Israeli settlements policies for more than a decade, but he had also been active in the Soviet Jewry cause. Eventually, he decided to keep quiet, in part because he saw other anti-occupation leaders like Saperstein joining in. He couldn't bring himself to go against the communal tides. "We didn't open our mouths at all. Now I am embarrassed about it. It's the one thing I regret more than anything else in my Jewish life," he says. "It was the most disgusting moment of American Jewish life."

"Knowing what I know now, seeing what has become of Israel," said a Jewish leader who actively participated in the lobbying efforts, "I probably wouldn't do it."

The only pro-Israel Jewish organization to support Bush and Baker was Americans for Peace Now. One of its presidents, Peter Edelman, testified on Capitol Hill on behalf of conditioning some American aid to Israel on a settlement freeze. For a Jewish organization to tell the American government that it should withhold any aid to Israel was extraordinary and unprecedented. Jonathan Jacoby, the group's executive director back then, remembers his nervousness about breaking away from the organized Jewish community. "I remember trembling as I left the hotel room that morning" on the way to Capitol Hill. "We were doing something that had never been done before. I was scared about what the community would say."

✡

All of these factors—fear, a dearth of information, lack of certainty, and me-too-ism—came into play during the run-up to the Iraq War in 2002 and 2003. With few exceptions, liberals in the organized American Jewish community with some connection to Israel kept their mouths shut as the Bush administration primed the nation to topple Saddam Hussein. This book is primarily concerned with the Israeli-Palestinian conflict. But there is much to be learned about the ethos and mentality of America's pro-Israel supporters by examining their role in, and reaction to, the Iraq War. Next, we will take an important little detour to find out what the community did—and didn't do—in the months leading up to the Shock and Awe campaign and the Iraq invasion, the most misguided military adventure in American history.

5

American Jews, Iraq, and the Fetish of Preemptive War

The American invasion of Iraq in March 2003 was a welcome gift to the bloggers and essayists who were obsessed with proving that Jewish fifth columnists had hijacked this nation's foreign policy.[1] It appeared to have everything they needed, a seeming perfect storm of evidence; it was as if the entire plot had been concocted by a Hezbollah activist who wanted to write like John le Carré. There were U.S. officials with apparently questionable loyalties, and apparent connections to a foreign government, who promoted and planned a war against an enemy they had been wanting to destroy for years. There was public support for the war from that same foreign government, aided by a mysterious, powerful network of grassroots supporters. And there was a docile media (controlled by you know who).

This notion kept smoldering in the war's early days. Yet it wasn't until Mearsheimer and Walt propounded the war-for-Israel theory that mainstream American Jewish leaders and other pundits poured their energies into refuting it. The two professors devoted a large swath of their paper to demonstrating that "the war was due in large part to the Lobby's influence, especially the neoconservatives within it."[2] They qualified the generalizations a bit in their book. They allowed that various reasons prompted the American invasion, such as the idea that "toppling Saddam would convince other rogue states that the U.S. was too powerful to oppose." But then they asserted, "There was another variable in the equation, and the war would almost certainly not have occurred had it been absent. The element was the Israel lobby, and especially a band of neoconservative policymakers and pundits who had been pushing the United States to attack Iraq since well before 9/11. . . . Pressure from Israel and the lobby was not the only factor behind the Bush administration's decision to attack Iraq, but it was a critical element."[3]

I am not persuaded by the war-for-Israel theorists. Protecting Israel was *one* of the Iraq War's anticipated benefits, but plenty of convincing essays and articles show that it was not one of the main motivations of the Bush administration's decision makers—i.e., Bush, Cheney, Secretary of Defense Donald Rumsfeld, Secretary of State Colin Powell, and National Security Adviser Condoleezza Rice. Some of those who dispute the war-for Israel theory are people who were bitterly opposed to the war and are not knee-jerk apologists for the conventional Israel lobby.[4] Also, Israel and its interests are barely mentioned in *Fiasco*, Thomas Ricks's magisterial account of the administration's thorough mishandling of the war,[5] or *Cobra II*, a similarly well-researched chronicle by Michael Gordon and Gen. Bernard Trainor.[6] For both books, the authors did hundreds of interviews with administration officials, including people intimately familiar with what was said, who said it, and what those in the inner sancta were thinking. When I asked Ricks via e-mail if the topic of Israel came up in his interviews but was not included in his manuscript, he responded, "Based on my research, I don't think Israel was an important factor. The trigger was 9/11."

But even if a small band of Likud loyalists *had* convinced officials above their pay grade to fight a war on behalf of a foreign country, this fact would not shed much light on the concrete obstacles to—and opportunities for—an alternative to the conventional Israel lobby. It is more important to examine how hard American Jewish organizations pushed for the war, how liberal Jews with a concern for Israel dealt with it, and whether there are lessons that can be learned from their behavior.

Mearsheimer and Walt made a vitally important point about the Iraq invasion that has been obscured in the ongoing war-for-Israel debate: "There was hardly any opposition to the war among the major American Jewish organizations," they wrote.[7] That is, alas, true. And those who try to absolve the organized American Jewish community of any and all responsibility for the Iraq War are engaging in strained revisionism.

More Silence from Even More Doves

Except for the Workmen's Circle, no group in the Presidents Conference publicly opposed the invasion.[8] None of the various dovish Jewish organizations with ties to Israel—except for the Tikkun community, led by Rabbi Michael Lerner, and the Shalom Center, led by Rabbi Arthur Waskow—lifted a finger to try to stop it.[9] I marched in New York City on February 15, 2003, as part of a worldwide protest to stop an invasion that made little sense to me. A few people from my Reform synagogue—but not many—were at my side.

American Jews with an attachment to Israel should acknowledge a truth that is hardly a secret: most of them, on the left and on the right, had a different relationship with Saddam Hussein than did most Americans. They felt more fear and loathing at the sound of his name. Their memories of his Scud missiles dropping on Tel Aviv were more vivid. That does not mean "dual loyalty" played a role in American Jewish attitudes toward Saddam, although bashers of the Jewish community toss out that charge casually and carelessly these days. If *dual loyalty* means American Jews consciously put Israel's interests *ahead* of America's, or that concerns about Israel's safety were more important—or equally important—to them as concerns about the safety of their own country, few, if any, were guilty as charged. But of course Israel's circumstances had *something* to do with their feelings about the war.

One reason why too few left-leaning American Jews in the organized community raised a peep against the rush to war was that Saddam was a bogeyman to them also. In fact, during Clinton's second term, the possibility that Saddam would acquire weapons of mass destruction was an important rationale for pursuing the peace process. To promote that process in the American Jewish community, the pro-Israel left relied heavily on the "periphery" theory of Yitzhak Rabin. One of his principal explanations and justifications for pursing peace with Israel's immediate neighbors, including the Palestinians, was that it would help to provide protection from far more dangerous threats on the periphery, notably Iraq and Iran. The idea was that progress toward solving the Palestinian problem would make it easier for relatively moderate Arab and Persian Gulf states to help Israel; it would give the leaders of those states more political cover to act as a buffer against Iraq or Iran and either openly or tacitly ally themselves with Israel. That was an article of faith to us. It still is.

Another article of faith was that Iraq was an existential threat to Israel. In 1998 I created an ad for Israel Policy Forum that appeared in the corner of the *New York Times* op-ed page. There was a photo of a nuclear-tipped missile. The headline read, "The U.S. and Israel are trying to develop a new anti-ballistic missile system. It's called peace." The copy was a reprise of Rabin's periphery theory, and it discussed how the peace process would help to defang and neutralize both Iraq and Iran. Given that legacy, when it appeared that the Israeli government either endorsed or didn't mind the Bush administration's frenzied preparations to topple Saddam Hussein, few left-leaning people in the organized Jewish community—whatever their doubts—could bring themselves to object.

What about the rest the community, that is, everyone else in the organizations in table 3? For the most part, the rhetoric used by the American Jewish mainstream was *not* the rhetoric of the people who provided an intellectual basis for invading Iraq, those preemptive war fetishists who openly mocked UN fecklessness and urged Bush to take Saddam out. With some exceptions, the Jewish organizations' positions generally sounded more like centrist Democrats than the neoconservatives who were eager for war, such as Richard Perle, Charles Krauthammer, William Kristol, and Robert Kagan.[10]

The organized American Jewish community—left, center, and right—was hoodwinked by false intelligence, like most Americans, like most of Congress. They swallowed the idea that Saddam had WMDs hook, line, and sinker. But the positions taken by most American Jewish groups indicated that they wanted to exhaust every diplomatic option to rid Iraq of those weapons and to use force only as a last resort.

Consider the Presidents Conference's statement in October 2002, arrived at after much wrangling between hawks and those who were much more cautious:[11] "Iraq must conform to the resolutions adopted by the Security Council and the other standards which President Bush has specified. We support the effort to enlist the United Nations and international cooperation to secure Iraqi compliance, including the use of international force as a last resort."[12] The JCPA released a similar statement during the same month: "Consistent with past JCPA policies on the threat of weapons of mass destruction in Iraq, the JCPA supports diplomatic efforts by the U.S., its allies and the United Nations to secure the elimination of weapons of mass destruction, with the use of force by the U.S. and its allies only as a last resort."[13] These statements were far too hawkish for my tastes, but they employed the logic of Hillary Clinton, John Kerry, and John Edwards, a logic that was—it turns out—dead wrong, yet distinctly different from the neoconservatives' enthusiastic rationales for war.[14]

Nevertheless, the sad truth is that the loudest and most strident voices in the American Jewish community were hawkish preemptive war advocates, and practically *no one* said, loudly and clearly, that they were wrong. Mearsheimer, Walt, and other war-for-Israel theorists are right on that point.

Regardless of where most of the organizations stood, powerful leaders of the American Jewish community such as Jack Rosen, chairman of the American Jewish Congress, loudly supported the Iraq invasion.[15] The chairman of the Presidents Conference at the time, Mortimer Zuckerman, wrote several columns that called for eliminating Saddam.[16] In the Presidents Conference's e-mail news bulletin, *Daily Alert*, which was—and is—sent out far and wide, the vast majority of stories and op-eds in the months before the invasion focused on the dangers Saddam posed to Israel and drummed up support for the war.[17] Liberal Jewish organizational officials made no effort to publicly refute or definitively peel themselves away from the neoconservatives whose reflexive contempt for conciliation was the dominant emotion of the Bush administration. Eventually, after the invasion, the Reform movement took a strong stand against the war, but it did not do so before the war began.[18]

It was the unwillingness of the mainstream Jewish community to protest the Bush doctrine of preemptive war, even when there was no immediate threat to the United States, that is the sobering lesson here. The fact that a small core of American Jewish neoconservatives—e.g., Paul Wolfowitz, Douglas Feith, David Wurmser, and Richard Perle—directly contributed to a disastrous war effort should not be blamed on the organized American Jewish community as a whole. But the fact that few American Jewish leaders or groups disassociated themselves from these people points to a need for major communal soul-searching.

The Muffled Voices of Reason

Critics of Mearshimer and Walt resent the way they conflated the American Jewish establishment with the neoconservatives in the Bush administration and their allies. According to Abe Foxman, "The neoconservatives, whom Walt and Mearsheimer discuss as if they were a tightly knit group, are in fact a loosely defined collection of intellectuals from various walks of life—academia, think tanks, government policy posts, journalists—who generally share a view the United States should take a forceful stance in international affairs. Some happen to be Jewish, some are not; some consider the alliance between the United States and Israel to be a cornerstone of American strategy; others lay less stress upon it."[19]

Foxman is correct, but the picture he paints is incomplete. Some Bush administration officials and advisers were associated with pro-Israel think tanks such as JINSA and the Washington Institute for Near East Policy.[20] More significant, the connection between the neocons' worldview and that of centrist and even some liberal American Jews should not be casually dismissed.

The early advocates of neoconservatism were cranky, former left-wing intellectuals, mostly Jews and Catholics, who became alienated by liberalism, détente with the Soviet Union, and the culture of the New Left in the 1960s and 1970s. Within the first generation of American neocons, only a few adherents, like Norman Podhoretz, devoted much energy to Israel.[21]

By the 1990s the movement had morphed into what ex-neocon Michael Lind has called "a kind of militaristic and imperial right with no precedents in American history or culture." To promote Wilsonian democracy and defend the world's people from tyranny, the neocons kept searching for and finding new sinister enemies to blot out. Their credo called for "waging World War IV," as Lind puts it, "against—well, against whomever—a revived Russia this year, China the next, the next year a vague 'Islamist threat' that somehow contains anti-Islamist Baathists and secular Palestinians along with Osama Bin Laden."[22]

Col. Karen Kwiatkowski (ret.), who worked with Feith and his people at the Pentagon from 2001 to 2003, told me it is "simplistic, not fact-based" to claim that the Bush administration's defense intellectuals were motivated *mainly* by concern for Israel when they helped to promote the Iraq War. Kwiatkowski is an intriguing source because she has written ferocious criticisms of the war that mention her discomfort at the "pro-Israel, anti-Arab" attitudes of political appointees in the Defense Department and their connections with the Israeli military. In an e-mail interview for an article I wrote for *Reform Judaism* magazine, she noted,

> The . . . preemptive war push is part of neoconservatism, but not particular to those neoconservatives, like Doug Feith or Wolfowitz . . . who also happen to be Jewish. . . . These folks . . . made their political bones as anti-communists. The so-called Islamists are seen by neoconservatives as the new communism. . . . Neoconservatives wish to see an "End of Evil" in a big, loud, decisive bang. We see a kind of predisposition for violent confrontation that isn't as much based on loyalty to Israel, but on something much closer to home.[23]

Nevertheless, Israel's situation clearly played a major role in defining the worldview of key officials who helped to sell the Iraq War to the American people, and who still want America to star in a never-ending Charles Bronson movie in which we go after bad guys wherever they are and by any means necessary.

Feith, Wurmser, and others in the Bush administration had deeply personal connections to Israel and the Likud Party. Their views were shaped in part by personal contacts with Israelis who had little faith in conciliatory diplomacy and, in times of crisis, much faith in shooting first and worrying about the UN and the TV cameras later.[24]

These habits of mind were hard for other American Jews, including those who otherwise detested what the neocons stood for, to counter. As with the Palestinian question, when the drums of the Iraq War were beating, the temptation to opt for diplomatic solutions was trumped by fear, by a craving for simple answers rather than ambiguities, by a reluctance to go against the communal grain, and above all, by uncertainty.

After 9/11 it was certainly possible to argue against those who claimed that the Middle East's dictators and nonstate actors understood only the iron fist and had nothing but contempt for the weak. But there was no way to be *certain* of these counterarguments. If Saddam had WMDs and the capacity to use them or hand them off to terrorists, it seemed much better to be safe than sorry. And that was another reason why there was much less resistance from American Jewish liberals than there should have been to the Bush administration's frantic rush to war.

Iran, American Jews, and More Silence

This brings us to the matter of Iran and its president, who has threatened Israel, hosted a conference of Holocaust deniers, and—as of this writing—refused to stop developing nuclear technology that could be used in weaponry. In the Bush administration's last eighteen months, the preemptive war fetishists were at it again: Michael Rubin, Joshua Muravchik, Norman Podhoretz, and others advocated an American attack on Iran, although the neocons were a bit quieter about it this time.[25]

Once again, major Jewish groups did not openly embrace the military option; although some, especially AIPAC, came much closer to doing so than they did in the run-up to the Iraq War. And once again, leaders of most American Jewish organizations were not willing to publicly denounce or even discourage the use of preemptive violence by the United States or Israel.[26] There were some prominent exceptions this time, including Americans for Peace Now and J Street, which did favor a mixture of less aggressive diplomacy and sanctions when dealing with Iran and stood out from most of the organized American Jewish community.[27]

AIPAC demonstrated its hawkish tilt in March 2007, when it successfully lobbied to eliminate a provision in a military spending bill that would have compelled the president to get approval from Congress before launching an attack on Iran.[28] It did so again in June 2008 by promoting a congressional resolution that many interpreted as calling for an all-out blockade of Iran. There was no dissent—none—from any of the Jewish groups on the center or center left, although APN, J Street and non-Jewish organizations like the National Iranian American Council objected, and eventually, the bill was withdrawn.[29]

Most American Jewish leaders and groups were reluctant to distance themselves from Israeli officials who made no secret of their hopes that the United States and the international community would take care of the Iranian problem. Above all, they were afraid of Iranian president Ahmadinejad, uncertain of whether to take his threats against Israel and his bluster seriously, figuring—as you've probably surmised by now—that it was better to be safe than sorry. Therefore, it is safe to predict that if, by the time you read this, Israel or the United States has attacked Iran, the bulk of the organizations in table 3 will either be busy justifying it or struggling to figure out what to say about it.

American Jewish organizations will do this mainly because there are credible arguments for keeping nuclear weapons out of the Iranians' hands. It is not only Israeli and American security experts who worry that nuclear capabilities could someday be transferred from Iran to terrorists or who are concerned about a frightening new arms race in the Persian Gulf and Europe, or who believe a "nuclear umbrella" would free Iran to be more meddlesome and venturesome in the region. Iran's other neighbors and the EU are also frightened by these possibilities. And yes, if there is even a slim chance that millions of people in Israel (and, therefore, Palestinians in the occupied territories) as well as Iranians could be obliterated because of recklessness by Iran's rulers, that should be a cause for concern for all reasonable people in the world.

But a good many convincing experts have also argued publicly that the United States, Israel, and the rest of the world can, if necessary, live with a nuclear Iran and that the dangers of attacking it outweigh the dangers of trying to contain it. And here is another sobering lesson: one searches in vain for these arguments in the websites and Iran-focused materials of the vast majority of American Jewish organizations. A tiny sample of these experts includes Ephraim Kam, former Mossad chief; Martin van Creveld, military historian at Hebrew University; retired Gen. Joseph Abizaid, former commander of U.S. Central Command for Iraq and Afghanistan; and Shlomo Ben-Ami. Their ideas are simply not part of the official conversation; they are ignored.[30]

Also ignored is the notion that a reliance on discredited, preemptive militarism won't help Israel in its struggle to cope with Iran. Those who say that Israel would be well served by diplomacy that goes beyond sanctions and threats, and who favor other options besides playing a dangerous game of chicken with Iran, don't find a place on many American Jewish podiums.

For example, Trita Parsi has written, "What will induce Tehran to play ball is not a threat, but the promise of achieving a legitimate regional role without surrendering its pride. For Israel, that could be a good thing. A tamed Iran—integrated into the region's political and economic structures and the forces of globalization—is much less dangerous than an angry and isolated Iran that defends its interests by fanning the flames of anti-Israeli extremism in the region. That's a concept supporters of Israel and AIPAC should find useful."[31] I certainly find it useful. If American Jewish leaders do, too, most have kept it a secret.

What does all this portend for alternatives to the conventional Israel lobby? Unsurprisingly, there is a difference between the positions of that lobby and the people it claims to speak for. Close to 70 percent of American Jews polled in June 2008 disapproved of the Bush administration's approach to Iran, which hewed closely to AIPAC's line. But the differences are not as broad as the no-war-with-Iran activists might hope. When asked their views of various statements by a hypothetical congressional candidate, 48 percent of American Jews said they were more likely to vote for a candidate who said America should attack Iran militarily if it pursued a nuclear weapons program (26 percent were "much more" likely and 22 percent were "somewhat" more likely).[32]

I am sorry to say that, when it comes to the American Jews and Iran, those who want to build a lobby for the rest of us need to be realistic and pragmatic. Catastrophic Judaism is unlikely to disappear when it is perceived to be based on an unpredictable head of state who has called for Israel's destruction. Rationally, American Jews might agree with Gal Beckerman that "it is not 1939. The enemies who wish us harm in this new century are more amorphous, scattered, complex. Armies alone cannot defeat them. We need to be strategic and nuanced, and, in this, Jewish memory will not help us."[33] But it is hard to believe that when they think about Iran, most Jews in the United States will be able to put Jewish memory aside and move on.

Still, it is one thing to be willing to get tough with a well-armed theocracy that has the power to wreak havoc on Israel and the region. It is quite another to apply the same logic to enforce an occupation in which Israel's power dwarfs that of the Palestinians. The two regional crises can and should be separated when analyzing American Jews' sentiments and potential for political activism.

More and more Jews inside and outside of the organized community understand that a reliance on the iron fist alone in the occupied territories has made matters worse for Israelis as well as Palestinians. Thus, more of them should, by all rights, be willing to join a political bloc in favor of changing American policy toward Israel and its *immediate* neighbors, even if there is confusion and hesitancy about what to do about one of Israel's *distant* neighbors.

If more American Jews do get actively involved in the pro-Israel left and try to help matters on the Israeli-Palestinian track, they won't be able to achieve their goals by themselves. Nor should they try to go it alone. The next chapter will look at the rest of the rest of us, non-Jewish Americans who are trying to pose moderate alternatives to conventional, pro-Israel forces in the United States.

6

THE SHARED EMERGENCY

In the wake of 9/11, people from many different religious and ethnic corners of America, in unprecedented numbers, began speaking with the same voice in defiance of right-wingers (and ultra-left-wingers) on the Israeli-Palestinian conflict. Sometimes working in tandem, usually separately, Arab-American groups, Catholic and mainline Protestant churches, some evangelical Christians, some American Islamic leaders, and pro-Israel peace groups are now calling on the United States to actively pursue a two-state solution while speaking out—with varying degrees of specificity—against the occupation and Palestinian terrorism.

Their shared views have become mainstream, as American as apple pie, frozen bagels, and pita bread. Perhaps that is an indication that they have found this common ground too late for it to matter much. But the possibility of two states hasn't yet been consigned to the burial ground of Middle East peace plans that has been filling up since Great Britain took over Palestine from the Ottomans. And the lack of any better alternative solution means any and all possibilities of hope on the American political landscape should be investigated.

Interviews with Arab-American activists and leaders of mostly non-Arab church groups convinced me that my hopes had to be modest and restrained. There is not exactly a love festival going on out there among Middle East peace activists from different faith communities. Far from it. For one thing, there are deep gaps between the narratives and rhetoric of left-leaning American Jews with ties to Israel and just about everyone else. There are ongoing disputes about specific tactics—e.g., divestment from American companies doing business in the West Bank. Right now, even moderates who agree sporadically don't have enough committed volunteers or money, and they have not coalesced into anything resembling a coherent, effective coalition. And those are the problems faced by activists. Even more obstacles must be overcome before there is broader participation from other Jews, Muslims, and Christians. So it is hard to believe any broad-based coalition will ever rival the Jewish and Christian Zionist right in terms of resources and political clout in the near future.

But, again, it may not be necessary to be so ambitious. A certain leap of faith is necessary here, as in all difficult political challenges: perceptions of the political landscape must be changed enough to reduce—not eliminate—executive inhibitions and muffle—not drown out—the cries of unrepentant hawks in Congress.

In a 1995 study of different foreign policy lobbies—including the conventional Israel lobby, Taiwan, South Africa, and Jonas Savimbi of Angola—former ambassador and undersecretary of state David Newsom noted,

> Lobbying illustrate[s] the persuasive power that images can create. The process is aided by the cohesion of enthusiastic supporters and by a polarizing ideological environment that admits no contrary views. . . . With individual leaders, the positive picture of a Savimbi or the negative one of Yasser Arafat became the conventional wisdom in the press and the Congress. *The climate of opinion is not open to balanced views. When circumstances bring a contrary picture into focus, it takes many months to change perceptions* [emphasis added].[1]

It has taken many years, not many months, to begin to change perceptions about the issue under discussion here. But the "climate of opinion" is certainly more open than it used to be to views on the Middle East that don't conform to those of the conventional Israel lobby. Perceptions can change. A different kind of noise, from a more broad-based—and better-funded—chorus, could alter at least some of the political calculations that help to shape American foreign policy making.

✡

"I would like to see a national alliance, with Palestinian and Jewish Americans at its core, an American alliance for two states, living alongside each other, in peace," said Dr. Ziad Asali, president of the American Task Force on Palestine (ATFP). "Our model should be the alliance formed against NAFTA. That involved a lot of strange bedfellows, people from the Chamber of Commerce, the unions, big agriculture. Why couldn't we gather together the same thing for peace in the Middle East?"

That is music to my ears, a new and different and sweet music that I wish I'd heard long ago. There have been Arab-Jewish or Muslim-Jewish "dialogue groups" in the United States for decades. Scattered around different urban centers, they have sought to foster understanding of the conflicting narratives of Israelis and Palestinians as well as different religious traditions. I've participated in two organized weekend dialogue projects with Arab Americans. They were moving and wonderful. They changed nothing, either on the ground in Israel and Palestine or in Washington.

At least by my reckoning, the possibility of *political* cooperation between Arab and Jewish Americans on the Israeli-Palestinian conflict was first discussed seriously by established communal leaders soon after 9/11. There was, among some organizational leaders, a conviction that it was time to put differences aside, not just for the sake of Palestinians and Israelis but also because it was in America's interests for them to cooperate. A few joint, unpublicized meetings of Jewish and Arab American notables were held in New York City apartments and hotels in 2002. The Jewish participants, brought together mostly by IPF, included current and former board members of local Jewish federations and leaders or ex-leaders of centrist organizations, as well as people from the Jewish peace camp. The Arabs included business leaders and some players in the American-Arab Anti-Discrimination Committee, the Arab American Institute, and other groups.

Just before a meeting at the Biltmore Hotel, the *Los Angeles Times* ran a joint opinion piece by George Salem, chairman of the Arab American Institute and treasurer of the United Palestinian Appeal, and Marvin Lender, then chairman of IPF and former president of the United Jewish Appeal. I ghostwrote some of it and still hope their joint vision can be made real. After describing searing television images of the second intifada and after calling upon the Bush administration to work much harder for peace, they noted,

> We are also motivated by other terrifying images, particularly the ones that linger in our minds from Sept. 11: the planes colliding into New York City skyscrapers, the firemen weeping over lost colleagues, the daily photos in the morning paper of people slaughtered for the "crime" of being Americans. These, too, are reasons why both our communities should endorse balanced, even-handed Middle East diplomacy by the administration. It is not only our Palestinian and Israeli brothers and sisters who need this kind of diplomacy: We Americans urgently need successful diplomacy as well, because ending Palestinian-Israeli violence and political stalemate is a vital element of the war on the terrorists who threaten our country.[2]

The meetings between Arab and Jewish leaders that year were polite and hopeful. Nothing came of them. Upon request after I interviewed him, Salem sent me an account that sums up both the opportunity and some of the challenges to Arab-Jewish cooperation: "I believe it is important for the mainstream of the Jewish community and the mainstream of the Arab American community to work together for the principles we all agree upon," he wrote. "I've been doing it a long time. Twenty years ago, when I was president of the National Association of Arab Americans, we had a press conference with Henry Siegman of the American Jewish Congress. People thought it was a bit odd then, but I thought it was very important that we send a signal that the mainstream leaders of both communities could coalesce on certain principles."

Referring mostly to more recent cooperation of the American Task Force on Palestine and the Arab American Institute with my camp, he said these efforts "have assisted both communities in their issue advancement. It gives us and our positions credibility when it is clear to the State Department and Congress that we are working with mainstream Jewish groups, like IPF and APN on issues of mutual concern."

Interesting, isn't it, that one of the principal benefits of joint activity is that the halo effect of politically connected American Jews helps Arab Americans in the crucial game of managing perceptions? The more one wanders around this issue, the more the settings for political decisions seem like a hall of mirrors.

At any rate, Salem wrote that the main reason the 2002 meetings didn't amount to much is that "the Jewish American participants wouldn't stand up to the right wing in their community. In a number of instances, we attempted to obtain bold, declarative statements with regard to the counterproductive nature of Sharon's response to the intifada, including the siege of [Palestinian Authority headquarters] in Ramallah. Although they were sympathetic, our Jewish colleagues were unwilling to confront the leaders of Israel or the right wing of the American Jewish political leadership publicly." Still, he affirmed, "political cooperation is possible. Ultimately, I believe any real political progress on this issue will depend on substantial cooperation of the center of the American Jewish community and the Palestinian and Arab-American leadership. Together, we can provide political cover for more evenhanded American policies."

✡

The American Task Force on Palestine was founded in 2003. It is a D.C.-based Palestinian-American advocacy group whose board members and supporters include Arab-American notables like Salem, a lawyer with close ties to the Republican Party. Ziad Asali, the current leader, is the former president of the American-Arab Anti-Discrimination Committee and his wife, Naila, is a former ADC chairperson and treasurer.

The ATFP has no grassroots to speak of and mostly targets the political elite and opinion leaders. It makes the case for active American engagement that could help foster a workable Israeli-Palestinian compromise and tries to raise money for Palestinians in the territories. The group has begun to garner attention in the Washington policy scene and in the media. Secretary of State Rice spoke at its annual dinner in 2006.[3]

As discussed earlier, the ATFP has worked on several congressional initiatives with organizations in the pro-Israel Jewish left, Churches for Middle East Peace, and the Arab American Institute. The staffers from these organizations all talk to each other, share position papers and strategies, and host joint programs.

It is a cliché that the experiences of Palestinians and Israeli Jews are in some respects mirror images of each other. Both experienced major catastrophes in the 1940s, both have diasporas, both have national narratives in which victimhood is an ever-present theme. In recent years, our respective moderate Middle East peace camps in the United States have also faced similar challenges. We are not exactly brothers and sisters engaged in the same struggle for the same reasons, but it is impossible not to feel a certain level of kinship.

Both camps are intent upon mobilizing passionate moderates, the hardest nut to crack in political organizing. Both must contend with extremist activists and passive, silent majorities. Out of a total of about 3.5 million Arabs in this country, there are about 275,000 Palestinians,[4] and "most of them are apolitical," said Ghaith al-Omari, the ATFP advocacy director who was on the Palestinian Authority negotiating team from 1999 to 2001 and has served in several senior positions in the Authority. "Those who are activists are hard-line." In their case, the hard-liners, many of whom are college students, believe in the democratic secular state and see no reason to comport with American Jews who worry about, let alone actively support, Israel. "It is easy to sit someplace in Chicago and call for a one-state solution and have intellectual purity," said al-Omari, who has spent most of his life in Jerusalem. "But the idea has almost no support in the West Bank or Gaza. Diasporas are always more militant than people on the ground in home countries."

People in both camps have been accused of being traitors to their own people, collaborators with the enemy. I don't know if al-Omari or Asali have ever been called "self-hating Palestinians," but it would not surprise me.

The ATFP has been publicly attacked in prominent Arab-American blogs. In the *Electronic Intifada*, Osamah Khalil lambasted them for supporting Fatah leaders in the Palestinian Authority, whom he called "thugs, collaborators, and corrupt and inept politicians." He also attacked them for criticizing Hamas and for their "defense of Abbas' strategy of deference and obsequiousness to the US and Israel, under the guise of 'political realities' and a 'realistic hope for the future of Palestine.'"[5]

Asali and company have endorsed the Palestinian right of return in principle, but in speeches and conversations, they have made no secret of their position that, in practice, unfortunately, the vast majority of Palestinian refugees will have to "return" to their homeland in the West Bank and Gaza Strip, not Israel proper. That is still a hard sell among many Palestinians and other Arab Americans.

"Our community, like the Jewish community, is divided into those who accept the consequences of 1948 and want to make the best of it, and those who don't," Asali said. His group accepts the consequences, much as they might be angry about them.

Palestinians in the territories as well as in the United States, according to al-Omari, have started to change their political goals and their approach to the conflict in a manner that makes it possible to contemplate a broad coalition that includes American Jews who want to help Israel. "There has been a new development in Palestinian thinking. It is more of an objective, goal-oriented approach. In the past, you had more of a posturing culture, obsessed with victimhood and justice and living up to ideals. There is more understanding now that the main goal should be to end the occupation and build a Palestinian state, so we need allies, we need to be practical. The old narrative of justice is good for intellectual purity, but it doesn't get us anywhere."

Political organizing is complicated by religious differences, since about 63 percent of Arab Americans are Christian and 24 percent are Muslim, as well as by the fact that Arab Americans have emigrated from twenty-two countries.[6] Moreover, as Palestinian Americans with direct links to people under occupation, the ATFP's leaders want to take the lead in any coalition and at times appear to be either leery of or cynical about making common cause with other Arab-American or Muslim groups.

"One of our goals as a people has always been to keep Palestinians out of the power politics of other Arab states," said al-Omari. "We don't want be subsumed by them there or here."

Still, these Palestinian Americans clearly understand that they can't do it alone. "Imagine the impact of a delegation of Jewish and Arab Americans visiting congressional offices together, saying the same things," said Rafi Dajani, the ATFP's former political director.

I would add an equally important, not unrealistic dream: Imagine if Jewish and Arab Americans (and others) consciously contributed to the same Middle East–related political action committees. Imagine if their collective targeted financial contributions put politicians on notice that support for territorial compromise and balanced American diplomacy in the Israeli-Palestinian conflict will be rewarded by both communities.

Judging solely from poll data, it should not be difficult for Jews and Arabs in this country to find common cause and push for peace in the Middle East. There is a remarkable degree of unanimity in the opinions of Arab and Jewish Americans about the conflict. A survey of both communities cosponsored by the Arab American Institute and Americans for Peace Now in May 2007 showed that almost all Jewish Americans (98 percent) and Arab Americans (88 percent) believe that Israelis have a right to live in a secure and independent state of their own and almost all Jewish Americans (90 percent) and Arab Americans (96 percent) believe that Palestinians have a right to live in a secure and independent state of their own.

Both groups were asked their views on a negotiated peace agreement between Israelis and Palestinians that included the establishment of an independent, secure Palestinian state alongside an independent secure Israeli state, and resolved final status issues of Jerusalem, refugees, and borders. Seventy-two percent of Jewish Americans strongly supported such an agreement, while 15 percent somewhat supported it. Eighty-seven percent of Arab Americans strongly supported it while 7 percent somewhat supported it.[7]

It has been difficult to take advantage of these shared sentiments, however. Salem provided one reason: mainstream American Jewish leaders with ties to Israel are reluctant to make joint statements with Arab Americans against Israeli military policies. But there are other obstacles.

George Gorayeb, the vice chair of the American-Arab Anti-Discrimination Committee and a board member of the Arab American Institute, has been organizing or participating in dialogue groups with American Jews for more than a decade. The ADC, with forty-one chapters around the country, is the largest self-identified Arab-American advocacy organization, and Gorayeb has run into stone walls when he has tried to stir the organization to work with Jews on concrete projects connected to the Middle East. There is too much rancor, too much bitterness in the United States, where Gorayeb faces the same duel of narratives that occurs between Israelis and Arabs in the Middle East.

"The ADC has found that if you put much effort into Arab-Jewish dialogue, you get a lot of push-back, a backlash from some members," he said. He tried to involve one local ADC chapter in a political coalition. The members reacted with skepticism and suspicions about the motives of American Jews who would work with them. "They thought it wasn't possible."

Another obstacle is sheer despair, especially among Palestinians and Lebanese who are recent immigrants. "There is a certain fatalism among people who come from Palestine. Also Lebanon. They have had the crap kicked out of them. They think, 'We'll never overcome this tide,' so they don't see much point in trying in this country."

The ADC—which merged with the National Association of Arab Americans in 2002—focuses mainly on discrimination against Arab and Muslim Americans, fostering Arab-American political participation and other issues. While of course the organization has weighed in frequently on the Arab-Israeli conflict, its government affairs operation has also addressed everything from wiretapping to immigration reform.[8]

Other groups that work on many of the same issues are Muslim, representing a population of more than 5 million people from many countries in addition to those in the Middle East. The Islamic Society of North America, the largest Muslim organization in the United States and Canada, is engaged in a formal dialogue project with the Union of Reform Judaism in local mosques and synagogues. When announcing this initiative, called

"The Children of Abraham: Jews and Muslims in Conversation," in 2007, leaders of both groups urged constituents to include the Israeli-Arab conflict in their conversations. Rabbi Yoffie specifically called on Jews and Muslims to "urge our government to commit itself to active, high-level engagement, in order to move the parties toward peace."[9] Working for improved mutual understanding is certainly a worthy and important task; it remains to be seen whether it will translate into anything with tangible political value.

Also in the mix are the Council on American-Islamic Relations (CAIR) and the Muslim Public Affairs Council, which mostly focus on domestic issues,[10] as well as smaller groups. Adding it all up, Gorayeb indicates the Arab-American and Muslim-American battleships are not ready. "I could find fifty savvy, politically active Arab Americans who would sign on" to joint political activity on the Middle East with Jewish Americans, under the right circumstances, he said. But "a real grassroots movement of thousands of people, that's hard to do. It's not insurmountable, but [it'll be] tough. There is a lot of suspicion between the communities. It will take a steady, plodding effort."

Of course, there is no time for steady or plodding efforts, as Gorayeb well knows. It would be wonderful if every Jewish American, Muslim American, and Arab American with any interest in helping to foster Middle East peace could participate in weekend dialogue workshops with trained facilitators to learn how to talk to the Other. But that is not possible. For now, what is needed is a collective willing suspension of disbelief about the impossibility of accomplishing something together, a process described by Hussein Ibish, a former senior fellow at the ATFP:

> Jewish and Arab Americans who are serious about peace . . . need to develop, insofar as possible, functional working relationships. I do not mean here simply Jewish and pro-Israel groups that oppose the occupation on moral grounds, but those that wish to end it for practical and selfish reasons as well. We are never going to convince each other to abandon the narratives that inform our support for Israel and Palestine respectively. But since, for different reasons, Israelis and Palestinians finally find themselves needing the same

> thing—an end to the conflict based on an end to the occupation—Arab and Jewish Americans ought and need to be able to build a working alliance to support that aim.[11]

Wise words. The sad truth is that the "functional working relationships" may never be sufficiently widespread to be much more than a powerful symbol, a bit of important imagery that politicians could invoke when giving speeches to defend themselves for doing the right thing. But at least some new institutional connections have been forged and another impetus exists that could encourage policymakers and politicians to be a bit braver.

If like-minded Jewish, Arab, and Muslim organizations aren't able to do it by themselves, what about Christian church organizations (most of them non-Arab) in the United States?

Other Voices, Other Sanctuaries

Mention America's "evangelical Christians" in the same breath that you mention "Israel," and most people will summon up the image of well-publicized, fire-and-brimstone, fundamentalist Christian Zionists. They believe the Jews have a divine right to every inch of the West Bank and Gaza Strip. Many—but not all—are dispensationalists, energized by an "end-time" theology in which the destruction of Israel will usher in the Apocalypse.[12]

Christian Zionists tend to be loyal and fervent supporters of some of the most fanatical Israeli settlers. Some not only send money to the West Bank but also to Washington. The movement has its own lobby in the capital: Christians United for Israel (CUFI), which was founded in 2006 by Reverend John Hagee. Hagee claims that CUFI has fifty thousand members. In 2007 more than four thousand (!) people showed up at a CUFI conference in Washington and pushed for what was on AIPAC's agenda—i.e., don't talk to Hamas, don't talk to Syria, ratchet up pressure on evil Iran.[13]

To the extent that political calculations entered into George W. Bush's decisions about the Middle East, it is likely that right-wing evangelicals mattered to him and political adviser Karl Rove more than American Jewish voters.

But Christian Zionism isn't the only strain of American evangelism, a broad catchword for communities or people that proselytize and try to convert others to their faith. In this country, there is an evangelical center composed of people who share some conservative social values with the likes of Hagee and 2008 vice presidential candidate Sarah Palin, but who are moderate or left of center on political issues involving the economy, health care, human rights, and foreign policy. Among this moderate group, said David Neff, editor of *Christianity Today*, "in recent times, there has been a reaction to the Christian Zionists in academic circles, relief and development groups and individual preachers." Although many are strong supporters of Israel, according to Neff, these people "have been getting the message that there are displaced brothers and sisters in Palestine who have problems. And they have begun to realize that we can't have peace without a viable Palestinian state."

Neff said that this line of thought is common within a large network of church-related independent colleges, including Wheaton and Gordon, and seminaries such as the Fuller Seminary. A second circle is made up of relief and development agencies that work in the Middle East and bring back an understanding of the Palestinian plight, including World Vision. Their disagreements with Hagee are part of a larger struggle on a wide range of social issues between moderate and left-wing evangelicals and followers of right-wing preachers like Pat Robertson, the late Jerry Falwell, and James Dobson. The former group, like nearly every other potential ally of my camp, tends to place a much higher priority on other political issues, such as preserving the social safety net.

Still, in July 2007 fifty-nine evangelical theologians, activists, pastors, and academics wrote to President Bush and insisted that "the American evangelical community is not a monolithic bloc in full and firm support of present Israeli policy." The group included pastors from so-called megachurches, such as Joel Hunter from Orlando, Florida. This group of pastors called for the United States "to move boldly forward so that the legitimate aspirations of the Palestinian people for their own state may be realized." Their letter condemned Palestinian suicide bombings and "violence against Israeli citizens" and also came down hard on "the continued unlawful and degrading Israeli settlement movement." Richard Mouw, the president of Fuller Theological Seminary in California, told the *Washington Post* that the letter "is going straight to the political authorities and saying: 'Hey, there are some of us who are not quite in sync with the loudest voices. And if you're motivated by a desire to please the evangelical community, you've got to know that some of us are not pleased by the heavy-handed favoring of the Israeli side in all of this.'"[14]

The contrast of their moderate language—which was echoed in a subsequent letter sent by more than eighty evangelical leaders to Secretary of State Condoleezza Rice—to the don't-yield-one-inch rhetoric of the Christian Zionists could not have been more stark, or more welcome. These moderate evangelists don't have a national television show to rival *The Seven Hundred Club*, on which Pat Robertson once blamed Ariel Sharon's stroke on the latter's willingness to withdraw from the Gaza Strip. Whatever political clout they have is derived from their individual leaders' relationships in Washington and a few smallish groups, including Evangelicals for Social Action and the Sojourners, which are on the community's leftward edge. Their particular battleship is the National Association of Evangelicals, which has not taken a stand on the Israeli-Palestinian conflict.

"I would like to see the new evangelical center, which is coming on strong, work hard for a genuine, pro-Israel, pro-Palestinian American policy," said Ron Sider, president of Evangelicals for Social Action, which has about five thousand activists. "If there really is a moment when there is a need for political activity, if a moment crystallized when it was clear that more American leverage on Israelis and Palestinians was necessary, the evangelical center would weigh in positively. . . . The danger, of course, is that these policies might be used to hurt Israel, so we would be very careful about the specifics of what needs to be endorsed."

"*If there really is a moment . . . if a moment crystallized . . .* " That was the refrain intoned in many of my interviews with non-Jewish and, for that matter, Jewish activists. Everyone was waiting for the moment, for promising signals from the region. Until then, understandably, not much energy would be invested in peace between Jews and Arabs.

At times, Sider sounded uncannily like George Gorayeb: "There would be no problem in getting a hundred distinguished evangelical leaders to sign a statement. But it's not at the top of the grassroots agenda. There is more passion here for overcoming poverty and HIV-AIDS." Left unsaid, I suspect, was that there is a much better chance to make a dent in poverty and even HIV-AIDS than there is to make much progress toward Israeli-Palestinian or Israeli-Syrian peace.

A much larger, or potentially larger, centrist Christian coalition group is Churches for Middle East Peace (CMEP), a coalition of twenty-two public policy offices of national churches and agencies. Most of them are "mainline Protestants"—as distinguished from the evangelicals—but the group does have Orthodox and Catholic representation. Founded in 1984, it began focusing intently on Congress in 2002.

At least nominally, its member organizations represent more than 30 million Americans, including the national Episcopalians, Presbyterians, United Church of Christ, Reformed Church, Evangelical Lutherans, United Methodist, and Unitarian Universalists. The individual denominations have their own staffs and carry out independent lobbying and educational activities. But, on its own, the CMEP has an e-mail network of about four thousand activists who e-mail their legislators or sign petitions to the executive branch and a much smaller cadre that meets with politicians.

Echoing reports from the Jewish peace groups, Julie Schumacher Cohen, the CMEP's legislative coordinator, said that since 2004 the reception afforded to her in Congress has become increasingly friendly. "If I went to a Hill meeting a few years ago, bringing up anything related to the Palestinians seemed off the wall. Now, a Palestinian state is accepted." Her subsequent choice of words was interesting: "There does seem to be more interest in Congress in acting differently," which is not the same thing as saying that Congress *will* act differently.

This church group has a major asset that its sometime allies among Jews or Arabs can't bring to bear: its volunteers have better access to Republicans in Tennessee or Wyoming or Arkansas, where there are few Jews or Arab Americans.

Stephen Collechi has another reason for optimism, or least for not giving up. He is the director of the International Justice and Peace Office for the U.S. Conference of Catholic Bishops, the most important Catholic body in the United States. The Conference is not part of the CMEP but tends to hold similar policy positions. Part of Collechi's job, he said, is to "encourage bishops and local clergy to partner with other groups on this issue." Collechi believes faith communities add something unique to the conversation about Middle East policies: an authoritative moral voice that has a political impact.

"I don't think the only way to get Congress to pass bills you want is with money and the prospect of delivering votes," he asserted. "Of course they're important. But sometimes, even when you can't mobilize large numbers of people, you can still motivate politicians. Moral arguments have an impact. [Members of Congress] are often moved by their own moral values. They do things that never promise to deliver money and votes." He cited the religious coalitions that helped to push for debt relief to developing countries and sanctions against the Sudanese government for its behavior in Darfur. That's encouraging, but when dealing with the Israeli-Palestinian conflict, one person's "moral" stance is another's unbalanced extremism.

✡

"For thirty years, the Presbyterian Church has been asking Israel to stop the settlements and appealing to the U.S. government to put curbs on Israel," said Donald Wagner. A Presbyterian, he is director of the Center for Middle Eastern Studies at North Park University in Chicago and an outspoken advocate of divestment from Israel. "There's been zero change. It's time to say we are not going to benefit from another people's suffering."[15]

Who can blame him for that frustration, that anguish? Nothing much has worked, has it? The political strategies of the past have not stopped the occupation. Some church activists don't care very much about offending American Jewish sensibilities. They want to get tough with Israel now and punish it until it changes.

By all rights, social justice activists in the mainline churches should be natural allies of the American Jewish peace camp. Their moral passion, their commitment to basic justice and fairness for both sides, are shared by many Jews with ties to Israel. A small minority veer close to the far left's vision of the conflict, but most who focus on this issue are two-staters whose ultimate goals are the same as—or very similar to—liberals in the organized Jewish community. But the tactics, language, and deep-rooted differences in perspective have led to raw feelings and an ongoing, untidy, depressing conflict that has not been good for anyone in the region.

Among some American churchgoers, the asymmetries of power, close ties to Christians in the Palestinian territories, and the brutal realities of the occupation have fed the conviction that this is simply a struggle between oppressors and the oppressed, power versus powerlessness. Some of that analysis is a holdover from the "liberation theology" of the 1970s, which put Israel in the same category as the rest of the imperialist, colonialist powers exploiting the wretched of the earth. So, Palestinians are treated as the meek who deserve to inherit that earth.

"Church activists on foreign policy issues use the politics of analogy," said Ronald Young, a Quaker who has been tirelessly working to organize alliances of different faith groups for Middle East peace since the early 1980s and is now the chief staffer of the National Interreligious Leadership Initiative for Peace in the Middle East. "They see certain similarities between the situations, and then they begin to talk as if Israel is South Africa or the junta in Nicaragua. That's just not true. . . . And it doesn't wash with many Jews. [The activists] can be insensitive to the importance of Israel to American Jews, to the sufferings that Israelis have also experienced."

It is also true that American Jews in the organized community, including relative moderates, can be insensitive to or defensive about the realities of everyday life under the occupation. They cannot bear it if other people become enraged when Israeli missiles or troops in the territories kill noncombatants.

One lightning rod for the American Jewish mainstream is Rev. Naim Ateek, an Episcopalian who is the director of Sabeel Ecumenical Liberation Theology Center in Jerusalem. Ateek has a devoted following of American coreligionists, and his center has partnerships and joint activities with mainline denominations like the United Church of Christ.[16] Ateek's defenders point out that he routinely condemns violence by both sides. But, according to the ADL,

> Ateek compares what he calls the "powers of darkness" against which Jesus fought to "the evil structures" that have dominated the Palestinians for the last hundred years.
>
> In his Easter Message in spring 2001, Ateek described the political situation in these words: "It seems to many of us that Jesus is on the cross again with thousands of crucified Palestinians around him. . . . Palestinian men, women, and children being crucified. Palestine has become one huge golgotha. The Israeli government crucifixion system is operating daily. Palestine has become the place of the skull."[17]

Such rhetoric does not exactly win friends in the American Jewish community.

It seemed almost inevitable that this tension would degenerate into open conflict when the Oslo process collapsed, the second intifada erupted, and Israel built its security barriers and set up its checkpoints. In 2004, a *battle royale* erupted when the Presbyterian Church USA's General Assembly voted to "initiate a process of phased selective disinvestment from multinational corporations investing in Israel." It was the first mainstream Protestant group in America to formally endorse this step, although others had been considering it. At the time, and in subsequent meetings, the Presbyterians tried to reassure American Jews and their own questioning church members by pointing out that they had endorsed the beginnings of a long process. Local church officials were urged to meet with representatives of Caterpillar and other companies active in the West Bank and push them to reform their practices. Then, if nothing was resolved, divestment was recommended.[18]

So what was wrong with that? It was not, Presbyterian leaders insisted, anything close to a wholesale boycott; it was targeted at companies that clearly contributed to the Palestinians' grim plight. "This is not an immediate divestment, nor a blanket divestment against Israel as a whole—I hope that gets heard," says the Rev. Marthame Sanders, a Presbyterian spokesman.[19]

If it was heard, it was not enough, not even close to enough, for the American Jewish Committee, the Jewish Council for Public Affairs, the ADL, the Union of Reform Judaism, and other groups. They treated it as a major crisis, both for Israel and for interfaith relations. American Jewish leaders were upset that the Presbyterians' resolution had called the occupation "the root of all evil" but did not give equal weight to Palestinian terrorism and threats to Israeli security. They wondered why the resolution categorically condemned the security wall in the territories without explaining that it had been erected in response to terrorist attacks. And they believed the choice of the divestment tool, which had been used to pressure the apartheid regime in South Africa, created an implicit comparison between Israel and what had been a pariah state—a comparison Jewish leaders rejected.

The hackles of American Jews in the organized community are raised when Afrikaners who enthusiastically enforced apartheid are put in the same category as Israelis, who are stuck with an occupation most of them don't want. They argue that, unlike blacks under apartheid, Arab citizens of Israel, despite some serious inequities, do have the same legal rights as Jewish citizens, including the right to vote. And they insist that Israeli policies in the West Bank and Gaza Strip are protective measures adapted for a violent conflict in territories that are subject to negotiations; those policies are not meant to enforce a permanent separatist system over an entire country. In my view, those arguments are increasingly difficult to make, given the West Bank checkpoints and security barriers that restrict Palestinian movement, given the segregated roads and separate legal systems for Israelis and Palestinians in the territories. But American Jewish leaders still make them, and most find the comparison to South Africa to be very offensive.

The Jewish groups fought back. They organized outreach to individual Presbyterian congregations and tried to show how much pain the national body's Middle East proposal had caused. "American Jews, especially liberals, were incensed. If Israel was South Africa, then what were they? The Jewish establishment tried to explain to their Protestant counterparts that Israel wasn't just another issue for them, but the very heart of their agenda," Ze'ev Chafets recounted.[20]

But divestment fever spread quickly. Within a year, other mainline denominations seriously considered it. So the Jewish groups met with them as well. Charges and countercharges clogged the mainstream and religious media, as both Jews and Christians, and members of the same Christian denominations, squared off. And there was also an incessant effort by some to calm everyone down.[21]

At their 2006 General Assembly, the Presbyterians voted to approve a toned-down resolution that, among other things, called for investments only in "peaceful pursuits" in the region. The move calmed the waters for awhile. The divestment movement slowed down in other groups as well.[22] But it keeps coming to the surface and sparking debates both locally and nationally in different denominations.[23]

Arguments about the language in church documents have also continued. One of the most ferocious fights occurred in June 2008, when the Presbyterian Church published an online resource document called "Vigilance Against Anti-Jewish Ideas and Bias." It was a revision of an earlier document that Jewish groups had praised. The earlier draft had admitted that "anti-Jewish theology can unfortunately be found in connection with PC(USA) General Assembly overtures." It had also cautioned against some of the rhetoric used by the liberation theologians. But the revised document removed much of the language that had eased tensions with American Jewish leaders, and it prompted more rage, more angry statements from Jewish groups and rabbis.[24]

I was not close to any of that action, just watched it from a distance with a mounting sense of anguish at all of the energy that was being poured into this dispute, which could have been devoted to more constructive endeavors.

"Ending the threat of Israel-focused divestment was never our final goal," wrote Ethan Felson, the associate executive director of the Jewish Council for Public Affairs, in the *Jewish Telegraphic Agency*. "Our goal was, and is, Israeli-Palestinian peace—an end to terrorism, two viable states living side by side in peace, an end to suffering—the same goal as our Protestant partners have."[25]

These disputes over divestment and language mirror similar conflicts that have erupted between the far left and the pro-Israel community on American college campuses. There, too, more time is devoted to arguing over whether Israel is comparable to apartheid-era South Africa than on searching for areas of agreement among people who are equally disturbed by the Palestinians' plight under occupation. Yet it would be a mistake to dismiss these disputes as simply matters of heated rhetoric, not substantive disagreements. Economic pressure on Israel is a policy matter. Groups on the pro-Israel left, for the moment, are decidedly uncomfortable with it, although I hear it discussed by people in frustrated, unofficial conversations from time to time. The principal objection is a tactical one, the same objection that has thwarted countless powerful statements and initiatives since Begin took power in 1977: "We will lose the community."

It might be possible—and it *should* be possible—to rally support for the kind of targeted financial penalties that the Bush-Baker team imposed on Israel under Yitzhak Shamir, if the Israeli government were clearly recalcitrant in the face of American demands and stood in the way of diplomatic progress. But a divestment campaign that treated the Israeli people like international villains and targeted the Israeli economy as a whole would not be effective.

If there were no American Jewish community, or if it were a substantially different community, I, for one, could see value in responsible church groups launching targeted divestment campaigns against American companies that profit from the occupation. If it helped to convince the Israeli government and Israeli people that there is a price to pay for not standing up to settler groups, it would be an important part of the anti-occupation arsenal. But, given the pain that it has caused potential American Jewish allies on the Middle East peace front, including the synagogue movements on the center left, the focus on divestment has done more harm than good.

"We do need some kind of new vehicle," said Ambassador Philip Wilcox. "Liberal groups should seek each other out. The Washington-based organizations [in the peace camp] should do more to lobby together." But the "credibility of Christian organizations is suspect in the Jewish community. The divestment initiatives are ill-advised. They provoke ancient fears of anti-

Semitism. . . . The divestment people do it with the best of intentions but they alienate American Jews who also oppose Israeli policies."

"In the church community, you have social justice people and you have interfaith people. Social justice people have tended to avoid being in the interfaith community," explained Ronald Young. "They don't have to worry about defending positions. The interfaith people do."

American Jews are hardly blameless, though. "The Jewish groups overreacted," said one church leader who was embroiled in the dispute. "They did a whole campaign that in some ways made the situation worse. It could have been a nonevent. One of the unfortunate things was that the focus was on divestment rather than the larger fight. That always seems to happen."

One time-worn habit of American Jewish communal leaders is to insist on "balance" in every statement made from non-Jewish peers about Israelis and Arabs. That is understandable. But, the fact is, there is an asymmetry of *suffering* as well as an asymmetry of power in Israel and the territories. Palestinians lose on both counts. American Jewish leaders sometimes find it difficult to acknowledge that, which can make interfaith efforts more difficult.

"It blows my mind that my Jewish brothers and sisters, who are with me on Darfur, who were with me on South Africa, can't bend themselves to deal with injustice to the Palestinians," said Reverend Dr. Susan Andrews, a former moderator of Presbyterian Church USA who dealt extensively with the American Jewish community during the divestment controversy. "I just never understood it."

Despite some fundamental differences, Felson seemed modestly optimistic about the ability of Jews and Christians to agree to disagree on some matters and to work together. As a result of the back-and-forth on divestment and language, he told me, "We can and must stand together on shared goals, as in 'this legislation will help yield peace, we support it.' . . . And we've also opened lines of communication between Jewish and Christian leaders. That helps us address concerns directly, often privately, with each other and with Israeli and Palestinian leaders."

Rev. Andrews shared Felson's take on the possibilities, up to a point. "I don't expect most of my Jewish friends to ever agree that divestment is appropriate. That doesn't mean that there can't be common ground on pulling back the 'wall' and talking about a shared Jerusalem." But the stark differences in perspective still rankled, still befuddled. "I don't understand why we can't have a common commitment to injustice *wherever* it comes from. My reading of Hebrew scripture supports that. Why is there such a gap?"

One reason is that both communities still lack a common language, a shared vocabulary, a way of discussing and analyzing the conflict that clearly demonstrates a commitment to the security and well-being of both Israelis and their Arab neighbors. Both communities need to work on it.

"Jews and Christians need to lock arms on this thing. . . . But we're caught in language that forces a choice between 'human rights' and 'security,'" said a former staff member of Presbyterian Church USA. "Right now, people are just passing each other in the night. . . . We need to change the conversation so that we have a more positive, shared language. One way to do it is focus on the need for two viable states and how to make that happen, figure out a constructive way to move forward."

In an op-ed targeted to American Jews, Felson wrote that one important lesson learned during the Presbyterian divestment fracas was that "tone and message matter. . . . Self-resonating messages sometimes fail. . . . If someone were to lecture you about the suffering of Palestinians before acknowledging Israel's right to exist, you might stop listening and start reloading. There is no reason to expect that our inclination toward recitation of lessons on history and Palestinian terrorism won't lead to the same communication failure." When I interviewed Felson, he insisted that both sides had learned from the other. The Protestant leaders, he said, "had a more nuanced perspective, a better understanding of the threat from terrorism. . . . And we've learned from them. It's time to stop ignoring Palestinian suffering."

That is an important and hopeful message. But there is still the problem of how to translate it into language that addresses the day-to-day realities of the region. Here is one suggestion: When confronted with accounts of the impact of checkpoints and the security barrier on daily Palestinian life, liberal pro-Israel American Jews would do well to state, clearly and convincingly, that the *experience* of Palestinians under occupation is as bad as the experience of South African blacks under apartheid. That doesn't mean they must accept that the political analogy is valid (at least not yet). But they would do a better job of building bridges and explaining why boycotts offend them if they also would explain why they are offended by much of what is inflicted on Palestinians every day in the occupied territories.

"Part of what needs to happen is a conversation about what justice means," said Rev. Andrews. "We need a conversation with the Jewish community, to get some specificity about what they mean by 'justice' and what we mean. In my circles, human rights is where it all begins. A political stance devoid of moral fiber can in no way be justified in either Christian or, as I understand it, Jewish tradition." From her mouth, as we say, to God's ears.

By the same token, Christian (or Muslim) American activists should realize that if they discount or minimize the centrality of Israel to many American Jews, if they *appear* to ignore Israel's need to protect its citizens from suicide bombings and rockets (even if that is not their intention), the possibilities of agreement on practical political action will be dramatically diminished. We all need to keep our eyes on that particular prize.

Lighting a Fire

The problems at the grassroots, interestingly, are not reflected among liberal religious leaders in America. The divestment issue has not been an obstacle to the National Interreligious Leadership Initiative for Peace in the Middle East. Formed in 2003, NILI is made up of thirty-two Christian, Islamic, and Jewish leaders who have managed to carve out some remarkably specific joint policy suggestions for the U.S. government. And they have tried to inspire churches, mosques, and synagogues to emulate their interfaith outreach or at least convey their positions, via e-mails to local congregations, sample sermons, and other outreach efforts.

The leaders involved in NILI include officials of most major mainline Protestant churches, two Roman Catholic cardinals, the president of the U.S. Conference of Catholic Bishops, and the primate of the Greek Orthodox Church in America. Evangelical leaders in NILI include David Neff and the president of the world's largest interdenominational seminary. The eight

Muslim leaders include those from the Islamic Society of North America and the Islamic Circle of North America. The Jews include key officials from Reform, Conservative, and Reconstructionist rabbinical associations.[26]

NILI's collective suggestions for Israeli, Palestinian, and American leaders have been far more detailed than the usual vague platitudes about the Middle East that come from people of different faiths, the kind that John Carr of the U.S. Conference of Catholic Bishops has dismissed as "lowest-common-denominator things: against violence, for peace."[27]

When the NILI leaders met with Undersecretary of State Nicholas Burns in December 2007, following the Annapolis conference for Middle East peace in November of that year, their position included demands of the Palestinians. They also called for "a comprehensive cease-fire in Israel, the West Bank and Gaza," which, at the time, was not what the Israeli government wanted, for fear that it would give legitimacy to Hamas. And they endorsed the "Government of Israel freezing expansion of settlements, withdrawing 'illegal outposts,' and easing movement for Palestinians by reducing the number of military check points."[28]

The agreement on these and other positions came after arduous negotiations, according to Young. "The fact that this group managed to get together and say these things, and the way they said them, ought to be a model for others. The purpose of this group is to light a fire under congregations and play a role in stimulating local work. It should goad them and be an inspiration for them."

NILI shows what might be possible. Below the leadership level, however, it is obvious that much more work needs to be done for an effective, energized, multireligious, multiethnic political bloc to take shape. "Everyone wants to end this," said Rabbi Douglas Krantz from Westchester, New York, referring to the Arab-Israeli conflict. Krantz has been engaged in interfaith dialogue for years and is now part of NILI. "They're all looking for a way to come together. They just can't figure out how to do it."

Next: how the Israelis could help.

7

The View from Israel

One by one, old paradigms that guided the organized Jewish community in its relations with Israel have been worn away by the changing realities in the region. It is now perfectly respectable to endorse the need for a Palestinian state and an end to the occupation, the importance of talking to former adversaries like Mahmoud Abbas and the Syrian leadership, and even the propriety of criticizing Israel.

But old paradigms linger. The toughest to change is the unwillingness to sanction tough love for Israel from the United States, including American proposals that make the Israeli government uncomfortable. This resistance persists mainly because, today, "there is still an underlying gut feeling in our community that Israel is still beleaguered, Israel is alone," according to Seymour Reich, former president of Israel Policy Forum. It is difficult for most communal leaders to get past the same raw fears that used to inhibit public criticism of Israel. The idea of even the most gentle American pressure on Israel calls up memories—or inherited stories—of Arab armies massing on Israel's borders, of Saddam Hussein's rockets falling on Tel Aviv, of a time when American support for Israel was not a given. There is also the worry of harmful precedents, the fear that once America grows accustomed to pressing Israel on specific issues, all bets will be off; there will be little to stop America from imposing a solution on Israel or turning its back on the Jewish state.

In November 2005 Reich praised Secretary of State Rice's efforts to forge a compromise between Israel and the Palestinian Authority over who should control the border crossing between the Gaza Strip and Egypt. He was vilified for backing Rice by some American Jewish leaders. It was obvious that Rice had leaned on the Israelis to give the Palestinians more control and to permit European Union observers to monitor the crossing. Yet in response to critics, Reich publicly insisted that "pressure on Israel is not part of my vocabulary" and denied that IPF had endorsed it.

In an interview with me, Reich urged extreme caution and measured deliberation before endorsing any American intervention that Israel would not care for: "I have a built-in inclination not to favor it. One has to approach it hesitantly, carefully. It depends on the specific policy issue, whether Israel should be leaned on or pushed. . . . In general, I think it sometimes needs to be 'noodged' along but not pressured or threatened. But we have to be very, very careful when we ask the administration to call for things Israel might not like to do."

The fact that even liberal American Jews in the organized community urge this kind of careful soul-searching before backing creative, bold American diplomacy is a political reality any administration must consider. The worries of people like Seymour Reich cannot simply be wished away or blotted out with complaints on the Internet by those who grumble about what George Ball called America's "special attachment" to Israel. No American administration can ignore those worries.

Another fact of political life: if a president comes up with grand diplomatic plans or wants to prod and press both sides of the conflict, the pro-Israel left and center left in the United States would be unlikely to line up behind those policies unless they were endorsed by at least some mainstream Israelis. American Jews who feel responsibility for helping the Jewish state would not back a president who pushed policies that the vast majority of Israelis abhorred.

Conversely, however, if Israelis asked for it, there would be less hesitancy from American Jews to support their government if it said "no" to Israel, especially on the issue of expanding and nurturing settlements. That, in turn, would make it easier to make common cause with non-Jewish groups and people who do not want Israel's core security interests to be compromised, but who are less timid about pressing for more aggressive American diplomacy.

Views from Israelis about the specific American interventions they would appreciate are rarely heard in the American and American Jewish media. To fill this void, I asked Israeli politicians and thinkers to share their ideas about how, precisely, America could help solve the Israeli-Palestinian conflict and how hard should it push Israel. These ideas are worth presenting not only because, coming from Israelis, they will have political utility in the nervous community of American Jews who want to do right by Israel; some of them are intriguing and should have a place in America's diplomatic arsenal.

The Israelis I interviewed for this book were not a representative group, just an impressive one. Most of them had supported or worked to implement the Oslo peace process. They had different ideas about how America could help Israelis and Palestinians (put twelve Jews in a room, the saying goes, and you will have twelve opinions). Some seemed to be engaged in a wrenching, private debate between different parts of themselves over how much open disagreement the United States should have with Israel (put one Jew in a room, and you will have three opinions) and were not well disposed to overt American pressure. But along with an unstated commitment to their country's security, they all shared a restrained yet palpable desperation, a conviction that Israel's divided polity and the settlers' power rendered their society incapable of coping with present disasters or fending off future ones.

It was not necessary to ask any of them if they believed that the Palestinians were also culpable for the complete mess both peoples were in. It was a given that the interviewees believed Palestinians had an obligation to stop exacerbating Israeli fears that withdrawal from the territories would lead to more violence, not less. But the topic of the moment was how the United States could help Israel to rescue itself.

Every one of their suggestions—no matter how modest—would be anathema to AIPAC, Hoenlein, ADL, and the rest of the conventional Israel lobby.

Follow through. Most interviewees expressed profound frustration with America's inability or unwillingness to actively help to bridge differences between the parties and stand up to successive Israeli governments. Reporter Danny Rubenstein said,

> The Americans didn't agree with the settlement project in the territories but didn't do anything about it. . . . After the Madrid Conference in '91, for ten years there was a golden opportunity for all of us. Israel was exhausted by the intifada. Israelis and Palestinians were like two boxers, ready to embrace each other. But, during Madrid, we had 100,000 settlers on the West Bank. By 2000 we had 200,000 plus. This was a mistake, a crime. The real Oslo criminals [referring to a right-wing publicity stunt that demanded the prosecution of "Oslo criminals," including Shimon Peres and Yossi Beilin] are those who destroyed Oslo by building more settlements. I can't say it was the Americans' fault. [But] if the U.S. had really insisted and said, "We don't want it," the situation would have changed. American policy was against the settlements for the last forty years but they didn't insist on it. They deducted the loan guarantees [in 2001], but it didn't mean much. The American government just paid lip service with its objections. The building continued. For that, I blame the Israel lobby [in the United States].

The lack of American follow-through on peace initiatives was also disappointing to Menachem Klein, a Bar-Ilan University professor and adviser to the Ehud Barak government on Jerusalem. "What the United States has been doing all the way back to the '67 war is to come up with peace plans and send senior envoys. Then the Americans see that the plans don't work, and they give up. The Americans are pragmatists. They get the cold shoulder from both Israelis and Arabs. And then they don't do much. . . . That has been the pattern. It hasn't helped us."

Don't rely on bilateralism. In September 2007 there was a depressing dearth of good ideas and bold thinking in Israel and the international community about the crisis in the occupied territories. In June Hamas had seized control of the Gaza Strip after bloody fighting with loyalists of Prime Minister Abbas and the Fatah Party, and Israel had imposed a blockade on the coastal territory. In September, with rockets from Gaza striking the southern Israeli town of Sderot nearly every day, Israel began to cut the Gazans' fuel supplies. The world was trying to figure out how to deal with the two feuding governments representing the Palestinian people, and it was difficult to find anyone with practical suggestions that offered a glimmer of hope. But former Israeli foreign minister Shlomo Ben-Ami, whom I interviewed that August, wouldn't give up.

Ben-Ami is the Israeli most closely identified with the premise that bilateral negotiations are doomed to fail and that Israeli-Palestinian peace won't be possible without a bold new international initiative led by the United States. The point of presenting his ideas here is not to endorse them. Different, new ideas will no doubt be necessary in one and three and ten years. The point is to convey the conviction of a veteran negotiator that "the Americans need to have more maneuvering room to discuss and suggest, as friends should do, what Israel needs." Ben-Ami urged,

> Don't let the parties try to reach an agreement by themselves. We tried this. This leads nowhere. The Israelis are incapable of achieving an agreement because of their dysfunctional coalition governments and political system. The Palestinians are too fragmented and too weak to meet Israel's security concerns without international assistance. Israel should expect the U.S. to support her not only with financial and military aid. The U.S. needs to lead an international coalition for Middle East peace.
>
> Normally, Israeli policymakers expect the United States to underwrite the process, to help us cut our losses, but never to be too involved in negotiations. That has proved to be very negative. It is up to the U.S. to create international support for the Clinton peace parameters. That means America needs to convince Russia, the EU, and key Arab states to support it. . . . The Clinton parameters

> should be brought before the parties as an international plan, as the international community's definition of UN Resolution 242. In the territories, only when there is a clear endgame in sight can legitimacy be created for a crackdown on terrorists."

What Ben-Ami wanted would not go over well with much of the mainstream American Jewish community, especially AIPAC. In the *American Prospect*, AIPAC spokesperson Rebecca Needler claimed that the Oslo process's "success," such as it was, "grew from direct negotiations between the two parties—exactly what AIPAC lobbies for today. . . . After the failure of negotiations at Camp David, American Jews became painfully aware of the inadequacy of a U.S.-imposed solution in the Middle East. While many Jewish organizations struggle to redefine themselves in the wake of this reality, AIPAC has long maintained that *only direct negotiations between the parties will result in peace* [emphasis added]."[1]

Daniel Levy disagrees. "That thought experiment has failed. We told ourselves that the occupier could negotiate the terms of a peace treaty with the occupied party. In the real world, it doesn't work. So we need something else to change the dynamic. . . . It has to be America."

Force Israel to ask itself questions. "It's an unreal situation because Israelis don't know the price they are paying for the settlements. Those costs should be put in front of the Israeli public, but they are opaque," said Gershom Goremberg, author of *The Accidental Empire: Israel and the Birth of Settlements, 1967–1977*. "In one way or another, the American government would help by making those costs transparent."

Goremberg, Peace Now activists, and others have tried for decades to get an accurate accounting of the occupation but have come up empty because, he said, "the settlement budgets are too many separate budget lines; all kinds of departments and entities are involved. No one in power has come along and said, 'I want a transparent democracy. I want to create awareness of the costs.'" The only person who did that, albeit indirectly, was George H. W. Bush, Goremberg said. In confronting Shamir on the loan guarantees and refusing to automatically fork over American money if it would be spent on settlements, "Bush showed Israelis there was a real price to pay. . . . It can't be proved, but many say Shamir lost the election in 1990 because Israelis couldn't forgive him for a confrontation with America."

The United States, Goremberg continued, should insist on learning the monetary costs. "You could say, 'Everything is fungible.' We are giving you money and even if it doesn't go directly [to the settlements], it frees up your budget and you are spending money on things we don't find helpful. . . . And if the Israeli public finally got that information, we would have a better chance of an informed debate."

Take advantage of the special relationship. Echoing Goremberg's comment about the fate of Shamir after the loan guarantees fracas, Ben-Ami mentioned that "an Israeli prime minister will have no problem getting elected if he argues with Europe. He will have a hard time getting elected if he argues with the United States."

Yossi Alpher agreed. A former Mossad operative, now a well-known strategic analyst and editor of *Bitterlemons.org*, he said, "It is extremely important to the Israeli public that there not be major disagreements with the United States, as we understand that the U.S. is our ultimate guarantor of security. If the U.S. has forcefully indicated that its highest priority interests are at stake, and if we are asked to do something, and there needs to be some push-and-pull with the [American] administration, the Israeli public will understand."

After George W. Bush presented the Road Map to the Israelis in 2003, "Sharon formally accepted it in order to keep Bush on his side," Alpher said. "He had a very healthy understanding of the need to maintain close ties with the United States." But "Bush capitulated," after Sharon's aides submitted a host of qualifications and Israel did not fulfill its promises, such as dismantling illegal settlement outposts. "Had Bush stood his ground," Alpher believes, "he had a good enough case that Sharon might have backed down."

Rely on the "freyer" factor. "Israelis don't want to be *freyers* [suckers, in Yiddish]. To be a *freyer* is a fate worse than death to most Israelis. . . . They understand that Americans don't want to be *freyer*s either," said Ephraim Sneh, a former Labor Party leader who has held a variety of cabinet posts. Sneh started his own political party in 2008. "From an Israeli perspective, from my perspective, American pressure should not cross certain lines. It should not dictate the formula of agreements, the future of the security regime or borders. But in order to make sure Israel fulfills its commitments, it's helpful for America to exert pressure." Therefore, he said, the Israeli public would support or at least not object too strongly if the United States prodded Israel to keep its promises.

According to Sneh, the demand that Israel keep its word and dismantle the illegal settlement outposts in the West Bank would be a productive use of American influence. He also said an insistence that Israel stop expanding more established settlements, as promised, would resonate positively in much of the Israeli public (although he clearly knew that the vocal right would be furious).

Precisely what constitutes "*expanded* settlements" has never been clearly defined or agreed upon by the Israelis and Americans. Israel has permitted new housing to be built relatively short distances from existing settlements and has called them "neighborhoods." But Sneh has little patience for that obfuscation. "It is clear what this means. If you build, if you expand, then you are violating the terms. The United States should say, 'Stop construction.' It's simple. Either you stop building or you don't."

Try tough love. But what if Israel doesn't listen? What if it doesn't keep its promises? What if it won't make commitments that the United States believes are necessary to keep the hope for peace alive? What if it doesn't stop taking actions that will make it much more difficult to achieve peace?

Among foreign policy experts who favor American evenhandedness in the Israeli-Palestinian conflict, it is difficult to find cogent, informed recommendations for precisely what kind of American leverage should be used and which diplomatic sticks should be available. Former American diplomats have been reluctant to wade into that political hornet's nest when discussing the Middle East.

In the report from the Kurtzer-Lazensky study group, a dry, matter-of-fact clause brings up an explosive topic: "Commitments made by the parties and agreements entered into must be respected and implemented. The

United States must ensure compliance through monitoring, setting standards of accountability, reporting violations fairly to the parties and *exacting consequences when commitments are broken or agreements not implemented* [emphasis added]."[2] Yet nowhere in the report is a range of possible "consequences" spelled out.

Aaron David Miller, in *The Much Too Promised Land,* notes that "we have demonstrated that we can be tough with the Palestinians on terror and violence. . . . We need to be tough with the Israelis, privately and publicly, on settlement activity. The fact is that the settlements are totally incompatible with creating confidence, let alone with generating an atmosphere for serious negotiations. Israel must freeze these activities. And we must impose costs if they won't."[3] Ah, but what "costs?" He won't say.

Some Israelis hope America will force Israel to pay a price for the settlement enterprise and other follies. In recent years, their anguish has occasionally prompted uninhibited, if impractical, pleas for help. In February 2008, for example, Israeli novelist A. B. Yehoshua wrote an editorial in *La Stampa*, the Italian daily, urging the United States to recall its ambassador until Israel removed illegal settlement outposts in the West Bank: "I can guarantee you that had [Bush] acted in this manner, Israel would have promptly dismantled the outposts, and the US administration would thus cement the faith of the Israelis and the Palestinians in the peace process."[4] Two months earlier David Landau, the editor of *Haaretz*, caused a stir at a dinner party attended by Secretary of State Rice, when he said, "Israel, after 40 years of failing to resolve its problem of occupation," needed America to "rape it into resolving the problem." After being criticized in the Hebrew press, he refused to back down.[5]

The Israelis I interviewed were no less anguished, but their suggestions were generally more practical. Some Israelis who actively supported the Oslo process are adamantly opposed to American interventionism. Alon Pinkas, a former counsel general for Israel in New York City, said, "I think it would be dangerous to endorse American pressure. There is a left wing that prays for American pressure, like Shlomo Ben-Ami, and a right wing that wants pressure in a different direction, to resist territorial compromise." He understood that since "Israel is the homeland of the Jewish people, you want American Jews to have a say. I can't say you should help me and then tell you that you can't speak out. If you think public discourse about Israel among American Jews has been right wing, you should balance it. . . . But I would not like an Israeli to actively encourage pressure."

But others, including experienced diplomats, have specific suggestions for diplomatic sticks America should be prepared to use, even though they hope that there will be no need to use them. Shlomo Gur was the director general of the Justice Ministry in the Barak government and deputy chief of staff of the Israeli embassy in Washington under Rabin. If Israel continued to plod along, changing facts on the ground in the territories and not stopping its creeping expansionism, Gur indicated the United States had a great many options that should be considered:

> The philosophy should be: prevention of every carrot is a stick, prevention of every stick is a carrot. The Americans could take the same approach to Israel as they take to China or Venezuela, [or] other countries that give it some trouble. What could be at stake are defense contracts, not contracts having to do with our security . . . , but contracts involving the sale of our arms to other countries. There are economic agreements related to agriculture; a certain percentage of American imports are produced in Israel, for example. There are the loan guarantees and other financial arrangements, financial ties. . . . Israel wants better connections with the EU. The United States doesn't need to be happy about it.

The warning that these economic and political agreements will not be sure things, he suggested, should be announced with a mixture of "private communications to the prime minister and public communications to Israel."

Another tool available to American diplomats is the United Nations, said David Kimche, the director general of Israel's Foreign Ministry in the Begin government and a former high-level official in the Mossad, who is now president of the Israel Council on Foreign Relations. "If Israel won't budge on the settlements, America should publicly denounce Israel's stand. It should say, 'If there are Security Council debates, we won't use our veto powers.' If the U.S. denounced Israel and stopped vetoing UN resolutions, it would be a powerful signal. It would be a major sign to the Israeli public that something was very wrong. If this happened more than once, I think the government [of Israel] would be under pressure to back down."

Menachem Klein was openly ambivalent about a forceful American role. On the one hand, he said, "I don't want the Americans to decide for us. It is our own decision. That is why we have an independent state. We should decide what is best for ourselves as a nation and a society." But, on the other hand, he sounded like a member of a left-wing church group that wants to put fierce economic pressure on Israel. "The United States should not support the settlement program," he said, and ticked off suggestions: "Tighten restrictions on U.S. funding for settlements. Label each product exported from the settlements so it is clear where it was manufactured . . . or put heavy taxes on those products. Boycott all of these products if you must. I am talking about *all* settlements beyond the '67 borders."

What these Israelis offered, collectively, were guidelines for the kind of American involvement that would help their country but would not in any way compromise or threaten Israel's security. The U.S. government needs *all* of these and more in its diplomatic tool kit. Of equal importance, Israel needs to know what is in that kit.

It would be a major leap into uncharted territory for self-styled pro-Israel American Jewish organizations to endorse some of the more bold suggestions from Gur, Kimche, or Klein. But what we are witnessing may be the latest example of "Diaspora lag"; if Israelis start talking more openly about American interventions, the ideas could begin to sway more American Jews who are worried about Israel's future as well as the security of their own country. Israelis who want American help, in other words, are also a piece of the jigsaw puzzle.

What will not work, what would be politically counterproductive, and what would not be right is for the American government to forcefully impose an agreement on the Israeli people. Mearsheimer and Walt, for example, offer the following recommendation:

> The United States has enormous potential leverage at its disposal for dealing with Israel and the Palestinians. It could threaten to cut off all economic and diplomatic support for Israel. If that were not enough, it would have little difficulty lining up international diplomatic support to isolate Israel, much the way South Africa was shunned at the end of the last century. Regarding the Palestinians, the United States could hold out the promise of fulfilling their dream of a viable state in the Occupied Territories coupled with massive long term economic aid. In return, the Palestinians would have to end all terrorism against Israel.[6]

Let's leave aside the fact that this prescription is unfair to Israel because it lays all the blame for what has happened at Israel's feet; it presumes that all an Israeli prime minister needs to do is withdraw from the territories, even if there is no Palestinian partner with the will or capacity to stop terrorist attacks and rocket launches. But even if that kind of diplomatic pressure were fair, it would be inconceivable for an American president to go that far. Not only would the entire panoply of Jewish and other organizations that are supportive of Israel find that course abhorrent, but so would many other Americans. Some polls, which Mearsheimer and Walt cite, have shown support for more American pressure on both sides. But none of them show that the American people want to treat Israel like a beyond-the-international-pale state that deserves to be "shunned like South Africa."[7] Americans, as a whole, still have a great deal of sympathy for Israel's circumstances.

Elsewhere in their tome, Mearsheimer and Walt offer suggestions for a new Israel lobby that represents the moderate majority of American Jews and garners support from other Americans. But the moderate forces they want to strengthen would want no part of their proposed tactics because they involve forcing the Israeli people to accept a solution, rather than find one on the basis of give-and-take negotiations buttressed with international support. That is what the American government must deal with. And whoever wants that government to overcome its inhibitions to press both Israelis and Palestinians hard must deal with it as well.

Fortunately, communal strictures prohibiting the kind of independent action envisioned by the Israelis are not nearly as strong as they used to be. More important, the negative consequences of doing nothing, of clinging to the status quo, have become clearer. "You need to galvanize other American Jews to change their idea about what it means to be pro-Israel," Goremberg said. "By supporting American engagement to bring about a peace agreement, they will be helping Israel. A peace agreement with the Palestinians would be one of the greatest gifts America could give to Israel."

It isn't likely that we will be seeing an America-Israel Interventionist League, a formal mechanism for Israelis to plead for American help in the near future (although that is a great idea). But a steady stream of public suggestions from Israelis would help immeasurably to change the nature of the discourse among American Jews. It would chip away at their timid reluctance to endorse the kind of American engagement that could, conceivably, change the deplorable facts on the ground.

8

Rhetoric (and Paradigms) for the Rest of Us

"There is no serious political debate among either Democrats or Republicans about our policy toward Israelis and Palestinians," wrote Nicholas Kristoff, asserting something only a little less obvious than the fact that the sun sets every evening. "And that silence harms America, Middle East peace prospects and Israel itself. . . . One reason is that American politicians have learned to muzzle themselves. In the run-up to the 2004 Democratic primaries, Howard Dean said he favored an 'even-handed role' for the U.S.—and was blasted for being hostile to Israel."[1]

One of the explanations for this state of affairs is obvious and well-known. Politicians and elected officials don't want to antagonize people who devote their lives to searching out and then attacking public figures who so much as hint that Israel bears some responsibility for the Palestinians' plight or the Middle East's problems. The power of these people to clamp down on those who lambaste Israel or its American supporters is often greatly exaggerated, but there is no doubt that the muzzlers are out there, doing their best. Jimmy Carter was hounded by furious objections after releasing *Palestine: Peace Not Apartheid*; some donors to Brandeis University reportedly threatened to withhold contributions when he was scheduled to speak there.[2] A scheduled play based on the writings of Rachel Corrie, a young

American who was run over by an Israeli bulldozer during a protest against the destruction of Palestinian homes in the West Bank, was cancelled by the New York Theater Workshop in February 2006 because of complaints that it wasn't "balanced."[3] During their book tour, Mearsheimer and Walt kept complaining that it was impossible to have an honest public conversation about the Israel lobby's power. A few institutions proved them right, like the Chicago Council on Global Affairs, which cancelled their scheduled appearance, supposedly because of complaints that their presentation would not be balanced.[4]

However, Carter did speak at Brandeis and received a warm reception. His book was a bestseller for a while.[5] Eventually, the Rachel Corrie play was performed in New York City.[6] And one thing that Mearsheimer and Walt certainly accomplished was to spark a no-holds-barred public conversation about the Israel lobby. Still, there are enough examples out there of attempts to quash critiques of Israel to warrant concern.

Perceptions, and self-censorship, probably play a role here too. Who knows how many plays have been cancelled, how many invitations for lecturers have not been proffered, for fear of angry reactions from American Jews? More important, that same fear prompts too many politicians to deal with the Middle East by either mouthing platitudes about undying support for Israel or saying nothing at all. They apply the same anticipatory vetoes to their stump speeches that State Department officials apply to policymaking. Both struggle to function in a rhetorical environment where the terms of the debate are still controlled by those who treat the Israeli-Palestinian conflict as a zero-sum game, in which anything good or sympathetic that is said about the Palestinians is automatically bad for Israel.

But there are other, less obvious reasons—besides the outright muzzling—for the dearth of candid conversation about Israel., Many people share the blame, including the pro-Israel peace camp, including me. It is time for some honest talk about the lack of honest talk: my camp exercises a self-censorship that often prevents us from saying what we believe and feel about Israeli behavior. This not only constrains the speeches, conversations, and thinking of elected and appointed officials. It also prevents passionate moderates—Jewish, Christian, and Muslim—from finding a common language, a shared set of rhetorical protocols about how to talk about the conflict and which topics to talk about.

Howard Dean and the Third Rail

In October 2003, I sat in a New York City boardroom with about twenty American Jews and listened to two of Howard Dean's campaign aides explain that he had often bashed Hamas, was dedicated to Israel's security needs, and not coincidentally, had a Jewish wife. The two had come to New York for a few meetings to shore up Jewish support for Dean during what they judged to be a major crisis during his run for the Democratic presidential nomination. Dean, in turn, was meeting with the Presidents Conference for the same purpose.

At a coffee shop in Phoenix, Arizona, in early September, Dean had played around with political kryptonite by making controversial comments about the Middle East. The intifada was raging. Israel and the Palestinian Authority were not talking to each other, at least not officially. Yasser Arafat was holed up in his battered Ramallah headquarters, besieged by the Israelis under Ariel Sharon, who refused to negotiate with the Palestinian Authority until it clamped down on terrorist cells. Asked if the United States should push for negotiations, Dean had said, "I don't believe stopping the terror has to be a prerequisite for talking. . . . I don't find it convenient to blame people. Nobody should have violence, ever. But they do, and it's not our place to take sides." The following week, he told the *Washington Post* that the United States should be "evenhanded." In other words, he advocated an American approach that was quite reasonable. But a shameful, now infamous storm erupted, a kind of noisy prelude to similar attacks on Barack Obama during his presidential run.

American Jewish organizational leaders were deluged with venomous e-mails complaining about Dean, probably sent by Republican operatives (although it has never been proved who sent them). Dean himself received an angry, well-publicized letter from congressional Democrats. He was denounced by his rival candidates, John Kerry and Joseph Lieberman, who told

Dean in a televised debate that his comments "break a 50-year record in which presidents, Republican and Democrat, members of Congress of both parties have supported our relationship with Israel based on shared values."[7]

Dean claimed, correctly, that he was advocating nothing more than the kind of diplomacy President Clinton had pursued and that Israel would always have his support. He told reporters he had mistakenly used "code words" that upset people and vowed never to use them again. But it was no use, he was tarred and feathered in the media as a candidate who had trouble with American Jews. The fact that much of the wrath against him came from politicians does not eliminate American Jews' culpability; the politicians clearly thought they were delivering what Jewish voters wanted *because no one told them otherwise.*

The meeting I attended included board members and supporters of left-of-center pro-Israel organizations, other professionals, graduate students, and staffers from centrist Jewish organizations. We were handed a document with red-meat, pro-Israel, anti-terrorist statements that Dean had made over the years. We were reminded that he had said that his positions were actually closer to those of AIPAC than Americans for Peace Now. But in that setting, the argument that Dean was unstinting in his support for Israel was a bit odd. The situation was almost surreal because I knew for a fact that at least a half dozen people in that room *agreed* with Dean. More than a few wanted the United States to be an honest broker and wanted the Bush administration to persuade Sharon to talk to the Palestinian Authority.

Yet no one at the meeting expressed support for what Dean had suggested or lamented the treatment he had received or discussed how Dean could make his case without alienating potential supporters. They simply asked polite questions about the candidate's views on Arafat and Israel's tough response to the intifada. They had bought into the assumption that Howard Dean's only problem was that he had committed a terrible political blunder and he had to fix it, quickly. No one was willing to imply or say that it was the political system that had blundered and had to be fixed, that the prevailing rules of political rhetoric had to change so that politicians like Dean could say what the people in that room actually believed.

I wanted to point out that Dean was, in fact, conveying a message most American Jews agreed with but couldn't get a word in before Dean's aides had to leave. The only message they had thought necessary to convey was one that placed Dean somewhere to the right of the late Yitzhak Rabin.

There were different cliques and claques in that room, and many of us had either not met one another or had met only casually. So it is likely that one reason why no one came to Dean's defense was the old bugaboo of me-too-ism, a worry about sticking necks out too far or offending people. It was hardly unusual, at that point in time, for mainstream American Jews to call for more balance in U.S. policies in the Middle East, but they tended to be hesitant to do so unless they knew their listeners. The same hesitancy exists today.

If American Jews who want to end one-sided diplomacy in the Middle East still censor what they say even among themselves, how can they expect America's political elite to push for a different American approach to the Arab-Israeli conflict? How can they expect anyone in the executive branch to avoid anticipatory vetoes and start showing more courage? And how can they expect to make common cause with non-Jewish Americans who share their goals and could add political impetus for change?

It is time for the anti-occupation wing of the pro-Israel community to wrest control of the conversation from those who cling to outworn assumptions about America's Middle East policy and what it means to be pro-Israel. The political elite should not be blamed for assuming that even tepid statements that favor robust American diplomacy or take exception to Israeli policies will be politically costly. They will cling to this assumption unless they receive clear signals that a different, more candid conversation is called for. It is up to us to give politicians, policymakers, and non-Jewish Americans the confidence that American Jews expect new approaches to the Arab-Israeli conflict and new ways of talking about it.

Other political movements have managed to seize control of public rhetoric, including the terms used to describe controversial topics and the ideas that are worth broaching in the public arena. As a result, politicians felt that they had more freedom to endorse the goals of those movements and to articulate concepts that were previously beyond the pale. The pro-choice movement did it. The fair trade movement has begun to do it. Surely the American Jewish peace camp, which includes some mainstream organizational leaders and political donors to both parties, should start trying to create an environment in which articulating what is manifestly true is not controversial or politically treacherous.

With that in mind, I will make a few proposals that will come across as heretical and dangerous to some in the American Jewish community and that might prevent me from getting invited to more than a few dinners.

Using the E-word

First, pro-Israel Jews on the left should start using the "e-word" (evenhanded) unabashedly and even the "p-word" (pressure), if Israel is being clearly and maddeningly recalcitrant. The pro-Israel peace groups in the United States that I have been involved with generally try to avoid using those terms or speaking honestly about the kind of American diplomacy that many of their members actually want. When they articulate goals for American Middle East policy, even the word *fair* is never used. Instead, they generally use punchless, innocuous euphemisms to describe what they would support: phrases such as *proactive diplomacy* or *energetic, creative American involvement.*

I don't mean to be self-righteous; I am also guilty. Over the years, when working or volunteering for Jewish peace groups, I have signed, ghostwritten, or edited letters to public officials and newspaper ads that have used similar tame, evasive language. The logic was that by not saying what we actually meant, by not advocating what we actually wanted to happen, we would not move "too far out in front of the community" and centrists would feel more comfortable associating with us. It was a reasonable strategy. As Dean learned, among certain listeners, code words like *evenhanded* and concepts like honest American brokerage evoke the same primal Jewish fears that have been discussed previously, the same conviction that Israel is still so vulnerable that the slightest disagreement with the United States is a direct and mortal threat. It was the so-called Arabists in the State Department, after all, who pushed for evenhandedness. In American Jewish lore, they were ready to desert Israel when it needed help.

But placating people with those fears has not accomplished much, has it? It has not prompted throngs of mainstream American Jews to actively support Jewish peace groups here or in Israel. All it has done is prop up the false perception that Jews in the United States do not trust their government to challenge both Israelis and Palestinians to make difficult compromises or even to express concerns about the Palestinians' plight. Even Churches for Middle East Peace and the American Task Force on Palestine, which understand the sensitivities of American Jewish allies—and potential allies—shy away from using the e-word or its equivalents.

Definitions and connotations can evolve. In the mid-1980s many of Israel's friends in the United States perceived the term *Palestinian state* as threatening; it was Arafat's goal, not Israel's. Now it is acceptable to endorse it, at least as a distant goal, in most Jewish settings. The same thing should happen to language that describes American diplomacy that is not automatically tilted toward Israel every time there is a disagreement with the Palestinians.

An *evenhanded* Middle East policy can mean whatever we want it to mean. It should mean being fair. Who can make a case against fundamental fairness? It should mean taking both sides' needs and aspirations into account. It should mean being ready to chastise and reward both Israelis and Palestinians. It should mean that if there are any diplomatic openings to Syria, it will be made clear to the Israelis that it is in America's as well as Israel's interests to explore them. An evenhanded American foreign policy should be defined as one that would be pro-Israeli, pro-Palestinian, and pro-American.

Now, I am not saying that many members of Congress or top administration officials are likely to use the e-word, the p-word, or their equivalents in public any time soon. Of course they won't. If they did, for the moment, they would pay a steep political price. But, remember, passionate Jewish moderates need to make just enough noise so that it registers on those trying to figure out the political calculus of this issue; completely drowning out more conventional voices is probably not possible. By clearly enunciating that it is sometimes appropriate for America to lean on both parties to this conflict, by calling for fundamental fairness, we can at least create a little more rhetorical space for politicians and policymakers, a little more room to talk honestly about controversial matters like the route of Israel's security barrier. As I've noted, these new, communal signals won't be received only by the political elite; they will also reach non-Jewish Americans and help to bridge the gaps that make coalition-building so difficult.

Within the organized American Jewish community, including those leaning leftward, the idea of balanced or evenhanded American diplomacy can spark fears of a slippery slope. It can call up the specter of precedents that eventually would lead to America siding with Israel's enemies. Those are worries that must be addressed, because an alternative to the conventional Israel lobby does need energetic support from part of the organized community.

To speak to those concerns, Jews and non-Jews who want more aggressive American diplomatic interventions in the Middle East should clearly assert that certain lines must never be crossed: (1) evenhandedness need not and must not mean imposing solutions on Israel, and (2) evenhandedness need not and must not mean turning America's back on Israel's core security requirements, its legitimate need to protect its citizens from hostile nonstate actors as well as nations that still threaten it. The pro-Israel left already has those lines, much to the chagrin of those who believe that punishing Israel will solve the region's problems. My camp should make it crystal clear that the lines won't change.

Another way to address American Jewish fears is to point out that the bonds between the United States and Israel are too strong to be sundered by sporadic disagreements. The American people think of Israel as an ally for many reasons other than the work of the conventional Israel lobby; there is a sense of a commonality of values and a shared commitment to democracy. That is not going to end simply because the United States presses Israel as well as its neighbors on specific policy matters.

Put another way, it is not impossible for Israelis and Palestinians to come up with mutually acceptable security arrangements. Those arrangements would require a unified Palestinian government—probably in combination with international peacekeepers and Israeli partners—to stop suicide bombers from slipping into Israeli cities and to thwart rejectionists who want to hurl missiles into Israel proper. All of that would need to be worked out via negotiations on a comprehensive agreement, one that gives the Palestinian government and people tangible incentives to uproot violent maximalists in their midst, once and for all, and one that incorporates lessons learned from previous security failures during the Oslo years. It is *inconceivable* that the United States would impose security arrangements on Israel by fiat.

So, what could possibly happen to Israel if the United States and the international community push harder to ask and answer tough questions about the occupied territories' future, the status of Jewish settlers beyond the Green Line, and the Palestinians' responsibility to enforce security agreements? Will Israel's army suddenly be ripped to shreds if the United States proposes that occupied territory be relinquished as part of a comprehensive peace agreement? Will it lose its formidable air force and navy and its long- and short-range missiles? Will it be expected to tolerate a situation in which its citizens are not protected from Palestinians who don't accept the authority of their new state's government? Of course not.

A new message, a clarion call, needs to ring out to the American Jewish community: too many people who care about Israel have selected the wrong reasons to be afraid; they are focusing on unlikely threats and ignoring real ones. They should be much more afraid of the intolerable status quo, an occupation that is an oppressive burden to both Palestinians and Israelis and that may well destroy Israel. And they should be much more worried about the dangers to America—our homes, our energy supplies, our soldiers overseas—that probably will grow if this conflict is allowed to fester.

Ending the Silence about Israel and Human Rights

A clearer, firmer, bolder message about American involvement would be reinforced by a clearer, firmer message protesting human rights abuses or questionable military actions by both Israelis as well as Palestinians. Before suggesting a prescription, a brief diagnosis is in order:

To many people who empathize with the Palestinians' plight under occupation, the most puzzling form of American Jewish silence is the kind that greets Palestinian suffering, especially suffering caused by Israeli actions that much of the world deems to be human rights abuses. Using the term *human rights* to question Israeli behavior in a public forum is enough to mark you as an outcast and Israel-basher in much of the organized American Jewish community. A whole industry exists to monitor and refute human rights NGOs whenever they set their sights on Israel. Worse, even mentioning Palestinian misfortunes is suspect in some quarters. When word spread during the 2008 presidential campaign that Barack Obama once said, "Nobody has suffered more than the Palestinians," he was roundly attacked by Jewish right-wingers as if he were calling for Israel's destruction.

But it is not only the right wing of my community that either defends or mutely accepts the way Israelis treat their neighbors. It is also American Jews who want the occupation to end. Some of us marched against the Vietnam War and even the Iraq War. Some of us give money to help victims in Darfur and fund shelters for battered women here at home. Few of us can bring ourselves to say much out loud about the battering of an entire people, if we are within the Jewish communal tent. Until very recently, I was in that category, looking back on my own reactions to sundry allegations of bad behavior by Israel.

"It hurts me a lot: when B'Tselem [a prominent Israeli human rights group] comes out with a report. I'm upset by the human rights violations. But I'm also upset by the *revelation* of the violation," said Ted Mann, candidly summing up an all-too-common dilemma. "I know everything has to be revealed. B'Tselem helps keep Israel a democratic society. Israelis need to see themselves in the mirror. But I worry about the way this information is used by people who hate Israel."

American Jews who tell themselves that they are committed to human rights as well as to Israel can often find justifications for Israeli activities the world doesn't care for. The core argument is that what appears to be cruel and unjust behavior is usually an unfortunate, unavoidable consequence of the situation that Jews and Arabs are mired in. Unlike much of the human rights advocacy community, people in the pro-Israel left generally view the region through a prism that reflects Israelis' sense of permanent vulnerability and their determination not to be vulnerable. If we object to the missiles that repeatedly killed innocent women and children in Gaza or Lebanon, we will be assured that Israel has done everything possible to avoid collateral damage, has been much more careful about shedding innocent blood than its adversaries, and is perfectly within its rights under the Geneva Conventions to go after enemy combatants that hide among civilians.

If Israel's supporters don't feel comfortable with endorsing hard-nosed Israeli military responses, it is difficult for them to come up with alternatives they themselves believe in. As has been true of the Zionist movement since the pre-state days, in an atmosphere where nothing seems predictable except the inveterate hostility of Israel's neighbors, it is much much easier to accept the preemptive strikes and targeted assassinations and to try not to think about the inevitably cruel civilian casualties. It is much easier not to argue with those who are convinced that Western humanistic values can't be applied to conflicts in the Middle East, where blame and shame rule the day. When Israel's defenders point out that the United States firebombed Dresden and Tokyo, NATO bombed civilians in Serbia, and U.S. bombers tried to obliterate Baghdad, and therefore armchair American moralists are in no position to criticize Israel from the comfort of their suburban homes, it is hard to come up with a persuasive response.

If pro-Israel doves object to almost anything Al Jazeera decides to transform into yet another symbol of Zionist bestiality, eventually we will hear evidence that Palestinian propagandists and their media allies have distorted the truth. When Israel assaulted the West Bank village of Jenin during the second intifada, at first the international media alleged that hundreds of innocent Palestinians had been massacred and that bulldozers had crushed houses and destroyed property for no discernible reason. Later, a UN report demonstrated that there had been no "massacre" and that most of the Palestinian casualties were armed combatants.[8] One could almost hear the sounds of Israel's friends around the world breathing sighs of relief. I certainly breathed easier.

Sometimes, however, what we read about or see on TV makes it difficult to counter and cope with allegations of indefensible Israeli behavior. When that happens, something other than logic and evidence kicks in, and we are left with little except a panicky unwillingness to believe Israelis are behaving as badly as people claim. We have a rooting interest for information and arguments that prop up our craving to believe in the Israelis

So, we try to look the other way when we come across tidbits like the following, from a B'Tselem press release in December 2007:

> A survey conducted by the Israeli military and published by leading Israeli daily, *Yedioth Ahronoth,* found that a quarter of soldiers serving at checkpoints in the West Bank perpetrated or witnessed abuse of Palestinians. In response, B'Tselem said that the numbers are shocking, but not surprising. The organization commends the military for initiating the survey, but states that physical and verbal abuse of Palestinians by soldiers, particularly at checkpoints, has long become routine. In spite of official condemnations, the military does not do enough to ensure accountability and to deter soldiers from engaging in such behavior.
>
> According to B'Tselem, most soldiers who harm Palestinians are never held accountable. Law enforcement authorities place numerous obstacles on Palestinians who try to complain against security forces personnel and only a small minority of complaints result in charges against those responsible for abuse.[9]

"There must be a reasonable explanation," we try to tell ourselves. "There must be something terribly wrong with the way this story is being told, even if it is the Israeli army itself that is telling it."

After a while, though, the evidence accumulates, and it becomes harder and harder to discard it or wish it away. The anguished testimony of the Israeli soldiers collected by Breaking the Silence makes a mockery of willful denial. Breaking the Silence is an explicitly nonpolitical organization that lets those who have served in the territories speak for themselves about the level of brutality and wanton cruelty there. They are not refuseniks. Most of them return to the Israel Defense Forces every year for reserve duty. They want their own society to wake up to what Israeli soldiers are being asked to do and, sadly, what some of them eagerly volunteer to do. In the organization's traveling exhibitions and on its website are firsthand reports of soldiers firing live ammunition, not rubber bullets, at teenagers; of barreling into a Palestinian village and shooting indiscriminately because a commander wants to send a message that he won't be pushed around; and of forcing Palestinians to be human shields during patrols in West Bank villages.[10]

"There must be a reasonable explanation for what is happening in the Gaza Strip," we tried to tell ourselves in December 2008 and January 2009, when confronted by news coverage of innocent civilians mauled, a UN school destroyed, and the rest of the terrible carnage that resulted from Israel's attack. "There must be a good reason why all of those people had to die or get maimed, why the Gaza hospitals had to overflow with the dead and wounded. The Israelis wouldn't have done that unless it was absolutely necessary."

After awhile, though, the evidence accumulated and for some of us in the pro-Israel peace camp, it was impossible to believe that the Israeli ends—stopping Hamas rocket fire—could justify the means, a disproportionate response that did not, and probably could not, draw adequate distinctions between military and civilian targets, which were crammed together in the houses and warrens of one of the world's most densely populated areas. It was impossible to take the official Israeli explanations or rationalizations on faith. In the midst of that Gaza Strip assault, I used words like *appalling* on my blog (www.realisticdove.org) to describe Israeli actions. Whether I was correct or not is beside the point. The point is that many other relatively moderate American Jews agreed with me, and once again, the vast majority of them said nothing and did nothing.

When people in my camp confront Israeli behavior that appears to be morally offensive, the standard response is that there is no such thing as a benign occupation or a war without bruality. Unless and until there is a political solution, according to this logic, morally grounded Israelis will be forced into circumstances in which it is difficult and sometimes impossible to be humane, it is difficult and sometimes impossible to be good. I have used that argument and it is true—up to a point.

The problem, however, is not merely that the brutality and humiliation inflicted on Palestinians is an inevitable consequence of occupation; the problem is that it is just plain *wrong*. I believe American Jews who support Israel should start saying that it is wrong. They must somehow find a way to stop suppressing their moral instincts, to stop ignoring what is best within themselves, and to start finding a vocabulary to acknowledge the moral horrors attendant on the occupation,without denouncing Israel as a whole or minimizing its need to defend itself.

Yes, those who focus only on Israeli behavior without putting it into context, without appreciating that steps must be taken to protect Israel's borders, have also lost their moral compass. Yes, the Palestinians have in many ways brought this situation upon themselves (e.g., if there had not been suicide bombers infiltrating Israeli cities, there would not be a security wall; there used to be a vocal peace camp in Israel, but it was shattered by the Palestinian intifada). But once that context is affirmed, the reasons for decrying the brutality and humiliation become compelling and the rationalizations for keeping our mouths shut become hollow.

When American Jews believe the explanations given by the Israeli government don't withstand scrutiny, when they think there is wrongdoing that has no justification, protesting loudly would not only be a moral necessity, it also would have political utility. American presidential administrations that agonize over whether to denounce Israeli behavior need to know that there is a broad base of American Jews who are not fringe leftists and are also upset by that behavior.

Articulating American Interests

This is the toughest new paradigm to persuade the Jewish community to accept: "If you are an American Jew, your first priority should be to lobby for what makes sense for America." That didn't come from Pat Buchanan or David Duke or any of the other Israel lobby bashers who are quick to accuse American Jews of dual loyalty. It came from Daniel Levy, the former Israeli negotiator. "Israel and its leaders have created conditions for a narrative that places policy within the frame of 'Is it good for Israel?' I don't think that is healthy for either country. 9/11 proves this is no longer a backwater issue you can ignore. We [Israelis] need an American president who would say,

'My point of departure would be to do what's best for me but also what's best for you. We have bigger fish to fry here. We have to deal with al Qaeda, the oil crisis, the entire Muslim world. What happens with the Palestinians is important to us. If you think a few kilometers of territory are worth wrecking the diplomatic process and the chance to calm regional tensions, you're wrong.'"

If a president were to make a case that compromise "was four square in American interests," Levy asked, "would there be a constituency out there for this? I hope so."

Unfortunately, one of the words that inevitably creates panic and alarm in much of the conventional Israel lobby is *linkage*, the self-evident connection between resolving the Arab-Israeli conflict and other American interests. In the introduction, I explained why what happens in Israel and the occupied territories is America's business too. This will be the case as long as, within the Muslim world, America's perceived support for Israeli behavior continues to make us appear to be an enemy of Islam. But, except among the small groups on the pro-Israel left, the organized American Jewish community does not want to acknowledge linkage, and even my camp doesn't talk about it as candidly as we should.

Fear of the l-word informed the conventional Israel lobby's reactions to Middle East policy recommendations from a commission led by former Secretary of State James Baker and former Congressman Lee Hamilton (D-Indiana). Released in 2006 and ignored by the Bush administration, their report made several suggestions for addressing America's failed military adventure in Iraq and threats from Iran. It noted that the "U.S. will not be able to achieve its goals in the Middle East unless the U.S. deals directly with the Arab-Israel conflict." It also called for American and international efforts to resolve the conflict as a means to help achieve regional stability.[11]

When the report was released, Iraqi insurgents were crossing the Syrian border back and forth to battle American troops in Iraq. There appeared to be at least a chance that Syrian-Israeli peace talks under American auspices would prompt Syrian president Bashar Asad to seal his borders and save American lives. There was at least a chance that jump-starting Israeli-Palestinian peace talks would be an incentive for Saudi Arabia, Jordan, and other states to use their leverage with Iraqi Sunnis to calm things down.

Whether or not those were the best diplomatic choices was worth debating. But Israel and the conventional lobby hoped to create a situation in which those options could not even be *considered* by U.S. officials. The Baker-Hamilton report may have overstated the connection between the Israeli-Arab problem and America's problems; Israel and some of its prominent supporters here denied that there was any connection at all.

In a conference call convened by the Presidents Conference to discuss the report, according to the *Forward*:

> leaders of most groups voiced reservations over this part of the Iraq Study Group report and called for action to block any Israel-Iraq linkage. Israel's consul general in New York, Arye Mekel, who took part in the discussion, reportedly said that while Israel will not try to intervene in an American decision-making process, it hopes to make clear that the two disputes are unrelated. Mekel, according to several participants, portrayed the report as negative from Israel's standpoint. . . . Other participants, including AIPAC executive director Howard Kohr, stressed the importance of ensuring that the recommendations seen as linking Israel and Iraq are not adopted.[12]

The *New York Times* reported that "Prime Minister Ehud Olmert, in turn, responded to the Baker-Hamilton report by affirming that 'the problems in Iraq . . . are entirely independent of the controversies between us and the Palestinians.' He said that Israel opposed any attempt to connect them. A senior Israeli official told *The New York Times*: 'Why should we want to link our own problem to a nightmare like Iraq? It's a terrible mess there.'"[13]

Why? Because America needed—and continues to need—every conceivable bit of help from its ally Israel to address a bloody disaster in Iraq. Because, shortly after that report was released, I spotted an American Iraq War veteran in a wheelchair in midtown Manhattan, with a metal cup.

The relationship in which Israel does the asking and the United States does the giving must change, and it is high time for those who are concerned about both countries to say so, emphatically. There needs to be giving and taking in both directions. Of course, the idea that Israel *owes* anything to America, or that it is time to start asking what Israel can do for America, is frightening to some. It is so frightening that it is not even on the communal agenda.

The relationship of Israel and the "Diaspora" is incessantly scrutinized in conferences and panel discussions, in commission reports and academic treatises. I have searched high and low in the archives of the Jewish People Policy Planning Institute, established by the Jewish Agency to wrestle with challenges to the Jewish future, and other prominent think tanks. There are references to the question of whether the Diaspora has a stake in Israel's future or the status of Jerusalem, or the propriety of American Jewish criticism of Israeli policy. But all of those discussions are based on the notion that Israel is a central part of Jewish identity. None of them address the question of whether American Jews have a stake in what happens in the Arab-Israeli conflict because we are *Americans*, because what happens in the Middle East directly affects us.

It is hard to believe that this question is going to be addressed in public communal forums—including synagogues—in the near future. Broaching it appears to leave open the possibility that Israel's interests are not the same as America's, or that the two countries' interests might diverge someday, and that possibility is too terrible to mention or contemplate. I would argue that the two countries' interests are identical right now. when it comes to solving the Palestinian question and addressing Israel's conflict with Syria. But allowing the conflicts to continue will make it *more* likely that someday Americans as a whole will stop supporting Israel or feel much kinship with it.

9

The Far Left's "Jewish Problem" and Why It Hurts the Palestinians

No doubt the following people want to help the Palestinians, but, in fact, they are doing the opposite:

- The 48,000-plus members of "Israel is not a country! . . . delist it from Facebook as a country!" The introduction of this group on Facebook, a social networking site, is one of the most bizarre in the history of polemics: "This group does not attack any groups or individuals. Our goal is to reach a peaceful solution. It simply states that 'Israel' is an apartheid regime. This group strongly condemns racism and does not tolerate it."[1]
- "The activist filmmaker welcomed by KPFA radio and La Pena Cultural Center for her work on Palestinian rights," as described by April Rosenblum in *The Past Didn't Go Anywhere,* a pamphlet on anti-Semitism on the left. "[She] sells videos on how Jews have designed everything from Marxism to neoconservatism to covertly advance their own interests, publishes articles on Jewish exaggeration of the Holocaust, and argues for quotas for Jewish journalists."[2]
- The college activists in "progressive movements" who, according to Tammy Shapiro, executive director of the Union of Progressive Zionists

(UPZ) campus group, won't accept or welcome students into their ranks until the newcomers say something nasty about Israel.

- "Cogit8," a commentator on Mondoweiss. His comment about violence in the Gaza Strip is alarming. Even more alarming is the fact that none of the other regular commentators saw fit to denounce it: "The recent killing of 120 Palestinians by a sophisticated war-machine has not produced even a ripple of empathy in America, whereas the death of one Jew by a crudely made rocket is trumpeted about the mother-land. Proof indeed of The Jewing of America—because most of 'your people' really don't give a rip about other human life."[3]

My purpose here is not to argue with such people about the realities of the region or American politics. One simply cannot win an argument with those who think that Israelis deserve to be singled out for human rights abuses above all other peoples on earth, or that American Jews are running the entire show in Washington from behind the scenes, or that there is nothing wrong with casually using the imagery and logic of Henry Ford or Christian blood libelists. In my experience, conversing with such people is like looking at a blue sky and being told by someone that the sky is black and that you are either being deceitful or lying to yourself if you describe the sky as blue.

My point here is that people who use such harsh rhetoric—and the much larger number of fellow travelers who ignore or refuse to challenge them—are unwittingly making matters *worse* for the Palestinian people. The central premise of this book is that American policymakers are unlikely to lose their inhibitions against an evenhanded approach to the Israeli-Palestinian conflict unless there is an effective political counterweight to the conventional Israel lobby. Left-leaning American Jews who are concerned with Israel's safety and well-being have a critically important role to play in developing this counterweight. But they will be much less likely to speak out for robust diplomacy or to criticize Israel if they think they are playing into the hands of people who—whatever their intentions might be—sound like they want Israel to disappear and embrace canards about Jews pulling the levers that control the world.

As the previous chapter showed, there are many, varied reasons for the silence of American Jews who are critical of Israel. But that is the psychological reality that helps to shape the political reality. So, the last thing anyone who has a problem with Israeli policies should do is give American Jews even *more* reasons to keep quiet. Too much of the far left does not seem to care about cutting off this supply of activists who could push for evenhandedness.

"It happens all the time. People will tell me, 'I can't join Brit Tzedek because those people [the far left] hate the Jews,'" says Christopher MacDonald-Dennis, director of the Office of Intercultural Affairs at Bryn Mawr and one of the leaders of Brit Tzedek v'Shalom in Philadelphia. "I have seen Jewish students deeply bothered by Israeli actions attend events criticizing Israel. They'll tell me, 'I agree on many things with the Palestinian solidarity people, but I can't say it. You don't know how it's going to be used against us.'"

There is a difficult free speech problem here, and I don't know how to solve it. Perhaps it is intractable. Silence about the occupation and objectionable Israeli behavior is not an option. And insisting that certain words and concepts cross the line from acceptable to unpalatable discourse only stirs up more anger at Israel and its supporters, whether on the right or the left.

In the spring of 2008 my synagogue, a local church, and a local anti–Iraq War group cohosted a screening of *Promises*, a moving documentary about Palestinian and Israeli children, their visions of each other, and attempts to open lines of communication between them. After the film, during a discussion period, a Jewish woman visiting from another town went into a long harangue against Israeli policy and concluded, "I think they are committing a holocaust against Palestinians." There were some gentle objections from Jews in the audience, including me, to the use of the word *holocaust* in that context. Later, a middle-aged man from the church said, "I'm sick and tired of being told that I can't call something a *holocaust*! Who are American Jews to tell me how to talk about something?"

Talking to him later, I explained why I thought terms like *holocaust* were needlessly inflammatory but also inaccurate. Despite the impression given by the Israelis' willingness to rationalize seemingly pitiless assaults on civilian neighborhoods, they were not going out of their way to deliberately exterminate an entire people. He didn't buy it. It was particularly infuriating to him, I suspect, that people who told him to measure his words carefully also concurred with him on a great many issues. That man had a good heart. He did not believe he was yelling "Fire!" in a crowded theater. Who can blame him for being frustrated?

For different reasons, Tammy Shapiro of the Union of Progressive Zionists is equally frustrated by the discourse on Israeli policies and actions. The UPZ was set up by a number of Jewish organizations—including Meretz USA and Ameinu—to provide a home for Jewish students who don't feel that "progressive" and "pro-Israel" need be contradictory, who are in the same or similar political spaces as national Jewish peace groups that retain at least some ties to the mainstream community. It was established because, on most campuses, political and educational activities focusing on the Arab-Israeli conflict force students to choose between two warring camps, between the Israel-right-or-wrong crowd and Israel-can-do-nothing-right activists.

"The more fuel people give to the [Jewish] right wing," Shapiro said, "the harder my job becomes." She told me that both dedicated bashers and supporters of Israel come after the kinds of students her organization tries to attract.

> The right tells people the only way to identify with Israel is to defend it. . . . The left won't let us defend it. . . . It's a big problem when Palestinian solidarity activists take one trip to the territories but don't get a chance to see how Israelis west of the Green Line live or hear their point of view. And they don't connect with progressive Israelis who are working against the occupation. Then they come back and they give lectures about Israel that are just wrong, one sided. If Jewish students hear them, a lot [of the Jewish students] figure they are just aiding these people if they speak out. Even if they agree with us, they are reluctant to get involved.

The notion that Israel is a racist and evil empire has long been a staple of the far left. But now this idea has been conjoined with the far right's traditional conception of international Jewry as a fifth column intent on hijacking the governments and economies of sovereign states. These two ideological strands, in turn, are becoming entwined with old forms of outright anti-Semitism that treat Jews as inherently bloodthirsty and dangerous. Tie them together, and sometimes the result is the kind of atmosphere that prompted pro-Palestinian demonstrators to crash a pro-Israel rally on May 7, 2002, at San Francisco State University, where they chanted, "Hitler did not finish the job" and "Go home or we'll kill you." In a widely distributed e-mail sent the day after the rally, San Francisco State professor Laurie Zoloth wrote, "I cannot fully express what it feels like to have to walk across campus daily, past maps of the Middle East that do not include Israel, past posters of cans of soup with labels on them of blood and dead babies, labeled 'canned Palestinian children meat, slaughtered to Jewish rites under American license.'" These icons of anti-Semitism have since been torn down and work is being done at San Francisco State and other universities to heighten sensitivities to this ancient, persistent prejudice, but such sentiments are still close to the surface on too many campuses.[4]

Leaders and activists in the mainstream American Jewish community are understandably alarmed by the tone and content of these messages. Still, some of their characterizations of what is beyond the pale are, to my mind, beyond the pale. It is certainly possible for someone to anatomize the considerable power of the mainstream Jewish community in the United States without intending to foment hatred against Jews as a whole. It is possible to denounce the idea of Zionism because it resulted in the expropriation of Palestinian land or to denounce Israel's military escapades, without loathing the Jewish people. The signs at a national anti-occupation rally in Washington on June 10, 2007, that read, "End the Israeli occupation of Congress," were, in my judgment, a misguided political tactic using senselessly overblown rhetoric. Those who held the signs were not necessarily blaming American Jews as a whole for the conventional Israel lobby's influence.

But I am fifty-four years old, and until I started visiting the neighborhoods of the blogosphere and the social networks that dealt with Israel a few years ago, I had never felt the tangible possibility that an unquenchable desire to blame the Jews might someday harm me and my family. Enter "Jewish thought police" and "Israel lobby" and "Zionists" on a search engine, and you will find tens of thousands of entries holding Israel's supporters accountable for everything from controlling the media to planning the attacks on 9/11 to the subprime mortgage crisis.

Until recently, I had also never realized the extent to which Israel has been transformed into a kind of totemic hate object, which prompts a kind of magical thinking "that imputes the demonic into a state and its people such that the reality of the political entity disappears into the symbol of human evil," as Eli Muller put it in the *Yale Daily News*.[5]

That is the context for the hypersensitive reactions of American Jewish interfaith groups to the insults hurled at Israel by left-wing Christian groups. When Reverend Ateek compares Palestinians to Christ and claims the Jewish state is crucifying them, he is not making the claim in a pristine intellectual vacuum. It is part of a continuum of alarming statements and analyses of Israel and American Jews that are casually accepted as truth in much of the world.

Ohio State linguist Michael Geis doesn't offer much hope in his blog, *The Language Guy*. He writes that

> Personally, I don't think a rational debate on the merits of Israel's actions in any given case or America's policy toward Israel is possible. . . . Being human and being fully rational at all times are mutually exclusive, in my experience. We do have emotions and I, for one, don't believe that how we feel about an issue can ever be fully separated from what we think about it no matter how objective we try to be.
>
> [Language has] both a conventional meaning and a meaning in context. The problem is that the speaker and the hearer cannot be expected always to assign the same contextual significances to what is said. How we interpret what each other says or writes depends on the beliefs we bring to the enterprise. To expect American Jews and American Muslims to interpret events such as the military

> confrontation between Hezbollah and Israel in similar ways would be quite unrealistic. And this fact alone makes civil discourse about the confrontation difficult if not impossible.[6]

Substitute hard-core American leftists—and a segment of the Christian church community—for "American Muslims" in Geis's formulation, and the problem is equally difficult to address.

The challenge has been compounded by its digitization and the nature of conversation on the Web. As Simon Schama puts it, "The triumph of the Web represents the overthrow, for good or for ill, not just of linear narrative but of the entire system of inductive reasoning, with its explicit commitment to hierarchies of knowledge, tests of proof and so on." The history and current reality of the Arab-Israeli conflict is complicated, but the blogosphere's format of largely unedited, call-and-response rants leaves little room for those who insist on pointing out nuances or gray areas. "Digital allegiances can be formed there not through any sort of sifting of truth and falsehood but in response to and in defense of a kind of cognitive battering," Schama writes.[7]

Similar allegiances are formed within some of the "Web 2.0" communities in the likes of Facebook and MySpace. They gather together like-minded people and tend to create narratives that are eventually accepted by everyone who stays in the group. That does not apply only to the explicitly anti-Israel or anti-Zionist groups. Mary X's personal Facebook profile might show that she is a college junior who likes old Steely Dan tunes, veggie Mexican food, and lolling on the sand in Rockaway Beach with her boyfriend and that she absolutely hates racism, child labor, WalMart, and anyone who tries to defend Israel.

One unfortunate trait of anti-Israel bloggers is that when they are accused of over-the-top rhetoric that foments hatred of Jews as a whole, *they*—the bloggers—often claim to be the victims, the aggrieved parties. To them, the only people who complain about anti-Jewish language and concepts are apologists for Israel who want to divert attention from Israeli barbarities. When I venture into left-wing neighborhoods of the Web (generally using pseudonyms like "Tough Dove" or "Salvage the Good") and object to remarks like those of Cogit8, I'm told that I'm just trying to hide Israel's crimes, even after I've expressed opposition to Israeli actions. I'm told that I am being oversensitive, a fig leaf for the Mossad, a useful idiot for Likud. Worst of all, I am told that prejudice against Jews or exaggerations about Israel's flaws are not problems anyone should be worrying about now, given the plight of the Palestinians, as if one cannot worry about all of these things at the same time.

MacDonald-Dennis was adopted by a Jewish mother and a Latino father. He is also gay. At least some of his background gives him street cred on the left. "When I tell people that what they are saying about Latinos offends me, they apologize and don't say it again," he said. "When I tell them what they are saying about gays offends me, they apologize. But when I tell them what they are saying about American Jews offends me, they don't care. . . . I never wanted to believe that anti-Zionism was the same as anti-Semitism. Now I'm not so sure."

✡

April Rosenblum has written, "The number of leftists with real anti-Jewish beliefs is tiny. What has a bigger impact is not those individual leftists who promote anti-Jewish beliefs, but the way that institutionally, people and organizations on the left are so silent, uncomfortable, defensive and even accusatory when someone brings concerns about anti-Semitism up."[8]

Rosenblum is part of a small group of self-styled progressives who are trying to demonstrate the dangers of modern anti-Semitism to their political allies. They are incorporating the Jewish experience into what lefties call "oppression theory," demonstrating the links between anti-Semitism and the oppression and liberation struggles of people of color, women, and gay people. Rosenblum, who told me she was a "progressive non-Zionist," is much more concerned with the fact that Jews are fleeing the non-Zionist left than with my quest for an alternative Middle East peace lobby that includes Jews. Both of us will be aided if she and her comrades make headway in left-wing circles.

People on the left who don't give American Jews the right to be upset or offended by anything are not going to listen to the ADL, APN, or me. Perhaps they will listen to political allies who may or may not believe there is any moral justification for Israel's existence, but who have accepted that the Jewish state is here to stay. While this latter group might not have enough patience to work in coalition with anyone in the organized Jewish community, some have begun to understand that the most vicious anti-Israel and anti-Jewish rhetoric causes too many Jews to keep their own counsel instead of objecting to Israeli policies. Plus, it can be deeply offensive.

According to Rosenblum's pamphlet, which is addressed to other non-Zionist progressives, the fact that Jews in many countries seem to be entrenched in the ruling class disguises their vulnerability to "a system of ideas passed down through a society that enables . . . scapegoating. . . . Jews are isolated, especially from other exploited groups—people who might normally team up with them and defend them in times of danger. Other oppressed groups get manipulated out of identifying and fighting the sources of their exploitation, instead being encouraged to channel their anger at Jews. . . . In hopes of gaining safety, Jews are pressured to cooperate with rulers, to silence themselves and to not rise up."[9]

Good luck, April. She has a tough road to travel. Convincing angry left-wingers that American Jews are victims of hidden or potential oppression won't be easy, but she is conveying messages that ought to stir the soul of progressives who are willing to take an honest look at their movements:

> At the very heart of the Palestinians' catastrophe lies anti-Semitism, the force that created the Jewish search for a modern state. And building a world that fights the oppression of Jews, and all humans, is the ultimate solution to today's condition, in which Jews cling to a tiny place of safety for themselves at the cost of oppressing Palestinians. Yet Palestinians don't have the luxury of waiting for anti-Semitism to be eradicated to struggle for their own freedom. So let's guarantee the short-term battle supports the long-term goals, by consciously building safeguards [for] Jews into tactics for Palestinian liberation.[10]

Rosenblum told me that her pamphlet, published in 2007, has been positively received. There is anecdotal evidence that at least some dents can be made in a prejudice that is not new to the left. Every dent helps to change the tenor and tone of the conversation.

Judy Andreas, a longtime activist for many left-wing causes in the Bay Area of California, has started a group called Catalyst to Coalition. She said it is "providing organizational and theoretical alternatives to the polarization" on the left because of this issue. In her circles, too often, "If you care about prejudice against Jews, that means you are pro-Israel, anti-Muslim. If you care about the pain and prejudice experienced by Palestinians, that means you are progressive, left-wing. That's the structure the left has built, and it needs to change."

MacDonald-Dennis does his bit for the cause in discussion groups he organizes on campus. He said, "More and more lefties I deal with are beginning to understand that Zionism was meant to be the national liberation movement of an oppressed people, and there was a logic to Israel's founding that they may not entirely accept. But they don't dismiss these ideas out of hand the way they used to. . . . They also understand that comparing Israelis to Nazis or Afrikaners offends me. I'm someone who agrees with them on a lot, and it doesn't accomplish anything to insult me." As a result, he said, "the way they speak can change . . . a little."

In the previous chapter, I suggested a role that American Jews can and should play in opening up the conversation about Israel and American policies that have bolstered an unacceptable status quo. I asked Professor Geis if he thought there were a way to make people on the left realize that certain words and attitudes are needlessly provocative to American Jews and to do something about it in their own movements. Somehow, African Americans found a way to change the way people described them or the comments people made about them by insisting that they were offended by specific words (e.g., *Negro*, *welfare mothers*). How did they do that, I asked? How can language be altered?

"One thing is clear. Unless you have walked in other people's shoes, you are not in a position to tell them how they should be talked about," Geis said. "That's true for Jews, African Americans, homosexuals. Jews have a right to say when something is anti-Semitic. . . . But the discourse [on this topic] is screwed up so badly you can't say *anything* without offending someone." One place to start, he said, is try to "establish red lines, criteria. Show different ways of criticizing Israel that can't be interpreted as criticizing Jews. Let us know what *you* think is anti-Semitic. I don't know anyone who has ever done that."

Doing so, of course, will provoke accusations that people in my camp are trying to control and suppress the discourse, thus proving that there is no substantial difference between left-wing and right-wing Zionists. But the discourse about the discourse is screwed up so badly that it can't get much worse.

Here are a few broad suggestions for those on the left who don't want to insult and alienate American Jews:

First of all, reasonable lefties, realize that you, too, are part of the jigsaw puzzle that must be completed if there is going to be a chance at Middle East peace.

Second, make sure your fellow travelers understand that commentators on Israel and American Jewry are playing around with historical forces much larger than the particular cause they are espousing. "If you are anti-Zionist and not anti-Semitic," urges Mitchell Cohen, a democratic socialist, in an essay called "Anti-Semitism and the Left That Doesn't Learn," "then don't use the categories, allusions and smug assertions that are all too familiar to any student of prejudice."[11]

Third, tell them that they are singling out for denunciation a group that has historically been the scapegoat for the world's ills and that it is irresponsible to ignore that. Even if they are convinced that Jews in the West are completely assimilated and will never be in any danger, tell them it is not their place to define what offends other people or to castigate people for their fears. When I stick my hand out and they slam it with a hammer and I cry out, "That hurts," they should not answer, "No it doesn't" or "It shouldn't hurt" or "Who cares?"

Fourth, urge them to listen to one of their own, April Rosenblum, in her tips for activists: "When people raise talk of anti-Semitism, *train your mind to not automatically* go to the Israeli-Palestinian conflict; consider the issue in its own right. Both are separate, vital issues that demand our concern."[12]

Fifth, when it is time to discuss Israeli or American policies, plead with them to accurately describe specific actions that they don't like. Urge them to provide a critique of those actions and policies, but not to say or imply that an entire people, or an entire nation, is intrinsically evil. Tell them that speaking and acting as if Israel is the worst human rights violator in the world accomplishes nothing except to make them feel better.

This is not exactly a matter of yelling "Fire!" in a crowded theater. Right now, the theater is already on fire. It's been burning for more than a hundred years. Many more Americans, including American Jews, need to be mobilized and recruited as firefighters. What the far left says about Israel will influence whether enough of these Jews will be available to help quench the flames.

10

Conclusion: A Lobby for the Rest of Us

First, some instructive words from none other than Theodor Herzl, the driving force behind modern Zionism and another master of power puffery. Just before the turn of the twentieth century, he had a growing number of enthusiastic European supporters but little money and absolutely no political power. Undaunted, he traveled to Constantinople and appealed to the Ottoman sultan to approve a homeland for the Jewish people in Palestine. Herzl claimed that, in return, a syndicate of Jewish bankers and financiers committed to a Jewish homeland—a syndicate that did not exist back then—would help to relieve the Ottoman Empire's debts. He failed, but he kept writing, organizing, proselytizing.

"At the very outset of his Zionist career, one of his friends expressed doubts about the wisdom and efficacy of making so much noise. Noise, Herzl replied in anger, was everything," notes the historian Walter Laqueur. "World history was nothing but noise, noise of arms and advancing ideas: 'Men must put noise to use.'"[1]

If the history of Zionism in the early twentieth century proves anything, it is that a small group of underfunded, ferociously determined people can make such a ruckus that eventually the world takes notice. The odds against effectuating major changes in the domestic political context of America's Middle East policies are not nearly as formidable.

Lessons Learned: A Summary

After showing how the conventional Israel lobby works, I have tried to take an honest look at the obstacles to—and possibility of—forging an effective alternative to that lobby. Certain aspects of the task seem a bit easier than I had presumed they would be when I started the interviews and other research for this book. The conventional Israel lobby, especially AIPAC, is not going anywhere. It will continue to wield considerable influence on Congress and, to a lesser extent, on the executive branch. But it is less than it appears to be, both a master of impressions management and a group that is lucky to benefit from wildly exaggerated notions of Jewish power. Those exaggerations are supported by an alliance that includes people who revile the lobby and revile Israel, the media, anxious politicians and their staffers, and the lobby itself. My hope is that this book will not be the only source of information about the conventional Israel lobby's reliance on smoke and mirrors and that others will question the myth of its unstoppable power. The more that happens, the less scary it will seem to America's political establishment and citizens who disagree with it.

Another encouraging lesson is that a stronger political bloc favoring evenhanded, pro-Israel, pro-Arab, and pro-American policies in the Middle East does not necessarily require as many resources as the conventional Israel lobby possesses. Our path is made easier by the hunger in Washington to speak more candidly about Israel and its neighbors and by rising anger at AIPAC and its allies.

This book will become available just after President Obama takes office. So, for at least a year, a third bit of encouragement can be found in political theorist John Kingdon's empirical observations of open "policy windows." Those are junctures when opportunities exist for decisive political action. That happens, Kingdon observed, when a problem takes center stage, ideas for solving it are readily available, and political winds are blowing in the right direction. Savvy political players need to be ready to take advantage of open policy windows. They don't open often, and they don't stay open long. But one reason they open is a change in presidential administrations, when, as Kingdon puts it, "the new administration gives some groups, legislators and agencies their opportunity—an open policy window—to push positions and proposals they did not have the opportunity to push with previous administrations, and it disadvantages other players."[2]

The challenges, though, are intimidating. A complex web of fears, tribal memories, me-too-ism, confusion, apathy, ambivalence about complex solutions, and ignorance militates against many American Jews rallying behind alternatives to the conventional Israel lobby.

Coalition-building between left-of-center, pro-Israel Jews and other Americans who mostly agree with them is hampered by the lack of a common language and by sometimes serious, substantive differences about tactics and goals. And it is hampered by a poisonous new environment in which offensive accusations against American Jews and Israel are not merely acceptable, they are de rigeur in certain circles. The biggest challenge, by far, is that the conventional Israel lobby is skilled and well funded and loud. That plays into the fear, ignorance, hunger for contributions, and other aspects of the congressional mentality. And it fosters habitual, almost instinctive inhibitions against balanced, creative Middle East diplomacy in people who matter in the executive branch. None of this can be changed without willpower, hard work, and new approaches to galvanizing political support for evenhandedness.

The political objectives are not difficult to identify. American presidents and their foreign policy teams need to be shielded from the slings and arrows of outraged legislators (or those who pretend to be outraged), citizen advocates for Israel who are stuck with obsolete paradigms, and the media they use as a bully pulpit.

What Might Be Done

There are plenty of tools available. In a realm where images and symbols have been manipulated to justify America's acquiescence to Israel's occupation, a misguided military adventure in Iraq, torture in American prisons, and a might-makes-right mentality, other powerful images and symbols are available to those who would use them. If, for example, a thousand truly prominent American Muslims, Christians, and Jews locked arms, even if temporarily and nervously, and called for the United States to stop coddling Israeli settlement construction *and* insisted on an end to Palestinian violence and incitement, the image might not have quite the same power as the image of seven thousand people at an AIPAC conference. But the former image would be powerful indeed.

More than a thousand American rabbis have signed statements from Brit Tzedek v'Shalom, and many deliver my camp's messages from their pulpits, at least once in a while. A few hundred members of the Christian clergy are actively involved with the likes of Churches for Middle East Peace. But a thousand rabbis and a thousand Christian clergy and as many Muslim religious leaders as possible, speaking loudly and clearly to the State Department and their congressional representatives, would be a new, important addition to the political scene.

So would the sight of a thousand, rather than a hundred, decidedly pro-Israel but left-leaning American Jews descending on Capitol Hill. So would cadres of peace camp supporters willing to reach out to and keep in touch with legislators in four hundred congressional districts. So would more donations flowing into the political system from our side of the fence, rewarding politicians who act independently of AIPAC and showing other legislators that there is a price to be paid for signing whatever "Dear Colleague" letter the conventional Israel lobby plunks in front of them.

So would 100,000 angry e-mails and letters from a newly energized grassroots (or Netroots) campaign when American politicians flirt with the likes of John Hagee. So would the same number of positive e-mails and letters when the White House takes a firm hand with both Israeli and Palestinian leaders. So would a concerted effort by this alternative political bloc, which should include the president's friends, to call for presidential courage and decry passivity. So would expanded efforts to give college students interested in the Middle East a home that is neither fanatically pro-Israel nor viciously hostile to it. So would using all forms of media to publicize each and every one of these actions and to criticize both sides of the Israeli-Arab conflict when both warrant criticism.

These ideas are all well and good, but how can we possibly get there from here? Suggestions for moving various puzzle pieces have been made throughout the book, and all of them won't be repeated here. A few will be noted and expanded on, and some additional observations will be offered. The ideas will be limited to the community I know something about. Some of what follows might have the feel of Inside Jewish Baseball, as I will discuss specific tactics for rallying American Jews that might not have much relevance to anyone who does not play that particular game. However, while my primary focus is on American Jews, I believe some of these suggestions would also help to develop a Middle East peace bloc that would include all Americans:

Transform individuals, not institutions. Some hope the conventional Israel lobby can be transformed from within. The suggestions from Mearsheimer and Walt include "convincing groups within the lobby to support a different agenda. . . . U.S. and Israeli interests would . . . be advanced by wresting power away from the hardliners who now control AIPAC, the Zionist Organization of America, the Conference of Presidents or the American Jewish Committee. Such efforts might also be strengthened by institutional reforms that would give the rank and file a greater voice in determining these organizations' policy positions."[3]

"Why should we care about all those old institutions?" a young Brit Tzedek activist and J Street supporter remarked to me. "We need our *own* institutions. Who elected Malcolm Hoenlein? I didn't! Who cares what they think?" (This woman wouldn't allow me to use her name, though, so, at some level, she obviously cares what they think.)

A less predictable source of similar ideas is Tom Dine, one of the people who transformed AIPAC in the 1980s as its executive director. Today, in what might be a sign of the American Jewish mainstream's transformation, he is a consultant for Israel Policy Forum. In no uncertain terms, Dine told me, "These people have to go," when I asked him what should happen within the organized Jewish community. "These people have stayed too long." He was too careful and too politic to mention exactly who needed to go and which organizations needed to be transformed, but he did say, "I am talking about the leaders who have led us down the wrong path. I almost never hear the word 'peace' from these organizations. They have made the mistake of aligning themselves with a narrow portion of the Israeli political scene. They're yesterday's news. They need to be replaced."

That might happen someday, but I wouldn't bank on it. The law of not-for profit survival obtains here. Staffers and board members who have guided organizations that shun any distance between Israel and America are not likely to "support a different agenda." They have had the opportunity to do so for years and have not taken it. A younger generation of Jewish professionals now getting involved with local Jewish federations and the defense agencies has, by and large, bought into a system that seeks to protect Israel from all blame at any cost. None of the large established centrist or center-right institutions depicted in table 3 are about to let anyone "wrest power" away from them without a ferocious fight. Nor are they likely to change their attitudes about the U.S.-Israel relationship.

Some new or restructured organizations might help, but a more important task at hand is to find and energize new individual activists and donors from existing Jewish organizations. Those who veer in our direction from mainstream groups need not desert established, important organizations like the JCPA; they simply need to acknowledge that on some issues related to Arab-Israeli conflict, the Jewish mainstream is not likely to create the kind of new political environment the president and Congress need. And they need to acknowledge that there is an emergency in the occupied territories, and while the American government can't rescue the parties by itself, they will continue to be trapped unless the United States takes a new hard-nosed, balanced tack. Those kinds of individual dovish affirmations occurred when Yitzhak Shamir was in power and small numbers of American Jews from the charitable federations and other parts of the organizational world helped groups like Project Nishma and Americans for Peace Now. They occurred during the Rabin years when mainstream leaders formed Israel Policy Forum. There is no reason they can't happen again, except now they need to happen on a much larger scale.

For any of this to happen, some lingering protocols that guide the relationship of affiliated American Jews with Israel must be discarded, without delay. Dine told me,

> In the way we deal with Israel, somehow we've forgotten about what is at the heart of being Jewish, which is to constantly question and argue until we get to the truth. I don't see that happening now. We're stuck. American Jewish organizations need to do some rethinking. The paradigms [author's note: this was his word choice, unsolicited and unprompted] of pre-'67 and post-'67, the period right after, are no longer valid.
>
> There is nothing wrong with criticizing Israel out loud. Israel is not a fragile flower. It is not going to fall apart. It has one of the strongest economies in the world. Israel has one of the most powerful militaries. What we should say to them [the Israelis] is, 'Get on with it! Create two states, with or without the wall. And we will engage with our own government and urge it to help even if you disagree with it!'

Find new blood. Among American Jews, the best hope for new sources of support for a Middle East peace bloc can be found in the unaffiliated or marginally affiliated. Beyond the reach of the established communal institutions are at least half of the Jews in the United States. That population, in turn, is more likely than affiliated Jews to have problems with Israeli policies.

Many but not all of them are young voters. As we saw in chapter 2, within this group are people who have retained at least some connection to Israel; their identities have been shaped in some way by the Jewish state, by what they were taught about it as kids and the stark contrast of current reality with those teachings.

Consider this: when American Jews thirty-five and younger were surveyed by Steven Cohen and Ari Kellman in 2006, they were given a choice of answers to describe their level of ambivalence about Israel. Forty-six percent said they were "sometimes" ambivalent. I think it is significant that they did not join the smaller percentage who said they were "often" or "always" ambivalent.[4]

Fifty-seven percent of American Jews from a broader age range affirmed in 2005 that "caring about Israel is a very important part of my being Jewish."

Yet, 37 percent agreed with the statement "I am often disturbed by Israeli policies," and 30 percent weren't sure how they felt about it (only 33 percent said they disagreed).[5] Do the math. It is clear that at least some proportion of the people who are disturbed or confused about Israel include those who *care.*

There they are. Hidden somewhere in that statistical thicket are young American Jews who aren't prepared to embrace—or attack—every Israeli policy, who know or suspect there is something wrong and even rotten in the occupation, who are somewhat alienated and sometimes ashamed, but who have not written Israel off completely. To them, the idea that Israel should be exempt from American criticism is not just obsolete; it is absurd. These are the people who ought to be lobbying Congress and e-mailing the State Department and urging a balanced Middle East policy, clearly identifying themselves as American Jews who don't always agree with the conventional Israel lobby.

I can hear the alarms clattering in the minds of those who are actively involved in the conventional Israel lobby as they read this. Over the years, when they've been confronted with polls showing that their positions are out of step with most American Jews, they've dismissed the dissenting respondents as people who are not involved in the Jewish community and don't have enough knowledge about Israel to be taken seriously. The prevailing attitude is that these respondents don't count, their opinions don't matter. It is time to ensure that their opinions matter. They have a right and an obligation to weigh in on American policy toward Israel because they are Americans concerned about their own country. They are also human beings who are appalled by suffering and injustice wherever they find it, including the occupied territories. Yet they are also self-described Jews. They understand, at some visceral level, that what is being done in the occupied territories is being done in their name too. And they don't like what is being done there. The strength of their ties to the Jewish state might not pass the litmus test of the guardians of the conventional Israel lobby, but that litmus test has created institutions that have hampered too many American presidents who have wanted to help both Israelis and Arabs.

Broaden the debate. One reason why too few American Jews who agree with the pro-Israel left have not gotten involved, said pollster Jim Gerstein, is that they don't pay much attention to the furious debates going on within the Jewish community and the organizations that are taking stands on Israel. He cited the responses from American Jews who were asked to convey their feelings about AIPAC in June 2008: 38 percent gave it a favorable rating, 21 percent gave it an unfavorable rating, *but everyone else had no opinion one way or the other*. Also, while they were concerned about the Israeli-Palestinian conflict, it was much a lower priority to them as voters than the economy, the Iraq War, health care, terrorism and national security, energy policies, and the environment.

One way to build a broader base, Gerstein suggested, is to "expand the issues, broaden the debate beyond the individual issues of the Arab-Israeli conflict. . . . We know from the data that other issues are much more important to them, so take advantage of it. . . . Open the door to them and engage them on the war in Iraq, on Iran. There really isn't any Jewish group focusing on Iraq; there's an absence of organizational activity." Gerstein also noted that most American Jews oppose the conventional Israel lobby's flirtation with John Hagee and right-wing Christian Zionists. "Once they walk through the door" and start speaking out or acting against policies that are of great concern to them, he said, it might be possible to build a larger, active, progressive, and explicitly Jewish base that would weigh in on the Israeli occupation and America's role in trying to end it.

In addition to capturing the attention and enthusiasm of more American Jews, focusing attention on a broader range of issues would have other benefits. Doing so would place more emphasis on America's priorities and interests, not just Israel's. That, in turn, would help to forge ties with non-Jewish allies. "I think if American Jews started talking about American interests in the region, it would have a broad appeal to everyone else," said Ron Sider of Evangelicals for Social Action. "It's something that could help to unify people."

Stop worrying (too much) about the "community." I have spent more than a few nights pushing the words of op-eds, ads, and press releases through a strainer, trying to catch the errant adjective, the provocative noun, the overly bold description of Israeli foolishness. The goal was to ensure that the left-leaning groups behind those documents would not offend too many people in the mainstream Jewish community. As discussed in chapter 8, any hint of the e-word or the p-word and their equivalents was off limits, as was any reference to Palestinians' human rights. We could not say, "The occupation is wrong, and Israelis' treatment of Palestinians is often against the Jewish values we cherish." No, that wouldn't do. We had to say, "Unless we end the occupation, Jews will be outnumbered from the Mediterranean to the Jordan; it will mean the end of the Jewish democratic state." Both were true, but only the demographic argument was permitted because we had to show we were not soft and naive humanists; we had to show we were as tough as any of the hawks, that we were Machiavellian doves, Rabin devotees. Well, we've done a splendid job of galvanizing the mainstream, organized American Jewish community, haven't we?

It has already been suggested that speaking more freely, more honestly, will create urgently needed rhetorical space for American politicians and make it much easier for the pro-Israel left to build alliances with non-Jewish Americans. But, of equal importance, it will broaden the base of American Jews, especially those who are young and ready and willing to take a stand against Israeli policies that trouble them. Erring on the side of caution hasn't worked very well. Erring on the side of boldness should be given a try.

There is nothing wrong with continually demonstrating concern for Israel and a commitment to keeping its citizens safe. On the contrary, that must be done. But instead of worrying *only* about what will offend the organized community, it would be worth worrying much more about what will capture the imagination and stir the moral fervor of American Jews who have little to do with that community.

✡

"Great political change often begins with the smallest of doubts," points out Washington columnist Gabor Steingart. "It was the Chinese philosopher Lao Tzu who said, 'A journey of a thousand miles begins with a single step.' The same can be said of political movements. In their embryonic state, they are often little more than doubts tugging at the corners of a political heart. The Cold War provides a ready example: Growing skepticism with the policy of confrontation eventually gave rise to détente. China today also owes its very existence to doubts. Communist Party leader Deng Xiaoping had stopped believing in the power of Mao and Marx to build a viable state."[6]

There are comparatively more doubts tugging at the hearts of many Americans about the wisdom of the U.S. government's passivity in the face of Israeli settlement expansion, the route of its security barrier, human rights violations, and other troubling policies and actions. Translating those doubts into a political atmosphere that encourages the U.S. government to reassure and protect both Israelis and Palestinians, while encouraging and pressing them to make the brave compromises necessary for peace, will be difficult. Not trying to do so would be unforgivable.

Acknowledgments

This book required an extraordinary amount of patience, shared knowledge, and even courage from a great many people.

Some of those interviewed were complete strangers who spoke to me only upon the recommendation of mutual acquaintances. Because the issues addressed here are so controversial, many of them must have wondered whether their words would be used for some nefarious project that would do more harm than good to American Jews, other Americans, Israelis, and Arabs. Most were on the record, others could not be certain that they would be off the record. But they took a chance. I am deeply grateful to them and hope that this book does more good than harm.

Many of the friends and acquaintances whom I interviewed patiently explicated the mysteries of American Jewish organizations, K Street, Capitol Hill, Foggy Bottom, the White House, Ramallah, and Tel Aviv. I am especially thankful to Lara Friedman, M. J. Rosenberg, Mark Rosenblum, Martin Bresler, and Ted Mann for the generous gifts of their valuable time.

My brother Aki explicated mysteries of Microsoft Word that had always been unfathomable to me and spent more than a few days fixing up the manuscript on his own. I am pretty sure that he disagrees with much of what is propounded here. So his work was a labor of brotherly love that I will never forget.

Both my agent, Rob Wilson, and my editor, Hilary Claggett, took a chance on a first-time author and deserve many plaudits.

Last but not least, I am more than just grateful to my wife, Lisa; my daughter Lillie; and my mother, Anna Tilow. I am in awe of them because they never stopped encouraging me to complete this book, even when it became clear that all of them would need superhuman patience and a willingness to forgo my company on too many nights and too many weekends. They deserve more appreciation than one man can possibly give.

Notes

Introduction

1. John J. Mearsheimer and Stephen M. Walt, "The Israel Lobby and U.S. Foreign Policy" (Cambridge, MA: KSG Faculty Research Working Paper Series, March 2006); a condensed version, sans footnotes, was published as "The Israel Lobby" in the *London Review of Books*, March 23, 2006.
2. See John J. Mearsheimer and Stephen M. Walt, *The Israel Lobby and U.S. Foreign Policy* (New York: Farrar, Straus and Giroux, 2007), 111–150.
3. Abraham H. Foxman, *The Deadliest Lies: The Israel Lobby and the Myth of Jewish Control* (New York: Palgrave Macmillan, 2007); Alan Dershowitz, "Debunking the Newest and Oldest Jewish Conspiracy: A Response to Mearsheimer and Walt" (Cambridge, MA: KSG Faculty Research Working Paper Series, April 5, 2006); David Gergen, "An Unfair Attack," *U.S. News and World Report*, March 26, 2006; and J. J. Goldberg, "In Dark Times, Blame the Jews," editorial, *Forward*, March 24, 2006.
4. Daniel Levy, "Is It Good for the Jews?" *American Prospect*, June 18, 2006.
5. Mearsheimer and Walt, *Israel Lobby and U.S. Foreign Policy*, 114.
6. Ibid.
7. Goldberg, "In Dark Times, Blame the Jews."
8. Joseph Berger, "U.S. Jews Found More Willing to Criticize Leaders of Israel," *New York Times*, April 29, 1987.
9. Norman Kempster, "U.S. Jews Back Push for Israel Peace, Poll Shows," *Los Angeles Times*, October 4, 1997.
10. Jim Gerstein, *Summary Findings: National Survey of American Jews*, July 16, 2008, http://www.jstreet.org/files/images/SurveyAnalysisfinal.doc.
11. Jimmy Breslin, *How the Good Guys Finally Won: Notes from an Impeachment Summer* (New York: Viking Press, 1975), 33–34.

12. Thomas Hobbes, *Leviathan: With Selected Variants from the Latin Edition of 1668*, ed. Edwin Curley (Indianapolis: Hackett Publishing Co., 1994), 51.
13. David Verbeeten, "How Important Is the Israel Lobby?" *Middle East Quarterly* 13, no. 4 (2006), 37–44.
14. Tom Segev, *One Palestine, Complete: Jews and Arabs under the Mandate* (New York: Metropolitan Books, 2000), 5.
15. Ibid., 41–42.
16. Yehudah Amichai, "Wildpeace," *The Selected Poetry of Yehuda Amichai*, ed. and trans. Chana Bloch and Stephen Mitchell (Berkeley: University of California Press, 1996), 88.
17. Quoted in Jonathan Curiel, "Taking of Iraq Could Create Wider Woes, Scholar Predicts," *San Francisco Chronicle*, February 28, 2003.
18. Shibley Telhami, *Does the Palestinian-Israeli Conflict Still Matter?* Analysis Paper 17 (Washington, DC: Saban Center for Middle East Policy, June 2008).
19. Steven Kull, "Negative Attitudes toward the United States in the Muslim World: Do They Matter?" testimony before U.S. House of Representatives Committee on Foreign Affairs, Subcommittee on International Organizations, Human Rights, and Oversight, 110 Cong., 1st sess., May 17, 2007.
20. Daniel Kurtzer and Scott Lasensky, *Negotiating Arab-Israeli Peace: American Leadership in the Middle East* (Washington, DC: U.S. Institute of Peace Press, 2007), 8–9.
21. Idith Zertal and Akiva Eldar, *Lords of the Land: The War over Israel's Settlements in the Occupied Territories, 1967–2007* (New York: Nation Books, 2007), xiii.
22. Shlomo Ben-Ami, *Scars of War, Wounds of Peace: The Israeli-Arab Tragedy* (Oxford: Oxford University Press, 2006), 304.
23. Aaron David Miller, *The Much Too Promised Land: America's Elusive Search for Arab-Israeli Peace* (New York: Bantam Books, 2008), 374–375.
24. Israel's Kahan Commission eventually found that Sharon bore "personal responsibility" for "ignoring the danger of bloodshed and revenge" and for "not taking appropriate measures to prevent bloodshed." See Ze'ev Schiff and Ya'ari, Ehud, *Israel's Lebanon War*, ed. and trans. Ina Friedman (New York: Simon & Schuster, 1984), 283–284. Over the years, other sources too numerous to mention have given Sharon more direct responsibility.

Chapter 1: Passion, Money, and Smoke and Mirrors: AIPAC and Congress

1. Dana Milbank, "AIPAC's Big, Bigger, Biggest Moment," *Washington Post*, May 24, 2005.
2. Ori Nir, "Leaders Stress American Side of Aipac," *Forward*, May 27, 2005.
3. Howard Kohr, keynote address, AIPAC Conference, May 2005. Transcript of speech retained by the author.

4. Judy Graham, personal e-mail to the author, June 8, 2008.
5. M. J. Rosenberg, "Congress Awakens," *IPFriday*, July 22, 2005, http://www.ipforum.org/display.cfm?rid=1751.
6. Americans for Peace Now, "Legislative Roundups and Other News," July 22, 2005, http://www.peacenow.org/roundup.asp?cid=1139.
7. Thomas Gorgussian and Anayat Durrani, "Freedom, Democracy and Israel," *Al-Ahram Weekly Online*, no. 585 (May 9, 2002), http://weekly.ahram.org.eg/2002/585/re63.htm.
8. Mearsheimer and Walt, *Israel Lobby and U.S. Foreign Policy*, 154.
9. Ted Lang, "Aipac's Power Base—America's Real Terrorists!" *The Price of Liberty*, no. 585 (September 6, 2004), http://www.thepriceofliberty.org/04/09/06/lang.htm.
10. Quoted in Jeffrey Blankfort, "The Israel Lobby and the Left: Uneasy Questions," *Left Curve*, no. 27 (May 2003), http://leftcurve.org/LC27WebPages/IsraelLobby.html.
11. J. J. Goldberg, *Jewish Power: Inside the American Jewish Establishment* (Reading, MA: Addison-Wesley, 1996), 268–269.
12. Ibid., 276.
13. Ibid., 272.
14. Center for Responsive Politics, "Top Individual Contributors to 527 Committees, 2004 Election Cycle," http://www.opensecrets.org/527s/527indivs.php?cycle=200.
15. Ron Kampeas, "Soros to Support Dovish Jews Seeking an Alternative to Aipac?" *Jewish Telegraphic Agency*, October 10, 2006.
16. Center for Responsive Politics, "Top Industries Giving to Members of Congress, 2004 Cycle," http://www.opensecrets.org/industries/mems.php?party=A&cycle=2004; Center for Responsive Politics, "Top Industries Giving to Members of Congress, 2006 Cycle," http://www.opensecrets.org/industries/mems.php?party=A&cycle=2006/.
17. Thomas Edsall and Mary Moore, "Pro-Israel Lobby Has a Strong Voice," *Washington Post*, September 5, 2004.
18. Goldberg, *Jewish Power*, 276.
19. Center for Responsive Politics, "Pro-Israel Money to Congress—House of Representatives, 2004," http://www.opensecrets.org/industries/recips.php?ind=Q05&cycle=2004&recipdetail=H&mem=Y&sortorder=U.
20. Center for Responsive Politics, "Top Industries for Dennis Hastert, 2004," http://www.opensecrets.org/politicians/industries.php?cycle=2004&cid=N00004781; Center for Responsive Politics, "2003–2004 Cycle Fundraising, Dennis Hastert," http://www.opensecrets.org/politicians/summary.php?cid=N00004781&cycle=2004.

21. Center for Responsive Politics, "Pro-Israel: Money to Congress—Senate, 2004," http://www.opensecrets.org/industries/summary.php?ind=Q05&cycle=2004&recipdetail=S&mem=Y.
22. Center for Responsive Politics, "Data Available for Kentucky Senate Race, 2004," http://www.opensecrets.org/races/summary.php?cycle=2004&id=KYS2.
23. Paul Findley, *They Dare to Speak Out: People and Institutions Confront Israel's Lobby* (Chicago: Lawrence Hill Books, 1989).
24. Thomas B. Edsall, "Impact of McKinney Loss Worries Some Democrats," *Washington Post*, August 22, 2002. See also Melanie Evenly, "Israel Lobby Sends a Wake-Up Call," *Atlanta Journal-Constitution*, July 26, 2002.
25. Steven M. Cohen, "Poll: Attachment of U.S. Jews to Israel Falls in Past 2 Years," *Forward*, March 4, 2005.
26. Jennifer Siegel, "Clinton, Giuliani Top Survey of Jewish Voters," *Forward*, December 12, 2007.
27. Bert A. Rockman, "Reinventing What for Whom? The President and Congress in the Making of U.S. Foreign Policy," *Presidential Studies Quarterly* 30 (March 2000).
28. Edsall and Moore, "Pro-Israel Lobby Has Strong Voice."
29. Joshua Runyon, "After a Heated Contest, an Incumbent Tastes Victory," *Jewish Exponent*, June 17, 2004.
30. Brit Tzedek v' Shalom, "New Senate Letter Calls for Proactive U.S. Engagement and Israeli Settlement Freeze," http://ga3.org/btvshalom/notice-description.tcl?newsletter_id=19342073.
31. Ron Kampeas, "New Wind in Washington Blows Ball Back into Israel's Diplomatic Court," *Jewish Telegraphic Agency*, February 1, 2005. Additional information on the role of Congress, the Bush administration, and AIPAC in this legislation came from the author's interview with Kampeas on November 3, 2005.
32. Rosenberg, "Congress Awakens."
33. Ron Kampeas, "Effort to Limit Aid to Palestinians Exposed Rifts in Congress, Community," *Jewish Telegraphic Agency*, May 30, 2006; American Task Force on Palestine, "ATFP Notes Significant Improvement in Senate Version of House Bill on Palestinians," June 23, 2006, http://www.americantaskforce.org/in_media/pr/1223504926_8; M. J. Rosenberg, "2006: The Year Pro-Israel Moderates Prevailed in Congress," *TPM Café*, December 29, 2006, http://tpmcafe.talkingpointsmemo.com/2006/12/29/2006_the_year_proisrael_modera/.
34. John W. Kingdon, *Agendas, Alternatives, and Public Policies*, 2nd ed. (New York: Longman, 1995), 168.
35. As of 2005 AIPAC's operating budget was "more than $40 million," according to the *Forward*. See Ori Nir, "Ex-Aide to Seek Dismissal of Case," *Forward*,

September 30, 2005. In May 2008 the *New Republic* indicated AIPAC's operating budget was "$60 million." See James Kirchick, "Street Cred?" *New Republic*, May 28, 2008, http://www.tnr.com/story_print.html?id=175293ef-7f70-408b-a68a-ffffdb56d7bf.

Chapter 2: American Jews and Their Lobbies

1. Mearsheimer and Walt, *Israel Lobby and U.S. Foreign Policy*, 120, 128.
2. Quoted in Foxman, *Deadliest Lies*, 15.
3. "National Jewish Population Survey 2000–01: Strength, Challenge and Diversity in the American Jewish Population," http://www.ujc.org/local_includes/downloads/3905.pdf.
4. For an overview of American Jewish organizations with information on, among other things, membership totals, see Jerome A. Chanes, *A Primer on the American Jewish Community* (New York: American Jewish Committee, 1999).
5. See, for example, David B. Ottoway. "U.S. Jewish Officials Disagree with Shamir," *Washington Post*, November 17, 1989.
6. Yossi Beilin, *His Brother's Keeper: Israel and Diaspora Jewry in the Twenty-first Century* (New York: Schocken Books, 2000), 78.
7. Jewish Institute for National Security Affairs, "Board of Advisors," http://www.jinsa.org/category/1/5.
8. Jewish Institute for National Security Affairs, "Baghdad and Annapolis," JINSA Report #722, November 21, 2007, http://www.jinsa.org/node/360.
9. J Street, *J Street 2008: Blazing a New Path*, December 2008.
10. Nathan Guttman, "Reform Leader Calls on U.S. to Pressure Israel, Jews to Pressure U.S.," *Haaretz*, November 24, 2003.
11. Eric Fingerhut, "Area Jews Rap Conservative Leader on Interfaith Initiative," *Washington Jewish Week*, March 22, 2007.
12. Michael Massing, "Deal Breakers," *American Prospect*, March 11, 2002.
13. Larry Yudelson, "Quiet at the Top: American Jewry's Leading Umbrella Organization," *Jewish Week*, August 4, 1994.
14. "National Jewish Population Survey 2000–01."
15. Gerstein, *Summary Findings.*
16. Ariel Beery and Hindy Poupko, "Contemporary Currents in the American Jewish Relationship with Israel" (final paper for the Taub Seminar, New York University, Robert F. Wagner School of Public Service, Program in Non-Profit Management and Judaic Studies, Spring 2007), http://www.scribd.com/doc/65480/Contemporary-Currents-in-the-American-Jewish-Relationship-with-Israel, 10, 13.
17. Ibid., 19.
18. Walter Laqueur, *A History of Zionism* (New York: Schocken Books, 1989), 402.

19. Union of American Hebrew Congregations, "Pittsburgh Platform," November 1885, http://www.jewishvirtuallibrary.org/jsource/Judaism/pittsburgh_program.html.
20. Melvin I. Urofsky, *We Are One! American Jewry and Israel* (Garden City, NY: Anchor Press, 1978), 17.
21. Peter Grose, *Israel in the Mind of America* (New York: Schocken Books, 1984), 45.
22. Urofsky, *We Are One*, 4.
23. According to AIPAC's first executive director, Sy Kenen, in 1959, "many of our contributors were active community leaders—self styled 'non-Zionists.'" Isaiah L. Kenen, *Israel's Defense Line: Her Friends and Foes in Washington* (Buffalo, NY: Prometheus Books, 1981), 100. For a description of a controversial and widely publicized anti-Zionist movement within American Jewry, the American Council on Judaism, see Urofsky, *We Are One*, 68–72.
24. Grose, *Israel in the Mind of America*, 178.
25. Urofsky, *We Are One*, 49–50.
26. Grose, *Israel in the Mind of America*, 172.
27. Kenen, *Israel's Defense Line*, 107.
28. Ibid., 70.
29. Ibid., 100.
30. Goldberg, *Jewish Power*, 153
31. Yossi Melman and Dan Raviv, *Friends in Deed: Inside the U.S.-Israel Alliance* (New York: Hyperion, 1994), 307.
32. For accounts of the lobby's structure, growth, and agenda during this period, see Goldberg, *Jewish Power*, 197–203; and Melman and Raviv, *Friends in Deed*, 306–327.
33. Goldberg, *Jewish Power*, 198.
34. Ibid., 202–203.

Chapter 3: Lamp Salesmen and Secretaries of State

1. Bert A. Rockman, "Reinventing What for Whom? The President and Congress in the Making of U.S. Foreign Policy," *Presidential Studies Quarterly* 30 (March 2000).
2. Etta Bick, "The Involvement of American Jews in Israel–United States Relations, 1956–57," *Middle Eastern Studies* 39, no. 3 (July 2003).
3. Donald Neff, *Warriors for Jerusalem: The Six Days That Changed the Middle East* (New York: Linden Press, 1984), 83, 156–158.
4. Melman and Raviv, *Friends in Deed*, 151. For other references to Fisher's role, see pp. 148, 160.
5. Goldberg, *Jewish Power*, 222.

6. David Lowery, "Why Do Organized Interests Lobby? A Multi-Goal, Multi-Context Theory of Lobbying," *Polity* 39, no. 1 (2007).
7. Melman and Raviv, *Friends in Deed*, 322.
8. David K. Shipler, "On Middle East Policy, a Major Influence," *New York Times*, July 6, 1987.
9. William B. Quandt, *Decade of Decisions: American Policy toward the Arab-Israeli Conflict, 1967–1976* (Berkeley: University of California Press, 1977), 20.
10. Daniel Levy, "Is It Good for the Jews?" *American Prospect*, June 18, 2006.
11. Kurtzer and Lasensky, *Negotiating Arab-Israeli Peace*, 16–17, 56–57.
12. "Jewish Vote in Presidential Elections," in *Jews in American Politics*, ed. L. Sandy Maisel and Ira Forman (Lanham, MD: Rowman and Littlefield, 2001), 153. Also available at http://www.jewishvirtuallibrary.org/jsource/US-Israel/jewvote.html.
13. For one of the many available descriptions of this well-documented press conference, see Melman and Raviv, *Friends in Deed*, 426–427.
14. David Howard Goldberg, *Foreign Policy and Ethnic Interest Groups: American and Canadian Jews Lobby for Israel* (New York: Greenwood Press, 1990), 62.
15. Steven L. Spiegel, *The Other Arab-Israeli Conflict: Making America's Middle East Policy, from Truman to Reagan* (Chicago: University of Chicago Press, 1985), 329–340.
16. Edward Tivnan, *The Lobby: Jewish Political Power and American Foreign Policy* (New York: Simon & Schuster, 1987), 119–120.
17. William B. Quandt, *Camp David: Peacemaking and Politics* (Washington, DC: Brookings Institution, 1986), 62.
18. For a brief overview, see *American Jewish Year Book, 1998* (Philadelphia: American Jewish Committee, 1999), 110–112.
19. "Thank You, Secretary Albright," advertisement, *New York Times*, August 10, 1997.
20. Norman Kempster, "U.S. Jews Back Push for Israel Peace, Poll Shows," *Los Angeles Times*, October 4, 1997.
21. *American Jewish Year Book, 1998*, 115.
22. Miller, *Much Too Promised Land*, 248.
23. Ameinu, "U.S. Jews Overwhelmingly Support Israel Gaza/West Bank Disengagement," press release, April 11, 2005, http://www.ameinu.net/news/pressreleases.php?pressreleaseid=14.
24. Gerstein, *Summary Findings*.

Chapter 4: The Silence of (Most) American Jewish Doves

1. Goldberg, *Jewish Power*, 212.
2. Arthur Hertzberg, *Jewish Polemics* (New York: Columbia University Press, 1992), 35.

3. Samuel G. Freedman, *Jew vs. Jew: The Struggle for the Soul of American Jewry* (New York: Simon & Schuster, 2000), 168.
4. Goldberg, *Jewish Power*, 212.
5. Mearsheimer and Walt, *Israel Lobby and U.S. Foreign Policy*, 122–128.
6. Anthony Loewenstein, "Denounced, but Jewish Dissent Grows," *Sydney Morning Herald*, February 6, 2007, http://www.smh.com.au/news/opinion/denounced-but-jewish-dissent-grows/2007/02/05/1170524024997.html.
7. Daniel Eisenberg, "AIPAC Attack? Charges of Pressure at a Jewish Weekly," *Columbia Journalism Review*, January 1, 1993.
8. Steven T. Rosenthal, *Irreconcilable Differences: The Waning of the American Jewish Love Affair with Israel* (Hanover, NH: Brandeis University Press/University Press of New England, 2001).
9. Ibid., 37.
10. Ibid., 54–55.
11. Paul Montgomery, "Discord Among U.S. Jews over Israel Seems to Grow," *New York Times*, July 15, 1982.
12. Cited in Tivnan, *The Lobby*, 173.
13. Ibid., 174.
14. Ari Goldman, "Shamir Assails His U.S. Jewish Critics," *New York Times*, March 21, 1988.
15. *American Jewish Year Book, 1990* (Philadelphia: American Jewish Committee, 1991), 260.
16. Ibid., 260.
17. Rosenthal, *Irreconcilable Differences*, 106
18. Thomas L. Friedman, "Warmth Does Not Mean Support, 41 Jews Write Shamir," *New York Times*, November 17, 1989.
19. Freedman, *Jew vs. Jew*, 169
20. "In the period between the Sinai campaign in 1956 and the Six Day War of June, 1967 . . . the initial honeymoon came to an end as American Jews no longer saw Israeli rebirth as the all-consuming passion of their lives, while Israelis wondered if they had been deserted," in Urofsky, *We Are One*, 323.
21. Kenen, *Israel's Defense Line*, 198.
22. Urofsky, *We Are One*, 359.
23. Barton Gellman, "At the Crossroads," *Washington Post*, May 26, 1996.
24. Howard Kohr, keynote address, AIPAC Conference, May 2005. Transcript of speech retained by the author.
25. Philip Weiss, "Are Pro-Israel Doves Part of the Lobby? Fleshler's Challenge," *Mondoweiss*, November 26, 2007, http://www.philipweiss.org/mondoweiss/2007/11/are-pro-israel.html.
26. Eli Leiter, review of *Planting Hatred, Sowing Pain: The Psychology of the Israeli-Palestinian Conflict*, by Moises Salinas, *Israel Horizons Magazine*, Winter 2008, 9.

Cattan, "Resolutions on Invasion Divide Jewish Leadership."

Mortimer B. Zuckerman, "A Question of Priorities," *U.S. News and World Report*, October 8, 2001; Mortimer B. Zuckerman, "Midnight for Baghdad," *U.S. News and World Report*, January 19, 2003.

Nacha Cattan, "Jewish Groups Press to Line Up on Iraq Attack: Conference Polls Its Members as Chair Urges War Forward," *Forward*, August 23, 2002.

Matthew Berger, "Reform Jews Step into Minefield with Opposition to Iraq War, Alito," *Jewish Telegraphic Agency*, November 22, 2005.

Foxman, *Deadliest Lies*, 76.

Jim Lobe, "Losing Faith," *InterPressService*, January 27, 2006.

Michael Lind, "A Tragedy of Errors: The Neoconservatives' War Has Proved a Disaster," *Nation*, February 23, 2004; Michael Lind, "How Neoconservatives Conquered Washington—and Launched a War," *Salon.com*, April 9, 2003, http://archive.salon.com/opinion/feature/2003/04/09/neocons/index.html.

Lind, "A Tragedy of Errors."

Fleshler, "Conspiracy?"

See for example, Lobe, "Losing Faith." Feith, Wurmser, and Perle were among the coauthors of an infamous paper that was sent to newly elected Likud prime minister Benjamin Netanyahu, "A Clean Break: A New Strategy for Securing the Realm," published in 1996 by the Institute for Advanced Strategic Studies. See http://www.iasps.org/strat1.htm. The paper is often purported to be a blueprint for the Iraq War. In my article on the war in *Reform Judaism*, I show that it is nothing of the kind; rather, it is "a grab-bag of Machiavellian fantasies" that the neoconservatives wanted to impose on many parts of the world, not just the Middle East. However, the paper does show an embrace of Netanyahu and a right-wing Likud approach to the region, including preemptive strikes on Lebanon and Syria and an uncompromising stance on the occupied territories. See Fleshler, "Conspiracy?"

5. Michael Rubin, "Now Bush Is Appeasing Iran," *Wall Street Journal*, July 21, 2008; Joshua Muravchik, "Operation Comeback," *Foreign Policy*, November–December 2006; Norman Podhoretz, "The Case for Bombing Iran—I Hope and Pray That President Bush Will Do It," *Wall Street Journal Online*, May 30, 2007, http://www.opinionjournal.com/federation/feature/?id=110010139.

6. Ron Kampeas, "Groups Defend Sanctions," *Forward*, December 4, 2007; Ori Nir, "Groups Push for Sanctions, Fear U.S. Will Falter on Iran," *Forward*, September 2, 2006; Ori Nir, "Jewish Groups Press for Iran Sanctions," *Forward*, September 23, 2005.

27. Americans for Peace Now, "Action Alert: 'Wanted: A Smarter Policy on Iran,'" July 9, 2008, http://www.peacenow.org/updates.asp?rid=0&cid=5093; Nathan Guttman, "Fearing Iraq Effect, Jewish Democrats Tread Carefully on Iran,"

27. Celestine Bohlen, "U.S. Plan Faulty, a P.L.O. Aide Says," *New* 1 13, 1989.
28. Quoted in Melman and Raviv, *Friends in Deed*, 425.

Chapter 5: American Jews, Iraq, and the Fetish of Preempti

1. See, for example, Justin Raimondo, "The Neocons' War," *A* 2, 2004, http://www.antiwar.com/justin/?articleid=2727; Je "War for Israel," *Left Curve*, April 22, 2004; and Kathleen Ch Christison, "Dual Loyalties: The Bush Neocons and Israel,' September 6, 2004, http://www.counterpunch.org/christison09
2. Mearsheimer and Walt, "Israel Lobby and U.S. Foreign Policy."
3. Mearsheimer and Walt, *Israel Lobby and U.S. Foreign Policy*, 23C
4. See, for example, Mitchell Plitnick and Chris Toensing, "'The Perspective," *Middle East Report* 243 (Summer 2007); Michell the 'Israel Lobby' Distorting America's Mideast Policies?" *Salon* 2006, http://www.salon.com/news/feature/2006/04/18/lobby/; "Conspiracy? Was Defending Israel the Motivating Factor Behin Invasion of Iraq?" *Reform Judaism*, Winter 2006, 54–58, 79.
5. Thomas E. Ricks, *Fiasco: The American Military Adventure in Ir* Penguin Press, 2006).
6. Michael R. Gordon and Bernard E. Trainor, *Cobra II: The Insi Invasion and Occupation of Iraq* (New York: Pantheon Books, 200
7. Mearsheimer and Walt, *Israel Lobby and U.S. Foreign Policy*, 241.
8. "Pharaoh in the White House," editorial, *Jewish Currents*, March
9. Julia Duin, "Changing of the Times: Jews Protested Vietnam, but War with Iraq," *Washington Times*, January 24, 2003.
10. For a summary of essays, op-eds, and letters to the president promo sion, see Mearsheimer and Walt, *Israel Lobby and U.S. Foreign Poli*
11. Nacha Cattan, "Resolutions on Invasion Divide Jewish Leadershi October 11, 2002.
12. Jewish Telegraphic Agency, "From 'Bomb Them' to 'I Want Proo Speak Out on War with Iraq," October 15, 2002. See also Jon "Attempt to Locate Advertisement Described by James Moran Flat," *GoodbyeJim.com*, January 17, 2004, http://www.jonathanmar 1074368601.
13. "JCPA Statement on Iraq," *Insider* 4, no. 35 (October 15, 2002), jewishpublicaffairs.org/organizations.php3?action=printContentIte 4&typeID=81&itemID=2514.
14. For background on the positions of the Reform movement, see Ur form Judaism Commission on Social Action, "The War in Iraq, Ba http://urj.org/Articles/index.cfm?id=8942&pge_prg_id=34230&pge

Forward, July 15, 2008; J Street, "Now Is Our Moment on Iran," Summer 2008, http://www.jstreet.org/campaigns/now-our-moment-iran.

28. Eli Lake, "Democrats Retreat on War Funds," *New York Sun*, March 14, 2007.
29. Guttman, "Fearing Iraq Effect."
30. Nathan Gardels, "Abizaid: 'Iran Is Not a Suicide State; Deterrence Will Work,'" *Huffington Post*, July 23, 2008, http://www.huffingtonpost.com/nathan-gardels/abizaid-iraq-is-not-a-sui_b_114575.html; Associated Press, "U.S. Gen. John Abizaid: 'World Could Find Ways to Live with Nuclear Iran,'" *Huffington Post*, September 18, 2007, http://www.huffingtonpost.com/2007/09/17/gen-abizaid-world-could-_n_64802.html?page=2; Martin van Creveld, "The World Can Live with a Nuclear Iran," *Forward*, September 24, 2007; Shlomo Ben-Ami and Trita Parsi, "The Alternative to an Israeli Attack on Iran," *Christian Science Monitor*, July 2, 2008.
31. Trita Parsi, "Mismarriage of Convenience," web exclusive, *Foreign Policy*, June 2008, http://www.foreignpolicy.com/story/cms.php?story_id=4330. See also, Kenneth Pollack and Ray Taykeyh, "Taking on Tehran," excerpt from *Foreign Affairs*, March–April 2005, http://www.foreignaffairs.org/20050301faessay84204/kenneth-pollack-ray-takeyh/taking-on-tehran.html.
32. Gerstein, *Summary Findings*.
33. Gal Beckerman, "The Neoconservative Persuasion, Examining the Jewish Roots of an Intellectual Movement," *Forward*, January 6, 2006.

Chapter 6: The Shared Emergency

1. David D. Newsom, "Foreign Policy Lobbies and Their Influence," *Cosmos Journal* (1995), http://www.cosmos-club.org/web/journals/1995/newsom.html.
2. George Salem and Marvin Lender, "The Only Hope for Peace," *Los Angeles Times*, March 24, 2002.
3. For Secretary Rice's address, see http://video.state.gov/?fr_story=FEEDROOM162445&rf=sitemap.
4. Arab American Institute, "Population Estimates of Americans of Palestinian Ancestry," October 17, 2006, http://www.aaiusa.org/issues/2550/population-estimates-of-americans-of-palestinian-ancestry.
5. Osamah Khalil, "The Politics of Fear," *Electronic Intifada*, October 2007, http://electronicintifada.net/v2/article9028.shtml.
6. Arab American Institute, "Arab Americans, Demographics," http://www.aaiusa.org/arab-americans/22/demographics. For more on the politics of the Arab-American community, see James Zogby, press conference, Foreign Press Center, Washington, DC, November 29, 2007, Federal News Service/Washington Transcript Service.
7. Americans for Peace Now and Arab American Institute, "Seeing Eye to Eye: A

Survey of Jewish American and Arab American Public Opinion," 2007, http://www.donteverstop.com/files/apn/upl/assets/AAI-APN2007Poll.pdf.

8. American-Arab Anti-Discrimination Committee, "Government Affairs," http://www.adc.org/index.php?id=2219.
9. Eric Yoffie, "Remarks to the 44th Annual Convention, Islamic Society of North America," August 31, 2007, http://urj.org/yoffie/isna/.
10. See, for example, the agenda of the CAIR Government Relations Department at http://www.cair.com/GovernmentRelations/IssuesandLegislation.aspx.
11. Hussein Ibish, "Sense, Nonsense and Strategy in the New Palestinian Political Landscape," American Task Force on Palestine, September 7, 2007, http://www.americantaskforce.org/policy_and_analysis/issue_paper/1223503715.
12. Rammy M. Haija, "The Armageddon Lobby: Dispensationalist Christian Zionism and the Shaping of U.S. Policy Towards Israel-Palestine," *Holy Land Studies: A Multidisciplinary Journal* 5, no. 1 (2006), 75–95. See also Ze'ev Chafets, *A Match Made in Heaven: American Jews, Christian Zionists, and One Man's Exploration of the Weird and Wonderful Judeo-Evangelical Alliance* (New York: HarperCollins, 2007).
13. Nathan Guttman, "Pro-Israel Christians Mobilize in Washington," *Forward*, July 18, 2007.
14. Caryle Murphy, "Evangelical Leaders Ask Bush to Adopt Balanced Middle East Policy," *Washington Post*, July 17, 2007.
15. Hasdai Westbrook, "The Israel Divestment Debate," *Nation*, May 8, 2006.
16. Michael Paulson, "Religious Tensions Flare as Mideast Conference Nears," *Boston Globe*, October 14, 2007.
17. Anti-Defamation League, *Sabeel Ecumenical Liberation Theology Center: An ADL Backgrounder*, April 18, 2008, http://www.adl.org/main_Interfaith/sabeel_backgrounder.htm.
18. For details on the controversy, see Chafets, *Match Made in Heaven*, 80–88; Neela Banerjee, "Jews Trying to Avert Protestant Divestment," *New York Times*, September 29, 2004; Pauline J. Chang, "Presbyterians Establish Divestment Criteria," *Christian Post*, November 10, 2004.
19. Jane Lampman, "Churches Raise Pressure on Firms in Israel," *Christian Science Monitor*, August 8, 2005.
20. Chafets, *Match Made in Heaven*, 82.
21. Rachel Zoll, "Presbyterians, Jews Try to Heal Rift over Israel Divestment Vote," *Associated Press*, November 24, 2004; Chafets, *Match Made in Heaven*, 81–88.
22. Laurie Goodstein, "Presbyterians Revise Israel Investing Policy," *New York Times*, June 22, 2006.
23. Rachel Pomerance, "Methodists to Weigh Divestment as a Tool to Shift Israel," *Washington Post*, February 16, 2008.

24. Nathan Guttman, "Jewish, Presbyterian Ties at New Low," *Forward*, June 17, 2008.
25. Ethan Felson, "Fight to Overturn Divestment Call Can Provide Lessons for Activists," *Jewish Telegraphic Agency*, June 25, 2006.
26. See National Interreligious Leadership Initiative for Peace in the Middle East, http://www.nili-mideastpeace.org.
27. Peter Steinfels, "Mideast Initiative Pushes Beyond Platitudes," *New York Times*, December 6, 2003.
28. National Interreligious Leadership Initiative for Peace in the Middle East, "Religious Leaders Call for Prayers on Days Before Annapolis Conference," November 21, 2007, http://www.nili-mideastpeace.org/downloads/2007_11PressRelease.pdf.

Chapter 7: The View from Israel

1. Rebecca Needler, "Deal Breakers (Correspondence)," *American Prospect*, May 6, 2002.
2. Kurtzer and Lasensky, *Negotiating Arab-Israeli Peace*, 43.
3. Miller, *Much Too Promised Land*, 375.
4. Menachem Gantz, "A. B. Yehoshua: Bush Should Recall Ambassador until Outposts Dismantled," *Ynet News*, January 20, 2008, http://www.ynetnews.com/articles/0,7340,L-3496354,00.html.
5. "Journalist: U.S. Should 'Rape' Israel," *New York Sun*, December 27, 2007.
6. Mearsheimer and Walt, *Israel Lobby and U.S. Foreign Policy*, 227.
7. See, for example, Steven Kull, "Americans on the Middle East Road Map," *Program on International Policy Attitudes*, University of Maryland, May 30, 2003, 9–11, 18–19; Jean-Michel Stoullig, "Americans Want Cutback in Aid to Israel If It Refuses to Withdraw: Poll," *Agence-France Presse*, April 13, 2002.

Chapter 8: Rhetoric (and Paradigms) for the Rest of Us

1. Nicholas D. Kristoff, "Talking About Israel," *New York Times*, March 18, 2007.
2. Jennifer Siegel, "Reform Rabbis Cancel Carter Center Visit," *Forward*, January 12, 2007.
3. Philip Weiss, "Too Hot for New York," *Nation*, April 3, 2006.
4. Cecilie Surawski, "Walt and Mearsheimer Censored: Chicago Council on Global Affairs Cancels Talk," *Muzzlewatch*, August 9, 2007, http://www.muzzlewatch.com/?p=222.
5. Nathaniel Popper, "Carter Wins Over Student Crowd at Brandeis," *Forward*, January 24, 2007.
6. Jason Zinoman, "The Week Ahead, Oct. 1–Oct 7," *New York Times*, October 1, 2007.

7. E. J. Kessler, "Lieberman and Dean Spar over Support for Israel," *Forward*, September 12, 2003; Needa Pickler, "Democrats Criticize Dean's Israel Remarks," *Associated Press*, September 11, 2003; Michelle Goldberg, "Howard Dean's Israel Problem," *Salon.com*, September 23, 2003, http://dir.salon.com/story/news/feature/2003/09/23/dean_israel/.
8. BBC World News, "UN Says No Massacre in Jenin," August 1, 2002, http://news.bbc.co.uk/2/hi/middle_east/2165272.stm.
9. B'Tselem, "The Israeli Army Does Not Do Enough to Combat Abuse of Palestinians," press release, December 16, 2007, http://www.btselem.org/english/Press_Releases/20071216.asp.
10. Breaking the Silence: Israeli Soldiers Talk about the Occupied Territories, http://www.breakingthesilence.org.il/index_e.asp.
11. James A. Baker III and Lee H. Hamilton, *Iraq Study Group Report* (Washington, DC: U.S. Institute of Peace, 2006), 38.
12. Nathan Guttman, "Groups Mute Criticism of Iraq Report," *Forward*, December 15, 2006.
13. Ethan Bronner, "Israel Is Not Linked to Iraq, Except That It Is," *New York Times*, December 10, 2006.

Chapter 9: The Far Left's "Jewish Problem" and Why It Hurts the Palestinians

1. "Israel is not a country! . . . Delist if from Facebook as a country!" http://www.facebook.com/group.php?gid=2221448894.g
2. April Rosenblum, *The Past Didn't Go Anywhere: Making Resistance to Antisemitism Part of All Our Movements*, April 2007, 12, http://www.thepast.info.
3. Cogit8, comment on "Hillary to Pounce on Obama's Comments to 100 Cleveland Jews (Hallelujah!)," *Mondoweiss*, March 5, 2008, http://www.philipweiss.org/mondoweiss/2008/03/obamas-meeting.html.
4. For a full text of the Zoloth letter and for sources on the rally and related incidents at San Francisco State University, see "A Quick Guide to San Francisco State University Events," *Yourish.com*, May 12–18, 2002, http://www.yourish.com/archives/2002/may12-18_2002.html. See also Melissa Radler, "San Francisco University Acts Against Anti-Semitism on Campus," *Jerusalem Post*, May 21, 2002.
5. Eli Muller, "Locating the Hate in Anti-Zionism," *Yale Daily News*, February 28, 2003.
6. Michael Geis, "Criticising Israel," *The Language Guy*, March 3, 2007, http://thelanguageguy.blogspot.com/search?q=israel+american+jews+and+muslims.
7. Simon Schama, "Virtual Annihilation," in *Those Who Forget the Past: The Question of Anti-Semitism*, ed. Ron Rosenbaum (New York: Random House Trade Paperbacks, 2004), 362.
8. Rosenblum, *Past Didn't Go Anywhere*, 12.

9. Ibid., 5
10. Ibid., 20
11. Mitchell Cohen, "Anti-Semitism and the Left That Doesn't Learn," *Dissent*, Winter 2008, http://www.dissentmagazine.org/article/?article=987.
12. Rosenblum, *Past Didn't Go Anywhere*, 20.

Chapter 10: Conclusion

1. Laqueur, *History of Zionism*, 116.
2. Kingdon, *Agendas, Alternatives, and Public Policies*, 168.
3. Mearsheimer and Walt, *Israel Lobby and U.S. Foreign Policy*, 352.
4. Steven M. Cohen and Ari Kellman, *Beyond Distancing: Young Adult American Jews and Their Alienation from Israel* (New York: Andrea and Charles Bronfman Philanthropies, 2007), http://www.acbp.net/About/PDF/Beyond%20 Distancing.pdf.
5. Steven M. Cohen, "Poll: Attachment of U.S. Jews to Israel Falls in Past 2 Years," *Forward*, March 4, 2005.
6. Gabor Steingart, "The End of Globalization," *Speigel Online International*, December 11, 2007, http://www.spiegel.de/international/world/0,1518,522 628,00.html.

Interviews

American Jewish Activists

Diane Balser, July 24, 2007
Jeremy Ben-Ami, January 31, 2007
Ken Bob, June 8, 2008
Martin Bresler, July 10, 2007
Charney Bromberg, November 15, 2007
Debra DeLee, September 20, 2006
Rabbi Jerome Epstein, April 20, 2008
Ethan Felson, January 8, 2008
Lara Friedman, January 31, 2006, and March 19, 2005
Marcia Friedman, November 26, 2007
Malcolm Hoenlein, November 16, 2007
Jonathan Jacoby, October 16, 2007
Victor Kovner, May 21, 2008
Rabbi Douglas Krantz, December 28, 2008
Rob Levy, May 27, 2007
Robert Lifton, 2008
Christopher MacDonald-Dennis, January 21, 2007
Ted Mann, March 22, 2008
Mitchell Plitnick, November 29, 2007, March 8, 2007, and February 3, 2009
Gail Pressberg, December 13, 2007
Seymour Reich, August 26, 2005
Mark Rosenblum, October 30, 2005, November 9, 2005, and February 2, 2006
Rabbi David Saperstein, November 19, 2008
Tammy Shapiro, December 14, 2007
Henry Siegman, November 30, 2005
Thomas Smerling, August 9, 2005
Rabbi Arthur Waskow, May 17, 2008

Rabbi Eric Yoffie, May 5, 2008
Anonymous activist, July 25, 2008 (quoted in chapter 10)

Former AIPAC Staff Members (and One Current)
Douglas Bloomfield, August 26, 2005
Thomas Dine, July 1, 2008
Steven Grossman, December 23, 2007
M. J. Rosenberg, January 24, 2007, and June 17, 2008
Elizabeth Schrayer, December 13, 2007
Neil Sher, September 16, 2005
Current AIPAC staff member, December 9, 2006 (quoted in chapter 1)
Former AIPAC staffer, July 27, 2006 (quoted in chapter 1)

Israelis
Yossi Alpher, February 14, 2008
Colette Avital, June 22, 2005
Yossi Beilin, December 10, 2007
Shlomo Ben-Ami, August 9, 2007
Gershom Gorenberg, June 15, 2008
Shlomo Gur, November 21, 2006
David Kimche, March 4, 2006
Menachem Klein, April 26, 2006, and March 18, 2008
Daniel Levy, December 20, 2007
Alon Pinkas, August 3, 2005
Danny Rubenstein, June 20, 2006
Ephraim Sneh, August 1, 2005

With Experience in Congress and/or the Executive Branch
Col. Karen Kwiatkowski (ret.), May 13, 2006
Ambassador Samuel Lewis, January 24, 2007
Robert Malley, September 20, 2006
Aaron David Miller, January 21 and 22, 2007
Jeremy Rabinovitz, January 27, 2005
Mara Rudman, February 5, 2008
Brent Scowcroft, January 4, 2008
Ambassador Philip Wilcox, November 10, 2005
Congressional aide, March 22, 2005 (quoted in chapter 1)
Congressional aide, May 16, 2006 (quoted in chapter 1)
Former State Department aide, November 21, 2007 (quoted in chapter 3)
Member of Congress, July 21, 2008 (quoted in chapter 1)

Official on the foreign policy teams of George H. W. Bush and Clinton, November 21, 2007 (quoted in chapter 3)
Official in the George H. W. Bush administration, December 1, 2007 (quoted in chapter 3)
Senate aide, March 24, 2005 (quoted in chapter 1)

Arab-American/Church/Interfaith Activists

Rev. Dr. Susan Andrews, May 17, 2008
Ziad Asali, December 24, 2007
Julie Schumacher Cohen, December 19, 2007
Stephen Collechi, January 29, 2007
Rafi Dajani, November 17, 2005
George Gorayeb, December 29, 2007
David Neff, January 8, 2007
George Salem, April 10, 2008
Ron Sider, February 1, 2008
Bruce Wexler, November 29, 2006
Corinne Whitlach, November 17, 2005
Ronald Young, December 3 and 10, 2006
Church leader, May 19, 2008 (quoted in chapter 6)
Former staff member of Presbyterian Church USA, January 8, 2008 (quoted in chapter 6)

Journalists

James "Jim" Besser, May 3 and 7, 2006
Larry Cohler-Esses, November 9, 2005
Ron Kampeas, November 3 and 5, 2005
Thomas Ricks (via e-mail), August 10, 2006

Other

Judy Andreas, April 9, 2008, and March 14, 2008
Michael Gies, March 1, 2007
April Rosenbloom, May 4, 2008
Steven Spiegel, November 7, 2007
Douglas Webber, September 16, 2005

Selected Bibliography

Amichai, Yehuda. *The Selected Poetry of Yehuda Amichai*. Edited and translated by Chana Bloch and Stephen Mitchell. Berkeley, University of California Press, 1996.

Baker III, James A., and Lee H. Hamilton. *Iraq Study Group Report*. Washington, DC: U.S. Institute of Peace, 2006.

Beilin, Yossi. *His Brother's Keeper: Israel and Diaspora Jewry in the Twenty-first Century.* New York: Schocken Books, 2000.

Ben-Ami, Shlomo. *Scars of War, Wounds of Peace: The Israeli-Arab Tragedy*. Oxford: Oxford University Press, 2006.

Blankfort, Jeffrey. "The Israel Lobby and the Left: Uneasy Questions." *Left Curve*, no. 27 (May 2003).

Breslin, Jimmy. *How the Good Guys Finally Won: Notes from an Impeachment Summer.* New York: Viking Press, 1975.

Center for Responsive Politics. *Open Secrets.org: Money in Politics*. 2008. http://www.opensecrets.org.

Chafets, Ze'ev. *A Match Made in Heaven: American Jews, Christian Zionists, and One Man's Exploration of the Weird and Wonderful Judeo-Evangelical Alliance*. New York: HarperCollins, 2007.

Chanes, Jerome A. *A Primer on the American Jewish Community.* New York: American Jewish Committee, 1999.

Findley, Paul. *They Dare to Speak Out: People and Institutions Confront Israel's Lobby*. Chicago: Lawrence Hill Books, 1989.

Foxman, Abraham H. *The Deadliest Lies: The Israel Lobby and the Myth of Jewish Control.* New York: Palgrave Macmillan, 2007.

Freedman, Samuel G. *Jew vs. Jew: The Struggle for the Soul of American Jewry*. New York: Simon & Schuster, 2000.

Goldberg, David Howard. *Foreign Policy and Ethnic Interest Groups: American and Canadian Jews Lobby for Israel.* New York: Greenwood Press, 1990.

Goldberg, J. J. *Jewish Power: Inside the American Jewish Establishment*. Reading, MA: Addison-Wesley, 1996.

Gordon, Michael R., and Bernard E. Trainor. *Cobra II: The Inside Story of the Invasion and Occupation of Iraq*. New York: Pantheon Books, 2006.

Grose, Peter. *Israel in the Mind of America*. New York: Schocken Books, 1984.

Hertzberg, Arthur. *Jewish Polemics*. New York: Columbia University Press, 1992.

Kellman, Ari, and Steven M. Cohen. *Beyond Distancing: Young Adult American Jews and Their Alienation from Israel*. New York: Andrea and Charles Bronfman Philanthropies, 2007. http://www.acbp.net/About/PDF/Beyond%20 Distancing.pdf.

Kenen, Isaiah L. *Israel's Defense Line: Her Friends and Foes in Washington*. Buffalo, NY: Prometheus Books, 1981.

Kingdon, John W. *Agendas, Alternatives, and Public Policies*. 2nd ed. New York: Longman, 1995.

Kull, Steven. "Negative Attitudes toward the United States in the Muslim World: Do They Matter?" Testimony before U.S. House of Representatives Committee on Foreign Affairs, Subcommittee on International Organizations, Human Rights, and Oversight. 110 Cong., 1st sess., May 17, 2007.

Kurtzer, Daniel, and Scott Lasensky. *Negotiating Arab-Israeli Peace: American Leadership in the Middle East*. Washington, DC: U.S. Institute of Peace Press, 2007.

Laqueur, Walter. *A History of Zionism*. New York: Schocken Books, 1989.

Levy, Daniel. "Is It Good for the Jews?" *American Prospect*, June 18, 2006.

Lowery, David. "Why Do Organized Interests Lobby? A Multi-Goal, Multi-Context Theory of Lobbying." *Polity* 39, no. 1 (2007): 26.

Maisel, L. Sandy, and Ira Forman, eds. *Jews in American Politics*. Lanham, MD: Rowman and Littlefield, 2001.

Mearsheimer, John J., and Stephen M. Walt. "The Israel Lobby and U.S. Foreign Policy." Cambridge, MA: KSG Faculty Research Working Paper Series, March 2006.

———. *The Israel Lobby and U.S. Foreign Policy*. New York: Farrar, Straus and Giroux, 2007.

Melman, Yossi, and Dan Raviv. *Friends in Deed: Inside the U.S.-Israel Alliance*. New York: Hyperion, 1994.

Miller, Aaron David. *The Much Too Promised Land: America's Elusive Search for Arab-Israeli Peace*. New York: Bantam Books, 2008.

Neff, Donald. *Warriors for Jerusalem: The Six Days That Changed the Middle East*. New York: Linden Press, 1984.

Parsi, Trita. *Treacherous Alliance: The Secret Dealings of Israel, Iran, and the United States*. New Haven: Yale University Press, 2007.

Quandt, William B. *Camp David: Peacemaking and Politics*. Washington, DC: Brookings Institution, 1986.

———. *Decade of Decisions: American Policy toward the Arab-Israeli Conflict, 1967–1976*. Berkeley: University of California Press, 1977.

———. *Peace Process: American Diplomacy and the Arab-Israeli Conflict since 1967*. 3rd ed. Berkeley: University of California Press, 2005.

Ricks, Thomas E. *Fiasco: The American Military Adventure in Iraq*. New York: Penguin Press, 2006.

Rockman, Bert A. "Reinventing What for Whom? President and Congress in the Making of Foreign Policy." *Presidential Studies Quarterly* 30 (2000).

Rosenbaum, Ron, ed. *Those Who Forget the Past: The Question of Anti-Semitism*. New York: Random House Trade Paperbacks, 2004.

Rosenthal, Steven T. *Irreconcilable Differences: The Waning of the American Jewish Love Affair with Israel*. Hanover, NH: Brandeis University Press/University Press of New England, 2001.

Ross, Dennis. *The Missing Peace: The Inside Story of the Fight for Middle East Peace*. New York: Farrar, Straus and Giroux, 2004.

Segev, Tom. *One Palestine, Complete: Jews and Arabs under the Mandate*. New York: Metropolitan Books, 2000.

Solomon, Morris S. *The Agenda and Political Techniques of the American Israel Public Affairs Committee*. Washington, DC: Industrial College of the Armed Forces, 1993.

Spiegel, Steven L. *The Other Arab-Israeli Conflict: Making America's Middle East Policy, from Truman to Reagan*. Chicago: University of Chicago Press, 1985.

Telhami, Shibley *Does the Palestinian-Israeli Conflict Still Matter?* Analysis Paper 17. Washington, DC: Saban Center for Middle East Policy, June 2008.

Tivnan, Edward. *The Lobby: Jewish Political Power and American Foreign Policy*. New York: Simon & Schuster, 1987.

United Jewish Communities. *National Jewish Population Survey 2000–01: Strength, Challenge and Diversity in the American Jewish Population*. http://www.ujc.org/local_includes/downloads/3905.pdf.

Urofsky, Melvin I. *We Are One! American Jewry and Israel*. Garden City, NY: Anchor Press, 1978.

Verbeeten, David. "How Important Is the Israel Lobby?" *Middle East Quarterly* 13, no. 4 (2006).

Zertal, Idith, and Akiva Eldar. *Lords of the Land: The War over Israel's Settlements in the Occupied Territories, 1967–2007*. New York: Nation Books, 2007.

Index

About the Author

Since the mid-1980s Dan Fleshler has spent much of his spare time and some of his professional life trying to convince American Jews to back Israel's peace camp and the American groups that support it.

He has fought this fight as a board member of Ameinu, Americans for Peace Now, and the Givat Haviva Educational Foundation. He is also a member of Brit Tzedek v'Shalom and is on the J Street Advisory Council. As a New York–based media and public affairs strategist, he has represented many clients who needed to communicate with the American Jewish community, American politicians as well as opinion leaders on issues related to Israel and the Middle East. He has also represented companies and trade associations with interests in Washington, D.C. So, he knows how the denizens of K Street ply their trade and has learned a thing or two about the sausage-making (or, if you prefer, kosher-hot-dog-making) that is involved in shaping foreign policy.

His public relations career has included stints as director of communications for the NAACP Legal Defense and Educational Fund and as an executive in several agencies based in New York City. He received a BA in general studies from Harvard College in 1976 and a master of fine arts in fiction writing from the Iowa Writer's Workshop in 1979. He was an assistant professor of English at Western Michigan University in 1980–81, before commencing his business career.